BWANA STOKESI

and his

AFRICAN CONQUESTS

BWANA STOKESI
and his
AFRICAN CONQUESTS

Nicholas Harman

JONATHAN CAPE
THIRTY-TWO BEDFORD SQUARE LONDON

First published 1986
Copyright © 1986 by Nicholas Harman
Maps copyright © 1986 by Richard Natkiel Associates
Jonathan Cape Ltd, 32 Bedford Square, London WC1B 3EL

British Library Cataloguing in Publication Data

Harman, Nicholas
Bwana Stokesi and his African conquests.
1. Stokes, Charles
I. Title
382'.4396'109676   HD9429.I862

ISBN 0-224-01998-8

Printed in Great Britain by
Butler & Tanner Ltd,
Frome and London

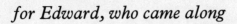
for Edward, who came along

Contents

Illustrations

My special thanks are due to the following for their help in obtaining photographs: Mr Erisa Kironde (29); *Punch* (22); Mr Donald Simpson, Librarian, the Royal Commonwealth Society (1-6, 14, 17, 23, 28, 30); the Librarian, the Royal Geographical Society (18); Mr Charles Stokes, jr (24).

Maps

Introduction

A century ago the powers of civilisation began their last imperial conquest of the habitable world. It took them fifteen years to carve up tropical Africa. In 1884, white people claimed sovereignty over a few islands and sandbanks around the coast. In Berlin that autumn the fourteen governments that really mattered in the world held a conference, and agreed upon rules for parcelling out the interior between them; by 1899 the job was done. A few thousand white men backed by the latest technology – quinine against fever, breech-loading rifles against the native inhabitants – had etched frontiers across deserts, forests and fertile lands, regardless of ethnic, geographical or any other logic.

The 'scramble for Africa' was quickly accomplished, and the results its pioneers achieved were quickly undone. The Germans were driven from their share of the spoil by the result of the first Great War in Europe. The empires of Britain, France and Portugal crumbled within a life-span, leaving behind a continent divided against itself by the heritage of its temporary masters. The tropical belt between Khartoum on the Nile, at 15° north of the Equator, and the Zambezi river, at 15° south, is now shared between thirty-four sovereign black states, which include fifteen of the world's twenty poorest nations. Europe's heedless strength was the father of Africa's present weakness.

Visiting Africa over the years, and journeying across those pointless frontiers, I wanted to know how the conquest felt at the time – to hear the story not only of the men who made history but of the people who suffered it as it happened. The conquerors wrote shelves of books, to justify their claims and to boast of their achievements. The historians have amply studied the European policies that lay behind the conquest. As I read their volumes, a name from the footnotes began to occupy the forefront of my mind.

Charles Stokes, of Dublin, was not a hero of the conquest – far from it. Nor was he in any way typical of the pioneering generation. But he was constantly present at the twists and turns of imperial rivalry, working with African rulers, or with the Arab traders who preceded the Europeans into the interior, or with whichever aspiring imperial power would pay him. He went to Africa as a lay missionary in 1878, before the empires took hold. When he married an African the mission threw him out. In association with his new family he grew prosperous as an independent trader, Bwana Stokesi, the caravan boss. In this role he was useful both to the British and to the Germans in the founding of their East African colonies; they employed him as a forerunner, then discarded him in favour of their own more orthodox administrators. So he advanced westward in search of trade, into the still unoccupied lands beyond the new dominions. But into that wild region at the very heart of the continent yet another rival empire was moving up its forces for occupation. A Belgian war-party from West Africa caught him, and hanged him from a tree.

His business was ivory, the only product of value the African interior produced, once the trade in human beings was banned. The people who killed the elephants wanted guns to do the killing, and to protect their tusks against their neighbours. So Stokes became an arms dealer, and he walked into his death-trap with a thousand muskets behind him. In the heart of Africa there was no such thing as peaceable commerce, whatever the missionaries, the soldiers and the company promoters claimed. Charles Stokes's simple, selfish attempt to make an independent living made him suspect to all other brands of imperialist. It also made him an incomparable witness to the process of imperial acquisition, with all its cant.

The man was tall, handsome, impulsive, with his great red Irish beard. He was full of patience in the months of marching across the limitless plains, and at journey's end he loved company. He soon abandoned the sweaty worsted

suit and revolver-belt of the conventional European traveller, and did his walking like an Arab, in a cool, white cotton
robe. When other white men came to a village they stood
outside the cane fence and gave orders. Stokes went inside
and sat down to talk. He exchanged polite greetings and
small gifts – some cloth from a porter's headload for a
peaceful passage, grain for the carriers, a goat for the armed
escort, maybe a fat hen for his own dinner. He drank thick
gruelly beer with the chief, and if he felt a touch of fever
coming on he took a pipe of *dagga*, or *kif*, or *bhang*, whichever was the local name for marijuana.

Captain Frederick Lugard, the freelance adventurer who
later won honour as the unifier and first ruler of Nigeria,
had a lot of trouble from Stokes, whom he condemned as
'casual about natives'; the trader loved his African wife, and
was proud of the children he had by at least two other
African women. Alfred Swann, the big-game hunter who later
settled down as senior resident magistrate of Nyasaland,
remembered Stokes's embarrassing hospitality: 'He was living in a small grass house, surrounded by hundreds of Wak-
umu. Bags of rupees lay scattered around under his bed,
and his happy disposition won for him hosts of both white
and black friends.' The money was kept under the bed
because, in camp, with a faithful woman always to keep
watch over it, that was the safest place.

The Germans were Stokes's most generous employers.
He did not like them as much as he liked their money: he
found them over-formal and given to obscure intrigues. But
they knew how to distill *schnapps* out of banana beer, and
given a sufficiency of that he danced on the Kaiser's birthday in 1891 with Feldwebel Kühne, under the stars that were
bright enough to see by, while on the one side the German
officers sat in a row beneath the flag-staff, and on the other
the drummers and the women looked on, all laughing. That
was beside Lake Victoria, the second largest sheet of fresh
water in the world, when Stokes had the only sailing-boat
on the lake and alliances on every shore. Then, so nearly,
he became rich and respected as he longed to be.

He never achieved his dream, which was to return to
Dublin as a gentleman of independent means, and to set up

his family in style. The marks he made on the literature of his time are indistinct. He was pretty certainly one of the models upon whom Sir Henry Rider Haggard based his central character, Allan Quatermain. In Joseph Conrad's *Heart of Darkness* he flits posthumously, obscure and unnamed, across the nightmare landscape. His death made him for a brief while famous, the centre of an international *cause célèbre*, the subject of parliamentary debates and official lies in three European nations, and of anxious messages between the old Queen-Empress of England and her greedy cousin, King Leopold of the Belgians. Then events moved on, and it was convenient to forget him. *L'affaire Stokes*, the row between Britain and Belgium that so delighted the governments of France and Germany, was wiped from the record. Lord Kimberley, the Foreign Secretary, wrote a note to the French ambassador in London just nine days after Stokes was hanged: 'I often ask myself whether these African disputes are worth taking seriously ... Northern and Southern Africa apart, they are a matter of barren deserts or places where white men cannot live, dotted with thinly scattered tribes who cannot be made to work.'

The times Charles Stokes lived through seem impossibly remote now. But in 1984 I called on his son, living in the best of health in his villa on Bungo Hill, on the outskirts of Kampala, on land presented in memory of his father's services to the royal family of Buganda. The British Empire swept up that ancient kingdom into the miscellaneous collection of territory and peoples called Uganda, and ruled it well-meaningly for over seventy years. The heritage of empire is politicians in London-tailored suits, and generals with the red bands of the British general staff around their caps, powerlessly presiding over a brutal anarchy, in the shining uplands where the Equator crosses the Great Lakes, and the crops come all year round.

In the plains and hills and forests of tropical Africa there are still people alive who were born before the white men came, and who saw them leave. The conquerors had thought – or their backers in Europe, statesmen, businessmen and bishops, had boasted – that they were bringing to the Dark Continent the blessings of a higher culture. Africa won. The climate killed many of the adventurers; fever and drink deranged the survivors. When the conquest was complete the colonial enterprises failed to show a profit, so the white men closed them down. The Africans accepted the tools and weapons and vehicles and medicines by which the invaders had gained their victory, and are using them now – for good or ill – in ways that Africans themselves determine. Charles Stokes was there, and bears witness to how it all began.

I

SPREADING
the
FAITH

Chapter 1

∼∽∾

Souls for the Saving

The main object of the Zambesi Expedition, as our instructions from Her Majesty's Government explicitly stated, was to extend the knowledge already attained of the geography and mineral and agricultural resources of Eastern and Central Africa – to improve our acquaintance with the inhabitants, and to endeavour to engage them to apply themselves to industrial pursuits and to the cultivation of their lands, with a view to the production of raw material to be exported to England in return for British manufacturers.

Dr David Livingstone, *An Expedition to the Zambesi* (1865), dedication to Lord Palmerston, Foreign Secretary

Queen Victoria's expanding empire owed almost everything to men from the disadvantaged Celtic regions of her domestic kingdom. Scottish missionaries opened the way to the heart of Africa, and Scotsmen ran the ships that served its coastal trade. H. M. Stanley, the most aggressive of explorers, was a Welshman by birth, although an American citizen at the time of his great adventures. Charles Stokes was an Irishman of a very special kind, which he defined himself during a particularly fierce row with a British official, who happened to be another Welshman: 'I want to tell you Captain Williams, I am a Britisher though not an Englishman born, I am Irishman born and bred and a true and loyal subject of Her Majesty the Queen of Great Britain ...'

By descent the Stokeses were purely English, of a family settled in Ireland during the 'plantation' of the seventeenth century. They intermarried exclusively with families of similar extraction, and never made their fortune. They

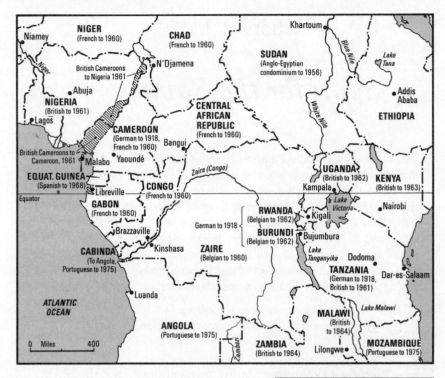

The European empires in tropical Africa lasted some 70 years. Quickly acquired, they proved on the whole unprofitable and unsuitable for white settlement. So, unlike the territories of southern Africa, they were easily abandoned. Yet the frontiers laid down around 1890 have survived (with a single exception, in the former German Kamerun), and are taken for granted by the continent's new masters. Charles Stokes played his part – sometimes very important, sometimes merely casual – in determining the present borders of nine sovereign nations. His purpose had been simply to make some money.

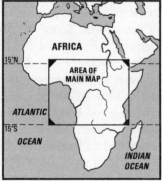

spoke with Irish accents and regarded themselves as Irish-
men, just as the English of the Virginia plantation in the
same period regard themselves as Americans. Like whites
in the American South, they prided themselves on their
difference from the majority of their neighbours. They were
a Protestant élite in an overwhelmingly Catholic nation,
which they nevertheless regarded as their own. The tradition lives on in Ireland's northern province.

As Protestants, the Stokeses had access to schools and jobs
to which most of their fellow-countrymen could never as-
pire. Charles Stokes's father was a supervising engineer
with the Irish North Western Railway. Of his six children
who survived childhood, Charles, born in 1852, was the
third. During his adolescence the family lived in Enniskil-
len, in County Fermanagh, on the northern side of what is
now the border between Northern Ireland and the Republic. Charles was therefore able to attend as a day-boy
the nearby Portora Royal School, then as now the most
prestigious of the Irish equivalents to an English public
school for the sons of the gentry. He was on the way to
qualifying as a gentleman himself, in the one genteel profes-
sion open to a youth of slender means, as a clergyman of
the Church of Ireland. But when Charles was twenty his
father died, probably from drink. The young man had to
find a paying job.

Through family connections he was fixed up with a clerk-
ship in a shipping firm, across the water in Liverpool.
There he set up house with his widowed mother, Louisa,
and learned about bills of lading and transport costs. No
doubt he picked up some general ideas about the Africa
trade. Liverpool, despite the collapse of its lucrative slaving
business, sent many ships to West Africa, exporting Manchester cottons, Birmingham guns and brassware, and
Dutch gin, in exchange for the palm oil which provided the
base for the food and soap industries that are still important
in the city.

In 1877, at the age of twenty-five, Charles Stokes heard
the missionary call. The dangers of the life he chose were
known to be appalling, the prospects of advancement slim;
like so many Victorian younger sons, he accepted them in

full awareness that death from fever was the most likely outcome. Perhaps he was moved by religious conviction (although there is not the slightest evidence of that). Or perhaps he thought a lay missionary, if not quite a clergyman, was at least near to being a gentleman. In Liverpool, as a clerk, he had no prospect of advancement, no chance of earning enough to marry on, nothing ahead but drudgery and boredom in drab lodgings with his mother. So he went.

He was recruited by the Church Missionary Society, the evangelical offshoot of the Church of England, for service in its new field in East Africa. At the CMS preparatory institute near Reading, west of London, he received a perfunctory training as a lay evangelist; but that he hardly needed. Any young man reared in the vigorously anti-Papist Church of Ireland would know the necessary doctrine anyway. What the CMS needed was Stokes's skill as a transport manager.

His fellow-trainees were also practical men – builders, mechanics, masons, carpenters, farmers – whose physical work would support the spiritual efforts of the ordained missionaries. They were not the gentlemanly companions Stokes believed he belonged among. But at least they were bound for an adventure, in which some might make their fortunes. In May 1878, Charles Stokes arrived at the island port of Zanzibar, twenty miles off the East African mainland, to join the mission to bring Christ to the African nation of Buganda, far in the interior.

The voyage out from England (through the brand-new Suez Canal, opened in 1869) had foreshadowed the hardships that lay ahead in the tropics. Stokes's companions on board were Alfred Copplestone, a builder, and Mrs Streeter, the wife of a farm expert already in Zanzibar, with her two small children. In the dreadful heat of the Red Sea Copplestone was incapacitated by fever. At Aden, the hateful, roasting coaling station at the entrance to the Indian Ocean, Mrs Streeter paid the penalty of the life thought suitable for white ladies in that climate – cooped up in her cabin, clothed in wool to 'protect' her from the sun, she died of apoplexy. It was the heat that killed her. There was a painful muddle about what to do for the children. Obviously they must be sent home. But to leave them in Aden to await the next ship from India would be to condemn them to death. Stokes took charge and escorted them to Zanzibar, where he presented them, motherless, to the distraught Streeter. 'Truly God's ways are not ours,' wrote the father. Obedient to the divine will, he sent the children back on the next ship and stayed at his post, alone.

So the young Irishman launched into his African career, in the service of that utterly Victorian blend of Christianity and cupidity which was the mission to Buganda. He knew practically nothing of what he was going for. The mission was, itself, motivated by true charity. But – as we shall see – the missionaries served as a ramp for commercial interests, and the funds behind them had been raised by a newspaper stunt. Nobody reflected for a moment that the millions of people in Africa might be living their own lives in their own way, and working out their own salvation. Nor did the self-appointed benefactors regret that the first tentative steps in the name of religion would be followed as surely as night follows day by the predatory discipline of imperial rule. But that harsh destiny was implicit in the mission's origins.

The man who unleashed the European invasion was as nearly a saint as any man can be who rejects the whole notion of sainthood. Dr David Livingstone, the Scottish missionary, was the first European to penetrate methodically into the heart of Africa. He walked into the unknown, to find and describe a continent of souls who had never heard the name of Jesus. He explained that these people, far from being untouched by the outside world, were being brutally exploited by invaders along whose well-established routes, and with whose help, he himself penetrated to the interior. The slave trade, suppressed on the west coast of Africa by British naval patrols, was still flourishing in the east and south. Livingstone, a powerful writer and a spellbinding public speaker, came back to describe its horrors and to call for the defeat of its profiteers. He thus opened the way for a new kind of exploitation.

The east coast slave traders were Arabs, supplying mar-

kets in the Middle East. The southern slavers were Portuguese, supplying Brazil and their own African farms.
They were subjecting the Africans' bodies to bondage in
this world. The Arabs were Muslims, the Portuguese
Roman Catholics. As the Scottish Protestant Livingstone
saw it, they were therefore also imperilling the souls of their
slaves for eternity. He called for a Protestant crusade to
Africa, a worthy successor to the moral campaigns that had
already freed the slaves first of the British West Indies and
then of the southern United States.

Livingstone argued that Africa must be freed not only
from slavery and human oppression, but also from the terrible harshness of daily life under the sun and rain of the
tropics, riddled with disease and danger of every kind. He
knew he would not have survived his journeys without
modern medicines; his great contribution to his own and
his successors' survival was the pill called Livingstone's
Rouser, a compound of quinine and calomel offering the
first effective means of suppressing the symptoms of malaria. He explained how pointless it was to send missionaries
into an environment that was bound to kill most of them.

If the Gospel was to prosper, it must be based on mission
stations supplied from the outside world with the necessities
for survival. That meant steamers to carry goods on the
rivers and lakes. It meant guns for defence (although Livingstone carried one only when it was unavoidable). It
meant producing a revenue to pay for these things, by
growing crops or digging minerals for export. His letters
home constantly, and often misleadingly, speak of the
potential riches of Africa – soil that looks just right for
cotton, rocks with what look like coal-bearing seams, people
ripe for recruiting and training into a reliable workforce.

To bring Africans into regular employment around com-
mercially viable mission stations would, said the doctor, be
good for their souls. The Bible, especially in the version
revealed to Lowland Scots, enjoined certain outward discip-
lines of life. A man must marry one wife only, and keep the
Sabbath sober and free from work. But if women died
regularly in childbirth, and if the unremitting burden of
daily labour was at some seasons unavoidable, such a Chris-

tian life was impossible. Good health, decent housing and steady, paid employment were the preconditions of salvation. With this message of godliness and profit he found a ready audience, and considerable funds, among far-seeing Victorian businessmen concerned that, as industrial production rose in Europe, the supply both of raw materials and of customers might run out. He went on to appeal for government protection over the new African missions he dreamed of. Karl Marx, then at work on *Das Kapital*, never saw as clearly the link from Christianity to capitalism, and from capitalism to imperialism. But at that time the British government, as devoted to liberal non-intervention in trade as Livingstone was to Christianity, would not move to support the missions.

In 1871 all trace of Livingstone was lost by his admirers. Half-crazed with sickness and exhaustion, he was living on the charity of Arab slave-traders in the region south of Lake Tanganyika. His disappearance became a sensation in the new popular press of the English-speaking world. A New York newspaper proprietor, James Gordon Bennett of the *Herald*, sent his most daring reporter to find the Scottish saint, regardless of expense. Henry Morton Stanley triumphantly completed his assignment. He was a rough sort of fellow, but some of the doctor's holy reputation rubbed off on him after publication of his articles from Ujiji, in which he attributed to himself the unforgettable greeting, 'Dr Livingstone, I presume?'

Stanley could not persuade the doctor to return with him to the coast. The old man wandered off on his obsessive quest for 'the fountains of the Nile', and died on his wanderings. His faithful African servants gutted the corpse and carried it down to Zanzibar, where it was pickled and shipped home for a state funeral in Westminster Abbey. Henceforth the conversion of Africa would proceed under the auspices of its own saint.

Stanley continued his African travels, with fees and expenses now so large that the New York *Herald* had to go halves on them with the London *Daily Telegraph*. Both papers got their money's worth. In August 1877 the great reporter emerged at the mouth of the river Congo, having completed in 999 days the journey from east to west across the equatorial line of the continent. The traveller's hardships and heroism were immense. He started with 355 followers, three of them Europeans; by the end the three other white men, and 111 Africans, were dead.

It was a wonderful true-life adventure story. It was also a political enterprise. On his way, in April 1875, Stanley visited and reported from an African nation of most unusual importance. Buganda, romantically sited where the headwaters of the Nile pour northwards out of the vast Lake Victoria, had been described by only one previous European visitor, the explorer Speke, in 1862. It contained a civilisation higher than any other yet known in black Africa.

Buganda had a king called the Kabaka, immensely rich in ivory. It had a complex political system closely resembling European feudalism, good roads, and extensive trade by canoe on the great lake. Now Stanley told how the Kabaka Mutesa, in the thirteen years since Speke's visit, had greatly improved the administration and prosperity of his realm. The improvement, said Stanley, was largely due to the introduction of writing and record-keeping, made possible by the arrival in the kingdom of teachers from the lower reaches of the Nile. They were Egyptian Muslims. There was an immediate possibility (said Stanley's article, written in his special style of barely suppressed hysteria) that the king and his people would shortly undergo a mass conversion to Islam. If so, the best hope for Christianity and progress in Africa could be lost for ever.

Egyptian penetration of black Africa, by way of Buganda, was indeed at this moment a serious possibility. By some climatic change, the immovable mass of floating reeds that usually blocks the upper reaches of the Nile had shifted, and the river became navigable over its whole length. This was demonstrated during Stanley's visit to the Kabaka's court, when one day a strange white man appeared and offered his greetings. Stanley was furious, fearing this visitor might grab a share in his exclusive story. The newcomer turned out to be a French mercenary soldier called Colonel Linant de Bellefonds, sent south along the Nile by his commanding officer, General Charles Gordon. Both Linant and

Gordon were safely Christian – Gordon devoutly so, a point made much of when he died, ten years later, at the hands of the militant Muslim soldiers of the Mahdi, in the Sudan – but the two European officers were in the service of the Khedive of Egypt, and their job was to extend Egyptian sovereignty to the source of the Nile. Egypt might be a European puppet, but it was a Muslim nation, and the Khedive's white officers commanded vast Muslim armies. An Egyptian conquest of Buganda would expose the country's people to the massive influence of Islam.

Stanley anxiously sounded out Linant's religious beliefs: 'The Colonel, though a Frenchman, is a Calvinist (fortunately, for the cause I had in mind).' As a Protestant, Linant could safely be employed to reinforce Stanley's plea for Christian evangelism in Buganda. Stanley entrusted his article to the colonel, for transport down the Nile and so to London. Linant died on the way, in a skirmish with tribesmen. But the letter got through, and in November 1875, only seven months after it was written, appeared in the *Daily Telegraph*. Its impact was strengthened by the news that General Gordon's Egyptian soldiers had already passed the rapids of the upper Nile, dragging small steamers that could bring the very source of the river under the authority of the government in Cairo. If Buganda were to be saved for Christianity, the obvious organiser of the rescue should be the Church Missionary Society, Livingstone's old employer. The CMS was rather embarrassed by association with a sensational newspaper fund-raising campaign, but it could hardly turn away gifts with a devout purpose.

Two days after publication of the article, a cheque for £5,000 came in. Its giver allowed himself to be known only as 'an unprofitable servant', but profit may not have been entirely absent from his motives. Word soon got around that the benefactor was William Mackinnon, the Glasgow shipping tycoon who had already befriended Stanley and knew in advance of his intention to visit Buganda. Mackinnon's British India Steam Packet Company, based in Bombay, ran a regular service to Zanzibar. He had everything to gain from an extension of British trade and influence on the African shore of the Indian Ocean.

Soon the CMS mission fund reached the large sum of £15,000, and the society was commendably quick in putting it to use. Only seven months after publication of Stanley's appeal – fourteen months after the writing of his despatch – the first missionaries arrived in Mackinnon's ship at Zanzibar, heading for the inland kingdom. They were heroic, but woefully ill-prepared for what they met in Africa. Of the eight men in that first party, one died almost as soon as he landed; two were sent home sick before they could leave the coast. The others blundered inland, to face the fierce climate and the unknown diseases, and the hostile indifference of those they had believed would be innocent tribesmen. Of the thirty-seven CMS men who left Britain in the 1870s and 1880s to found the Anglican Church in Buganda, twenty-two died in Africa, ten retired sick within five years, and just five survived – including Charles Stokes, listed noncommittally as 'retired to trade'.

The sacrifice of these men was admired, and publicised, among Christians everywhere. The Roman Catholic Church reacted fast: the charismatic Pope Pius IX was passionately committed to the world struggle against Islam, and against Protestant heresy too. His enthusiasm was incarnated in the new missionary order of the White Fathers, based in Algiers, whose priests were recruited in France and were encouraged to regard the expansion of the French empire and of the Roman Catholic Church as the same thing. French politicians who opposed the church at home were keen to back its imperialist work abroad. The socialist leader Gambetta suppressed church schools in France, but insisted that 'Anti-clericalism is not for export' ('L'anti-cléricalisme n'est pas article d'exportation').

In Germany, too, the missionary societies were active in urging the government to acquire colonies overseas – and Africa was the place where they believed the Germans should find their place in the sun. The message of Livingstone, then of Stanley, was closely studied among the devout and the influential. One of the first wave of CMS lay missionaries was the Scottish engineer Alexander Mackay. He had done his training in an engineering plant in Berlin, where he was active in a group of militantly evangelistic

Protestants patronised by rich society ladies. With one of them, the Countess von Arnim, he kept up a correspondence from his arrival in Africa in 1876 until his death in 1890. She was the beloved sister of the German Chancellor, Bismarck. Buganda was from the very start of the missionary drive the subject of European interest, which soon became European political rivalry.

East Africa itself was far from being the political vacuum that the first missionaries had assumed they would find. Buganda was in a class of its own as a wholly African kingdom with its own political structure. But Zanzibar, the missionaries' coastal base, was itself ruled by an Arab Sultan whose overlordship was acknowledged – as Livingstone had made plain – by heads of towns and districts as far inland as the headwaters of the river Congo, half-way across the continent. The missionaries took Zanzibar as their base for the push towards Buganda precisely in order not to approach the interior along the Nile, by way of Egypt, a Muslim nation. But Zanzibar was Muslim too. Its leading citizens described themselves as Arabs, although after many generations of interbreeding with Africans they often did not look it. They had a language of their own, with a Bantu African form but a largely Arabic vocabulary, called Swahili, meaning the coast language; it was (and remains today) the most powerful cultural and commercial unifier of East Africa.

Swahili people had dominated the East African coast for centuries. They were long-established in 1496, when Vasco da Gama, the first European to visit their ports, described their pride in their Islamic faith, and their contempt for the darker-skinned inland peoples, whom they called *Kafirs*, 'unbelievers'. They owned slaves and traded in slaves for export.

In the 1840s the Royal Navy, based on the port of Bombay in India, closed down the slave trade to Arabia, and Zanzibar seemed destined to become a mere backwater on the Indian Ocean, clear of the main trade route round the southern tip of Africa. But with the opening of the Suez Canal in 1869 the island was back in the commercial mainstream once more. Three years later William Mackinnon started his British India steamship service between Zanzibar and Bombay, the terminus of commerce between Britain and India. German trading firms arrived to compete with the British for the island's commerce. Sultan Bargash, who succeeded to the throne of Zanzibar in 1870, could not cope with all this change. He was torn between the influence of the British consul-general, an old friend of Dr Livingstone called Dr John Kirk, and that of the German merchants. Both Kirk and the Germans had warships to reinforce their influence.

In the interior, the Swahili merchants still swore allegiance to the Sultan. They traded in ivory, and affirmed their alliances with the inland African chiefs by marrying (or at least having children by) their daughters: the male children, brought up as Muslims and trained as soldiers, bred a new generation to perpetuate Arab power. The merchants continued to take slaves: the export trade was small and risky, with the British navy on the seas, but people could still be profitably sold for household service, or for work in the clove plantations of Zanzibar or the sugar plantations of the French island colonies in the Indian Ocean. Domestic slavery was such a matter. It was tolerated by Islam, deep-rooted in local custom, and indispensable for all commercial activity. Trading in the African interior meant trading in people. There was no alternative.

Tropical Africa produced only two marketable items for export, human beings and elephant tusks, and you could not get one without the other. In that terrible climate, man was the only beast of burden strong enough, and tractable enough, to be employed to carry loads. The camels of the Sahara, the oxen of southern Africa, the donkeys of the Middle East, lay down and died. African elephants and zebras could not be tamed to carry or pull burdens. But human beings could be tamed by other men with guns. And once they had carried their loads down to the coast the unwanted people could be sold off for cash, making two profits instead of one from a cargo of ivory.

The scale of this business was immense, in human terms. There were no roads, so no wheeled vehicles (although both Arabs and Africans knew perfectly well how to make them).

The normal limit of what a man can carry as a daily burden over long distances is about thirty kilograms, or seventy-five pounds in the old English weights. To carry one tonne of goods for barter – there was no money in the interior – meant employing thirty-three porters. For every four porters an extra carrier was needed for food and water. Every caravan needed an escort of at least twenty musketeers. The escort needed its own porters; the caravan leader needed half a dozen more again for his personal effects. To transport ten tonnes of goods inland required at least 500 people; most caravans were much larger than that.

For the return journey the caravans were larger still, swollen by slaves captured or acquired from local allies. Once out of their home districts these poor people could not escape, since they had no chance of finding their way home. Mostly they marched humbly along, disciplined by the whip and the gun, beneath their loads. Selected prisoners – young boys and girls chosen for the high price they would fetch in the sex trade in Arabia – were taken specifically for sale, not as porters. Caravan managers took care not to scar them with shackles, or to allow their escorts to pass on avoidable diseases.

There are of course no reliable figures on the human cost of the trade in slaves and ivory. Dr Livingstone – naturally inclined to exaggerate the horrors – claimed that only one captured slave in ten survived the journey to the coast. His friend and editor, the Reverend Horace Waller, put the survival rate at one in five, and underlined the point with this chilling description: 'It is like sending up to London for a large block of ice in the summer; you know that a certain amount will melt away before it reaches you in the country, but that which remains will be quite sufficient for your wants.'

In quest of ivory and slaves the Arabs penetrated ever further into the interior. They armed the men of their outposts, and their African allies, with guns for the hunt and for protection. The ivory trade became the arms trade, at a time when the armies of the white man's world were re-equipping themselves with the new breech-loading rifles whose mass production had been developed by the Americans to kill each other more effectively during their civil war. Hundreds of thousands of army-surplus muskets flooded the African market, mostly from the old stock of the British armies at home or in India.

The Indian empire, at the start, provided both the motive and the model for British actions in Africa. The significance of Zanzibar was as a safe haven for the Royal Navy on the opposite shore of the Indian Ocean. And, as in India, the expense of direct administration was spared by putting in British 'advisers' to tell local Muslim rulers how to run their countries. Dr Kirk was consul-general in Zanzibar and the Sultan's principal adviser; a young lieutenant of the Royal Navy, Lloyd Mathews, was installed to run the Sultan's army. The Sultan received, and accepted, their advice on foreign affairs and commercial questions. On internal affairs, including the question of domestic slavery, the British advisers were careful not to interfere. But the pretence that the Sultan of Zanzibar was free to run his island's internal affairs could not survive the arrival of the Protestant missionaries, who detested both Islam, the spiritual basis of his government, and slavery, its economic basis. They were perfectly ready, if Dr Kirk would not compel the Sultan to abolish domestic slavery in his domains, to lobby their friends in London until a gunboat was sent to sort the matter out.

Behind this façade of power stood the great mass of the African people. Of them, no reliable record survives. They did not write until outsiders came among them. Even where their oral history is preserved, it is in the writings of Africans taught to think as the missionaries wanted them to think. They did not build in stone. Their artefacts were made of iron, bronze, wood and clay, and have almost all been melted down or have perished through decay. Far to the west, the great civilisations of Ghana and Benin left behind their art. To the south, the ruins of Zimbabwe proved that Africans could build as well as anyone. But in the tropical belt the only certain thing about the African people is that, when the Europeans arrived, their conditions of life were already changing fast.

Above all, despite the appalling depredations of the slave

trade, the black population of the interior was rapidly increasing. The Portuguese, who started raiding the West African coastline for slaves in the late fifteenth century, had brought in the reverse direction, from the Americas, a wealth of previously unknown food crops. The staples of African peasant farming are yams, maize, potatoes of many kinds, cassava, groundnuts, tomatoes. All are American; all are immensely more productive under cultivation than the indigenous grains and roots that were there before. Even earlier, Arab and Indian traders had brought in from Asia plantains and bananas – which may have arrived as early as the eleventh century – and more recently rice. The Arabs had brought marijuana, the Europeans tobacco.

These new crops had spread by gradual diffusion to regions where no Portuguese or Arab had ever visited. They made possible the development of farming settlements on a scale quite new to Africa. Surplus crops could be stored through the long dry months, releasing labour from year-round drudgery on the land, for trade, for arts and crafts, and for war. The Africans were working out their own development. The result was an amazing diversity of peoples, often living side by side, or actively competing for land. On the high plains there were pastoralists, wandering and living with the herds of cattle that moved with them. In the low lands, wherever there was year-round water, the tsetse flies were fatal for cattle; but there the new crops made real farming possible. Trade was developing in many products found only in specific places: salt, copper, iron.

The most complex of these emerging tropical cultures had grown up in the lakeland country to the north of Lake Victoria. Plantains grew luxuriously in the wet valleys. Fish were plentiful. Pastoral people had migrated down with their cattle from the north, to mingle with the farmers. On that wealth of food and human talent the civilisation of Buganda had grown steadily richer and more complex, without any significant contact with non-Africans.

To the south of Lake Victoria the people called the Wanyamwesi had recently become powerful for quite different reasons. They lived on the plateau country across which all Arab trading caravans had to pass on their way to the great lakes of Victoria and Tanganyika. Their staple crop was maize, which is easily stored and ground, and can be conveniently carried and cooked by travellers. The Arabs, rather than enslaving the Wanyamwesi, employed them as porters; in time, the porterage teams were given guns and enlisted as guards and escorts for the caravans.

Once armed, the Wanyamwesi developed a certain independence of the Arabs. They were regularly paid for their work. They charged agreed prices for the food they supplied to passing caravans. They began to levy passage dues – known as *hongo* – on travellers through their territory. In 1871, when Stanley passed through, he found the Wanyamwesi in a state of war with the forces of the Sultan of Zanzibar, who was trying to enforce free passage for his officials. The supreme chief of the Wanyamwesi, Mirambo, was insisting on his people's sovereign rights, and he had a real army with muskets and spears to back him up. Stanley, with unusual prudence, refused to take sides in the fighting: he hoisted the Stars and Stripes at the head of his caravan, and took refuge in the nearest town. Mirambo carried on his resistance for six or seven more years, winning recognition as an independent ruler.

The Baganda were the target of the Christian drive into East Africa. The Wanyamwesi were indispensable to anyone wanting to travel in the region. With both these peoples Charles Stokes, as soon as he arrived in Zanzibar in 1878, formed instant and lasting alliances. It was his African alliances that gave him the exceptional position he retained for seventeen years, until his death.

Chapter 2

The Race for Buganda

The reverend ministers ... practised the superstitious cere-
monies of a religion as bad or worse than Islamism.

Monsignor Hirth, Vicar-Apostolic of the Nyanza, of his
Anglican rivals (1890)

Casting aside the maundering cant which labours to main-
tain that Rome is a portion of genuine Christianity, she
should be recognised in her true aspect as its avowed and
persistent antagonist.

Report by the CMS on the activities of the Roman
Catholic priests in Buganda (1882)

Charles Stokes set foot in Zanzibar with poor Streeter's
orphan children in his charge almost two years after the
arrival of the first missionary pioneers. In that time, for all
their prayers and their devoted efforts, the evangelists had
made no significant progress towards the interior. Even the
task of establishing a base seemed beyond them. The
clergymen of the mission had welcomed the task of saving
souls, and faced with courage the prospect of martyrdom.
But they were quite unfitted for the practical work upon
which their spiritual endeavours were to be founded. They
wrote home, to the bafflement of their organising committee, for books on carpentry and brickmaking and how to
operate a forge, and for extra copies of Paley's *Evidences of
Christianity* to replace those lost, or torn by careless servants, or eaten by termites.

Nothing worked as planned. The loss of men was dis-
heartening: no sooner did a much-needed specialist crafts-

man arrive from home than he went down with fever and had to be shipped back. Machinery did not work either. The mission had bought a small steam-launch, the *Daisy*, planning eventually to take her apart and have her carried up by porters to sail on Lake Victoria. Meanwhile she was set to work ferrying people and goods between Zanzibar island and the mainland. Her high boiler made her unstable, and she constantly went aground on the filthy mudbanks of the harbour. 'Stinkibar', the old hands called the over-crowded town: the windless streets were crammed with vile odours.

William Mackinnon, the Glasgow millionaire, had do-nated a larger yacht, a steamer with auxiliary sail, for longer journeys up and down the coast in quest of the best route for the interior. The *Highland Lassie* burned a ton of coal a day, costing $17, or £3 8s., which the mission had no funds to buy. The Reverend E. A. Praeger welcomed the resignation of her first skipper, Mr R. J. Canham: 'Every-thing on board is in a fearfully dirty and deplorable condi-tion – plainly betokening that it is a heathen concern. I sincerely trust that for the future it will be commanded by a true Xtian, who will doubtless then engage a Christian crew.'

But there were no Christians for hire in Africa. Such men as could be trained as craftsmen and foremen were Mus-lims, and obstinately persisted in their error despite the proofs of Paley's *Evidences*. The missionaries did indeed have several hundred nominal Christians in their care, liv-ing in the settlement of Frere Town, on the mainland coast opposite Zanzibar. They were ex-slaves, some freed from slave-dhows bound for Arabia, some bought from their Zanzibari owners. Consul Kirk deplored the practice of purchasing people's freedom, pointing out that the pros-perity of slave-owners was guaranteed if there was always a Christian customer ready to buy their chattels. He also stated that some slaves, having been bought into freedom, promptly absconded back to slavery and pleaded to be bought once more – sharing, meanwhile, the purchase money with their former owners. Be that as it may, once free and living on mission rations, the new freedmen pre-ferred leisure to hard work.

An élite group of ex-slaves was meant to be the mainstay of the mission labour-force. They had been liberated as children on the high seas, by Royal Navy patrols. They could not be sent back to their far-off homes in the bush, so the CMS had established a refuge for them at Nasik, near Bombay, across the Indian Ocean. There they were taught the essentials of Christian behaviour and the skill to read the Bible. Now it seemed right to put them to work in the service of their fellow-Africans.

The Nasik boys were a disaster. Having been taught to read, they classed themselves as clerks. In India, clerks were debarred by the rules of caste from manual work. The Nasik girls would not even wash clothes, leaving that duty to an Indian *dhobi-wallah* whose caste-bound destiny was to do nothing but laundry. The freed slaves were as incapable of looking after themselves as were their superiors, English clergymen brought up in households full of servants. Mr Streeter, the widower, was made superintendent of Frere Town, and described the Nasik people as a disgrace. He thrashed five or six of the men and women, 'after all other means had failed'. Reporting to his supervising committee in London the missionary chose his words with tact. But it is obvious that the problem was sex.

One of the most promising of the Nasik pupils was one Moses Willing, a clever lad and (as his name may indicate) an ingratiating one. He did so well at his studies that, when installed at Frere Town, he was made a teacher at the mission school there, and then (all available Europeans being sick or absent) promoted to the headship of the school. In March 1880, Mr Streeter reported on the fate of Mr Willing: 'For some time past it was known that he was leading an immoral life, and was kindly remonstrated with, but to no effect, until being caught in the act he was brought up in front of [the superintendent] and punished as he deserved.' After his flogging Mr Willing swore that he was repentant, and Mr Streeter confirmed that he had been a very good teacher. But he did not get his job back. Instead he took employment where his sexual morals would not be called in question, and where his skill in keeping records and accounts would earn good money. He became, and remained until 1895, a confidential clerk in the service of Charles Stokes, transport contractor.

Charles Stokes's first assignment for the mission in Zanzibar was to make progress towards the far interior, with the supplies and trade goods indispensable for the expedition to convert the Kabaka Mutesa of Buganda. Stokes and his companion William Penrose, a builder by trade, were charged with the management of a caravan of porters, whose loads had been obtained by the CMS's commercial agent in Zanzibar, the firm of Smith Mackenzie. Its local partner, E. N. Mackenzie, had indeed bought the necessary goods – bolts of bright Bombay and Massachusetts cloth (*merikani*, American cloth, they called it in Swahili), coils of brass and copper wire, boxes of brilliant Venetian glass beads in assorted colours, specially ordered through Messrs Levin and Co. of Bevis Marks near the old synagogue in the City of London.

Organising the porters was another matter. Mackenzie was used to supplying goods to Arab traders, who themselves ran caravans to the interior. Now he was trying to act as a caravan operator himself, employing an Arab contractor to get the necessary men together. The contractor was idle, and most of the usual porterage teams were already employed. Stokes had to use his own initiative to recruit a team. No European had tackled such a job before.

The first requisite was luck, and Stokes had it. The Kabaka of Buganda had sent down a dozen men to act as guides to his inland kingdom: at least one of them was a court official, empowered to act to some extent on behalf of the king. Stokes got on well with them, and asked their help. They put him in touch with the Wanyamwesi team that had carried their baggage to the coast – including, no doubt, ivory to pay their expenses. The men were anxious to get home, and to be paid for it, so Stokes had no problem hiring them. Only 300 men were available, too few to transport the large quantity of goods the mission would need inland, so Penrose stayed behind, to bring up the rest of the stuff as soon as more porters could be hired. By mid-July

1878, only two months after his first arrival in Zanzibar, Stokes was on the way.

Caravan work was hard and weary, trudging under the sun across the plain that stretched endlessly ahead into the heat-haze. Most Europeans in those early days privately laughed at Africans, and publicly bullied them. Stokes did neither. He did not pay his porters above the going rate, nor did he hobnob with them except when he was drunk. He could not even talk to them much: three years after his arrival in Africa a missionary colleague noted that even his Swahili – the easiest of languages – was sketchy, and pronounced with a powerful Irish accent. But he hated the routine of discipline, enforced by flogging, that was the usual caravan regime. Charm, a natural resistance to fever, and a degree of prudence bordering on cowardice, were the secrets of his survival. Better men walked into trouble, while Stokes walked around it.

The plan was for his caravan, followed by Penrose's, to meet up with the leader of the mission's advance guard, the fanatical Scot Alexander Mackay, at Mpwapwa in the highlands of Unyamwesi. Mackay, who had arrived in Africa in May 1876, liked to think of himself as careful and calculating: he wrote home claiming for himself the German qualities of '*Vorsicht, Probiren, Muth*', which he translated as foresight, experiment, courage. His first attempt on the interior had been in July 1876, when a severe attack of fever forced him to turn back. He convalesced aboard the filthy steam-yacht *Highland Lassie*, then headed inland again in May 1877, trying forlornly to build a road. The attempt was useless.

The caravan route was a narrow strip of bare earth, kept free of thorns and undergrowth simply by the pressure of passing feet. Tidy-minded Europeans found the paths infuriating: they twisted round quite small bushes, curled up watercourses to a crossing-point and down the opposite bank to start again on the other side. The overnight halting places were badly sited, right beside the drinking-pools, which were therefore foul with human waste. It seemed only reasonable to hack away obstructions, build bridges, straighten the path and establish well-chosen camp-sites.

Mackay could not see why, with a bit of widening, the track could not be made suitable at least for wheeled hand-carts, maybe eventually for bullock-wagons.

As soon as the rains came the watercourses rose and swept away Mackay's improvised bridges. Bushes, hacked down, sprang up again in spiny brambles. There were no draft animals, no wheelwrights to fix a broken cart, no carts, no suitable timber to make one of. But the time lost on the roadworks saved Mackay's life. He was still well behind the advance guard, led by the mission's best men, when they reached Lake Victoria and hired canoes for the trip north to Buganda. Lieutenant Shergold Smith and the Reverend Thomas O'Neill landed from their canoes on Ukerewe island in the lake. They did not know that six years previously H. M. Stanley had landed here, had a row with the island's chief, and ordered an indiscriminate slaughter of the inhabitants. This time the natives, seeing white men arrive, prudently attacked first. Both Smith and O'Neill died of their wounds.

By the early months of 1878, when Stokes was landing at Zanzibar, Mackay had established an inland base-camp at Mpwapwa. It was a fairly healthy site in the hills, where a cool breeze blew in the evenings, but it was well off the established Arab trade-route to Lake Victoria, and this was deliberate. Mackay was in deep trouble, with a warrant from the Sultan out for his arrest. The problem had arisen from his zeal to put down the slave trade. Whenever he heard of an Arab caravan travelling in his vicinity, he would inquire whether it included any slaves. The answer was almost always yes: domestic slavery was, after all, still lawful in the Sultan's domains, with the agreement of the British consul. But Mackay would not tolerate it, and made a practice of attacking anyone he had reason to believe was a slave-holder. In one such fracas he and his missionary colleagues were seen to fire a shotgun at the leaders of a caravan, influential Zanzibar merchants on what was by their own standards legitimate business. The injured men reached the coast and complained to the Sultan of the unprovoked outrage. The ruler, as he could hardly fail to do, issued a warrant for the arrest and questioning of Mackay on a charge of assault. The outcome under the Zanzibari system of conciliation would doubtless have been nothing much more than a reprimand and an order to pay compensation; but Mackay refused to answer the summons, staying out of reach of the Sultan's soldiers and sleeping, melodramatically, with his Colt revolver always under his pillow.

Consul Kirk, the Sultan's official British 'adviser', was in a real difficulty. Faced with the refusal of the missionary to obey the law of the land, he issued a formal letter disclaiming all connection between the mission and the British government. This letter was addressed to the Sultan's governor at the principal inland town of Tabora, to the quasi-independent 'Sultan' Mirambo of Unyamwesi, and to the Kabaka of Buganda, the target of the missionaries' zeal.

Holed up inland, Mackay had saved his own skin at the price of the mission's good relations with the men upon whom its progress most depended. The first casualty of his rash behaviour was William Penrose, bringing up the goods left behind from Stokes's first small caravan. It had taken Penrose four months to collect the porters he needed. Unable to recruit the necessary armed escort, he started on his long march in company with an Arab caravan. On the way from the coast the party had to pass through land occupied by the Wagogo people, wandering cattle-owners well known for their propensity to fight. The Wagogo demanded *hongo*, or passage-money, from the passers-by; as usual, there was a dispute over the amount. The Arabs made off sharply into the bush, leaving Penrose and his undefended party to face the Wagogo. Penrose was killed. According to the survivors of his party, the Arabs and the Wagogo then settled the question of *hongo* by sharing between them the goods Penrose's people had been carrying.

Stokes, unlike either Mackay or Penrose, got through and kept the peace. He too was asked by the Wagogo for excessive *hongo*. He argued, bargained, then paid up quietly. On another occasion one of his porters wandered off to buy food on his own account, and took the opportunity to molest a local woman. The villagers attacked him and left him quite badly hurt. Stokes's men got ready to avenge their

wounded comrade; Stokes produced his revolver and
threatened to shoot the first man who moved. The village
chief was summoned, and came to see Stokes with his followers standing menacingly in the background. Stokes
shouted at the chief, blamed his people for the incident,
and threatened to have him flogged. But shouting was as far
as it went. The honour of the caravan was preserved,
further bloodshed was prevented, and the mission's goods
got through. Thus Stokes began to show the skill in compromise that African travel demanded.

The first stage of the journey took just over a month,
marching ten miles a day out of the scorching coastal plain
into the foothills at Mpwapwa. The impetuous Mackay had
decided not to wait for his supplies, and had moved on up
country. Stokes was greeted by his shipboard companion,
Alfred Copplestone, and the two men combined to pursue
their journey in the wake of Mackay. The usual route on-
ward led to the provincial capital of Tabora. But the Christians could not go there. The new governor, Abdullah bin
Nasib, was a stout defender of the Sultan's interests, and
had received both the Sultan's order for the arrest of
Mackay and Consul Kirk's letter disclaiming a British interest in the protection of the missionaries.

The alternative was to seek help from a well-known ally
of the Europeans. In the previous year, Said bin Salim had
been dismissed by the Sultan from his post as governor of
Tabora, probably because of his excessive friendliness to
the missionaries. The old man had been employed by the
very first European visitors to the region, the explorers Bur-
ton and Speke, in 1862, and from them had acquired a taste
for white men's company and white men's drink. Said had
gone into retirement in the village of Uyui, a couple of
days' march north-east of Tabora, and to that place Stokes
and Copplestone headed.

At Uyui they established a depot for their goods and built
a small thatched house: for years it was to be the nearest
thing Stokes had to a home. But for now the two missionaries had no idea how to proceed. Their objective was to
move up to the shores of Lake Victoria, hire some of the
big long-range canoes suitable for moving goods over the

lake to Buganda, and there make contact with Mackay.
They knew their predecessors Shergold Smith and O'Neill
had tried to do the same, and been killed on the lakeside.
And they had no notion where Mackay had got to. There
were no messages from him, either because his messengers
had been intercepted, or because he had sent none for fear
that the Sultan's officers would intercept them and thus
track him down. Anyway there was tension between the
Zanzibaris in the mission caravan and the local Wanyamwesi people. The porters hired at the coast had completed their contracts, and went off home. There were no
replacements available in the area.

For five months the two men hung around Uyui, waiting
for news from Mackay, working on their house, shooting
game and getting to know the local people, with whom
Stokes in his usual careless way established excellent relations. It was January 1879 before Stokes and Copplestone
set off together for the lakeside, to cross if possible into
Buganda. They took fewer than sixty porters on the
month-long march to the lake, which they joined at the tiny
harbour of Kagei, where Arab traders into Buganda usually
hired their canoes. There they had a bitter shock. In Kagei
village they encountered three strange, deeply sunburnt
men, dressed in cool, white robes like those of the Arabs.
They were White Fathers, French priests of the Society of
Missionaries of Algiers, the militant order whose aim was
to save the people of Buganda from the poison of Protestant
false doctrine. Their leader, Father Livinhac, explained that
two other White Fathers had already crossed the lake, hot
on the heels of Mackay.

This was desperate news. First, the Roman Catholics had
beaten the Protestant missionaries to Kagei, and so had
prior call on such long-range canoes as might be available.
Second, Mackay and the party carrying his supplies now
had a quite unexpected sort of opposition to face. There
was nothing for it but to wait until Mackay got a message
through and canoes became available.

Stokes was not as upset as he no doubt should have been.
He had no particular objection to Catholic priests as long
as they were good fellows, and the White Fathers were

no-nonsense, practical men. He managed to hire some small canoes, and explored the nearby coastline and islands. In particular he went over to Ukerewe island, where Smith and O'Neill had met their deaths. Tactfully approached, Chief Lukonge proved to be reasonable enough: he and Stokes became quite friendly, and the chief helped to find the remains of the dead missionaries. Stokes was eventually able to reclaim their bodies and give them Christian burial at Kagei, along with John Smith, dead of the fever there in May 1877.

Alexander Mackay was already in Buganda, learning something of that nation's proudly independent life. He had dreamed of arriving as a spiritual master. Instead he came as a suppliant, to live on the charity of the Kabaka. On arrival at Kagei in June 1878, he had found a large cache of stores carried up in the caravan of Shergold Smith and O'Neill. Nothing had been stolen, but everything was in disarray; in particular, the engine of the little steamer *Daisy* was all in bits, with rats' dung in the pressure gauge and books in the boiler. The boat herself was lying out of the water, assembled by Lieutenant Smith and in theory awaiting the arrival of Mackay, the engineer, for the installation of her motive power. Unfortunately the time spent in the open had sprung her planks apart, and the white ants had attacked them. There was no question of fitting the rusty engine. Eventually she was patched together, rigged up with makeshift sails, and put to use. But the swift and reliable transport the missionaries had expected to rely upon was not available on Lake Victoria for many years to come.

Lake Victoria was a far more formidable obstacle than anyone had expected in Europe. A stiff south-east wind blows regularly across the water, raising a fierce chop. The shores are mostly shelving, lined with great reed-beds that make landing impossible – and where there are steep-sided inlets there are usually rocks beneath the water, making sailing risky. All around the available landing-places such trees as there may once have been had been chopped down to make canoes, or huts, or to burn as fuel in cooking-fires. If efficient boats were to be placed on the lake, timber would have to be carried up from the coast. The idea of using a steamer was quite impractical, since wood for fuel was not available. (The present groves of eucalyptus, and the shady mango-trees on the tributary streams, are of course the result of planting by European or Arab settlers: the lake shore had much less wood before the days of colonisation.)

So it was in hired canoes that Mackay at last made the journey of 250 miles across the great lake to Buganda, where he stepped ashore in November 1878. There he was at once taken to meet the Kabaka Mutesa, whose intelligence and curiosity were at once aroused by the missionary's mechanical skills. His Christian faith was another matter.

The Kabaka had long been attracted by Islam, seeing that the teachers of that faith possessed access to books and to practical skills that were beyond his own people's experience. Quite possibly Mutesa would have accepted conversion by those teachers, but for one absolute obstacle. Conversion to Islam involves circumcision. The operation would have kept the Kabaka away from his wives (he had about 700 at this time) for several weeks. Moreover, his traditional advisers – and Buganda was, in its way, a constitutional monarchy, where power depended on the assent of the ruling barons – forcefully reminded their king that a Kabaka had to be physically perfect. Deliberate mutilation of a part of the body employed in securing the succession to the throne might, they said, disqualify the patient for kingship.

Mutesa had long and anxious conversations both with the Muslim teachers and with his councillors to see if there was a way out of the problem. None was found, and he remained formally unconverted to Islam. So the details of conversion to Christianity were eagerly examined, to see if there was a snag hidden there too. Mutesa became something of a theologian, asking awkward questions about the nature of the Trinity ('But if there is one God, how can there also be three?'), and generally taxing the wit of his would-be spiritual guides.

Mutesa was, frankly, more interested in Mackay's guns and machines, including the printing press the missionary quickly set up to produce samples of devout literature –

first in Swahili, then, as soon as he learned the new language, in Luganda. This very much irritated Mackay's companion and nominal superior, the Reverend C. T. Wilson. He saw no point in Mackay's long talks about technology with the Kabaka, and appears to have decided quite early on that missionary efforts would be better directed at the simple pagans of other tribes rather than at the subtle Mutesa, who saw Christianity mainly as a means to increase his own material power.

The politics of the conversion of the Buganda soon took on a new complexity, with the unexpected arrival of two fresh waves of missionaries. The first to join Wilson and Mackay were sent by their own organisation, the Church Missionary Society. They arrived in February 1879, not by the east coast of Africa at all, but up the Nile by courtesy of General Gordon Pasha, governor of the Sudan on behalf of the Khedive of Egypt. They were the Reverend C. W. Pearson, Dr R. W. Felkin and the Reverend G. Litchfield.

The CMS in London had grown impatient at the slow progress of the parties sent towards Buganda by way of Zanzibar. They did not know that Wilson and Mackay had got through to their destination – but they were aware that the Zanzibar base was a whirlpool of intrigue, and that Mackay himself was wanted by the Zanzibari police. The new party, which had travelled by way of Suakin, on the Red Sea, across the Sudan to the Nile, then up the river to Buganda, had been told that its orders superseded those of the east coast team led by Mackay.

Pearson carried, and delivered to Mutesa, a letter signed by the British Prime Minister, Lord Beaconsfield, assuring the Kabaka that these missionaries were genuinely under the protection of the Queen. (Mutesa was fascinated by the idea of this far-off Queen, wondering always whether, since she was so wise and powerful, she was also very fat.) Mackay, from whom Consul Kirk had specifically withdrawn protection, was furious. Mutesa observed the squabble, and understandably formed the view that one or other of the two Protestant missionary parties must be deceiving him: he, after all, had to rely upon their translations of letters that said quite different things.

But that was by no means all of it. Just three days after
the arrival of the Pearson party a small flotilla of canoes
arrived at the Buganda lake port of Entebbe, containing yet
another group of European Christian missionaries. These
were the first two White Fathers, Father Lourdel and Brother Amans. They were dressed as Arab merchants in long
white robes; they spoke no Swahili or other East African
language, but since their order was based on Algiers they
had some command of Arabic. Mutesa called them in and
interrogated them. He found to his astonishment that they
spoke no English, the only European language he had heard
of. They denied fervently that the Christianity they advo-
cated was the same religion the Protestants swore was the
one true faith.

To Mackay, who had gained the Kabaka's interest, if not
yet his confidence, the Catholics were creatures of evil, the
'cursed leaven of Rome'. Mutesa's interest in the three var-
ieties of monotheism now presented at his court – Islam,
and the two versions of Christianity – was dispassionate.
He was a monarch devoted to the unity of his people, and
he was determined that they should not be divided by the
introduction of rival alien faiths. His kingship was unequi-
vocally supported by his own people's traditional religion,
in which he himself, as the latest manifestation of the ancestral tradition of the Baganda, had a priestly, if not a
godlike, status. The king (according to Mackay) expressed
concern that by tolerating both Islam and Christianity in
his realm he would be contributing to its division. Mackay
replied that tolerating the presence of both Protestant and
Roman Catholic missionaries would divide it even more
gravely.

The rows between the missionaries became ever more
open, observed by the Kabaka with what (reading between
the lines of the rival missions' accounts) seems to have been
a certain amused contempt. Father Lourdel was invited to
say Mass before the court; Mackay stalked out, muttering.
The following Sunday, Mackay was invited to lead the
court in prayers, and afterwards reported that Lourdel
jumped up and exclaimed, in a mixture of bad Arabic, Swahili, Luganda and French, 'For hundreds of years they were

with us, but now they believe and teach only lies.' The priest's linguistic powers cannot have been as poor as Mackay made out, for the Scot records that the Kabaka solemnly translated his meaning to the court. Meanwhile the king infuriated both sorts of missionary by inviting them to explain in what their beliefs differed, then refusing to accept that the differences were meaningful: their quarrels helped to confirm him in his opinion of his own superiority.

Such was the climate of evangelism in which Charles Stokes arrived in Buganda, in April 1879. The missionary leaders – with Mackay the only exception – were tempted to believe they would do better to leave Buganda. But Mutesa was far too shrewd simply to let the white men move out. He suspected, rightly, that they would use their absence to prepare a new onslaught on his kingdom. Moreover, he liked the material things they brought with them. Mackay's technology was fascinating, and the French Fathers had brought toys of other kinds. They had presented some muskets, which did not greatly impress Mutesa, since he knew by now that rifles were better, and might be obtained if only he managed the Europeans craftily. The priests had also come prepared with the surplus stock of a Paris theatrical costumier: cheap but gaudy uniforms, fragile swords with fake jewels in the handles, mirrors and bright trinkets – the traditional gifts to chiefs on the West African coast. Mutesa was far too sophisticated to value them for himself, but if the Europeans could produce stuff like this, what more might he not get by patient long-term bargaining?

Stokes, with Copplestone, was the latest arrival in Buganda, and was rather well treated by the authorities. They took most of his trade goods as *hongo*, then allowed him to wander around the country, visiting in particular the source of the Nile at Ripon Falls, where the river charges in a cloud of spray out of Lake Victoria (a sight still thrilling, even now that the water races through the dam of a power-station). Among the missionaries he refused to take sides, remaining on speaking terms even with the ferocious Mackay, whom everyone else was now keeping clear of.

In June, Stokes managed to get permission to leave Buganda, travelling with Copplestone and Pearson. Felkin left about the same time by the Nile route. On his return Stokes wrote a report to the CMS, in which he revealed the subject of his conversations with Mutesa: 'Poor fellow, his only thought is to get guns and powder ... I pray God every effort to bring guns up country may be stopped.' Felkin gave this remark his own interpretation: he told the CMS that Stokes had got permission to leave by promising to send the Kabaka guns from his store at Uyui. If true – and it seems more than likely – this was Stokes's first step into the illicit arms trade that was to become his livelihood.

Quarrelling was not his style: he might blaze into a row, but soon all would be forgotten and his easy generosity came out again. This was amiable, but not always to his colleagues' advantage. His first act on getting back to Kagei was to lend the mission boat, the patched-up *Daisy* with her makeshift sails, to the rival White Fathers for a trip of exploration. The Fathers ran the boat on the rocks, and that was the end of her. The engine which would have made her the mission's lifeline remained useless ashore at Kagei.

Chapter 3

The Caravan Master

A manly and excellent fellow, strong in body and will, and
yet if that will not have its own way, he sulks and pouts and
can kick against all authority. He has a fine tenor voice and
is a great favourite in Zanzibar, but he is fickle and does not
know his own mind for one hour. He is mentally lazy, will
not learn kiSwahili or any other language, he has no missionary spirit, never will settle down in Buganda.

> The Reverend Philip O'Flaherty, reporting on Charles
> Stokes to the CMS (1880)

In eighteen months of African service Charles Stokes had
proved his worth. He had successfully led his caravan up
country, and won his way through to the ultimate destination of Buganda. Above all he had survived where so many
of his colleagues had died. But his moral qualities by no
means matched his physical achievements. He was not
particularly Christian, let alone sternly Protestant. He took
things easy. That was why he managed his African followers
so well.

For the rest, neither the men nor the equipment provided
out of the charity of England had stood up to the African
test. The fierce climate and the unfamiliar people had
soured the schemes of the devoted. Faced with their own
internal quarrels, the active rivalry of the French priests
and the indifference of the indigenous peoples, the tiny
group of Protestants began to lose heart. They embodied,
but could hardly have articulated, the absurdity of the
attempt to impose the standards of Victorian churchman-

ship in a continent whose material values and moral standards were so utterly alien.

Within Buganda, the CMS people had divided into factions – those who had arrived by way of Zanzibar, led by
Alexander Mackay, and those who had come up the Nile,
led by Robert Felkin. Each sent discreditable reports on the
other's conduct to the CMS headquarters in London.
Felkin and his party gained a notable advantage by setting
off home themselves. The Kabaka, curious as to whether
Britain was due the physical and moral authority its missionaries claimed, decided to send a party of court officials
with them, to see London for themselves. Felkin and the
Reverend Charles Wilson decided to return as they had
come, following the river down to Khartoum, and then
journeying east by the camel-route across the desert to the
Red Sea port of Suakin to take ship home by way of the
Suez Canal. They preferred this journey, even though the
Nile route was said to be threatened by a militant Muslim
movement, following one Muhammad Ahmad, who had declared himself to be the Mahdi with the divine mission to
purge the Sudan of all Turkish and Christian influence.

Stokes was on Mackay's side in the argument; moreover,
he wanted a trip home. He therefore suggested to the CMS
in London that he would make a far better guide for the
Baganda party than Felkin and Wilson possibly could, and
proposed to headquarters that he should go to Zanzibar,
there to await a telegram saying, simply, 'Come'. Then he
would take a boat up to Suakin, join Felkin, Wilson and
their charges, travel with them to Britain and escort the
Baganda on their visit before taking them back home via
Zanzibar. Since he spoke no Luganda at all, and precious
little even of the *lingua franca*, Swahili, this was a crazy
idea, even if the journey had been feasible, which it was
not. The CMS office in London simply disregarded his
letter. Felkin and Wilson reached home safely, without
Stokes's protection.

Mackay himself was virtually a hostage in Buganda. He
was short of almost everything he needed – trade goods, to
free himself from absolute dependence on the Kabaka's uncertain charity, and technical equipment with which to

carry on the practical work that he rightly believed to be the best instrument for winning the Kabaka's friendship, or at least toleration. Stokes was instructed to bring the necessary goods across the lake, from the large store of mission property stocked in the base-camp he and Copplestone had established at Uyui.

Stokes did nothing of the kind. Mackay was an awkward man to be allied with. The Zanzibari court summons against him had been lifted – thanks to some conciliatory work by Consul Kirk, the CMS had paid a forfeit of only $200 in order to have the case dropped – but Felkin's personal reports, after his arrival in London, were deeply disturbing. (Some thought them deeply malicious: it was Felkin, not Mackay, who resigned from the CMS in 1880.) Mackay was ordered home to explain himself. Either he ignored the instructions, or just possibly he never received them. He certainly believed that if he were to be withdrawn at this stage – and if the Kabaka allowed him to leave, a far more ticklish question – the Protestant cause would be lost for ever in the kingdom.

The safest place was on the sidelines, and that is where Charles Stokes stayed. He did nothing about transporting the goods Mackay had ordered for Buganda. Instead, with Copplestone, he repaired and extended the house and store at Uyui, and improved his relations with the Wanyamwesi people of the area. After a while he travelled down to Zanzibar; it is possible that he took advantage of the trip to do a little business in ivory from Buganda, but this is not clear. Then he took a sea trip along the coast to the old Arab port of Mombasa. There was not much else to do.

From time to time, perhaps to prove he was still a useful man, Stokes sent off a proposal to his chiefs in London. His notions were often eccentric; even when they were sound he couched them in terms that made their rejection certain. For example, he suggested the transport of a 'good strong boat' up to Lake Victoria, to replace the wrecked *Daisy*. Oak planks, although far heavier to carry and therefore requiring a far larger number of porters than those for a light, deal boat, would be resistant to termites and to rough usage by inexperienced African crews. Then he spoiled the whole thing by pointing out – once more, accurately enough – that the new boat would pay for itself 'by trading in Karagwe, Buganda and Kagei, as Arabs are settled in these places'. The good committee members in London were hardly likely to be attracted by the idea of profiting by trade with the very people they were determined to root out. But Stokes never let ideological objections stand in the way of a notion for making money.

He was also longing for female company. In November 1879, he wrote to the CMS asking leave to marry Miss Rachel Cochrane, of 'The Hollies', Moseley, Birmingham. The same letter assured the CMS that he firmly intended to stay in Africa, and asked for approval of his plan to make a permanent base at Uyui. There is no further reference in the correspondence to the young lady, other than the inevitable rejection of the marriage plan by the CMS.

Even if he was condemned to a bachelor life, Stokes was making himself comfortable. Early in 1880 a senior missionary, the Reverend J. W. Handford, wrote to the CMS committee seeking approval of his arrangement to rent for himself and his wife the upper floor of a spacious and airy house on the mainland coast opposite Zanzibar. The rent was a modest-sounding one rupee a day, and the landlord was Charles Stokes, who had himself rented the whole house from its Arab owner. It would seem that Stokes was making some money on his own account by now: at any rate he was living in some style, and there is no record that the CMS took him to task for exceeding his expense allowance.

The CMS, deeply concerned at the lack of progress in Buganda and the dissension among its people in East Africa, now decided to pull things together for one last try. The party of envoys from Buganda had completed their tour of Britain, and were now ready to return with an account of its wonders: Felkin remained their companion and guide for the journey home. Whatever he might have preferred, the journey by the Nile route was now no longer possible. The Mahdi's Islamic soldiers had begun the campaign that would defeat the Egyptian army under its British generals, and install their leader in Khartoum as head of the Muslim state of the Sudan. No unbeliever was permitted to pass through the country. (The route into Buganda from the north was to remain closed until 1898, when a vast British-led army, supplied by a purpose-built railway across the desert, at last defeated the army of the Mahdi's successors at the battle of Omdurman.)

So Felkin and the Baganda envoys arrived back in Africa by way of Zanzibar, in July 1880. Felkin had handed in his resignation to the CMS: he took the ship straight back to England as soon as he had delivered his charges. Stokes believed he would at that point take over, escorting the envoys back to Buganda and there presenting them to the Kabaka with their accounts of the wonders they had seen in Britain. This, surely, would establish Stokes once and for all as a friend and ally of the Kabaka, with all the power of England at his back. The opportunities for influence, and maybe for trade, would be almost unlimited.

But the CMS committee realised full well that the Buganda mission could not be entrusted to the same men who had hitherto made such a mess of it. They had appointed a senior and responsible clergyman to carry forward the work – the Reverend Philip O'Flaherty, a man in his mid-forties who had proved his worth on mission service in Turkey. The attempt to convert the Turks had been a failure, but O'Flaherty had shown himself a good organiser, had got on peaceably with the established authorities, and had learned fluent Arabic. Equally important, he had worked in Turkey alongside Roman Catholic missionaries, and had avoided direct rows with them. He, if anyone, seemed likely to be able to work out a reasonable relationship with the French Catholics in Buganda, as in fact he did.

Unfortunately, for Stokes, O'Flaherty was also an Irishman, and a sharp observer of humanity. He at once spotted and described in letters home the peculiar qualities and defects of his fellow-countryman: he respected Stokes's charm, but shrewdly identified his vanity and impulsiveness. Stokes had organised a small caravan of his Wanyamwesi allies to travel down to Zanzibar to meet the

returning Baganda and escort them promptly home. Not
until later did O'Flaherty report his suspicion that this
caravan had carried a cargo of ivory to the coast on Stokes's
personal account. But clearly he had taken the measure of
his subordinate at once.

Far from being the chief escort to the Baganda envoys,
Stokes now found himself under the firm authority of an
older and more prudent man. Once in Buganda, O'Flaherty
was to be head of the Protestant mission. Mackay was to go
to London to clear himself, if he could, of the charges
arising from his aggressive conduct, bolstered as they were
by Felkin's reports. Stokes was to be the baggage-master and
administrative officer of the mission, a subordinate role far
from what he had dreamed. Mackay was a loner, who could
have been relied on to leave Stokes to carry on his own
work in his own way – including work on his own account.
O'Flaherty was certain to be an energetic and understanding supervisor, exactly what Stokes did not want. The one
consolation was that the CMS gave Stokes leave to consolidate his base camp and depot at Uyui, where he could carry
on his personal life and trade free of intrusive supervision.

The journey up country was tiresome. The Buganda
party could not simply be ordered about by Stokes, the
caravan leader, because O'Flaherty was in charge, while the
great pile of stores brought by O'Flaherty from England –
many of the things desperately needed by Mackay, some
presents for the Kabaka, a stock of trade goods to enable
the mission to function without constant begging from the
Kabaka's court – could not be handled by the small team of
Wanyamwesi porters brought down by Stokes. Extra men
had to be recruited in Zanzibar market: they demanded
higher wages than the inland people, and did not willingly
follow the daily routine and discipline of caravan work.

It took three months to walk to Mpwapwa. There
O'Flaherty fell ill. Hardened as he was by years in the
Middle East, he was as vulnerable as any newcomer to the
sicknesses of Africa. Stokes took the opportunity of the
delay to conduct some private diplomacy of his own. A
series of dangerous incidents had lately taken place in Wanyamwesi territory: their supreme chief, Mirambo, long re-

cognised as the chief opponent of the Sultan of Zanzibar's authority in the interior, was now opposing the Europeans too. The Christians feared that he might be on the point of conversion to Islam. His demands for *hongo* from passing caravans had risen to embarrassing heights.

So Stokes went to visit the great chief, and reported to the CMS on their conversations. Mirambo, he said, was in truth friendly to European influence. The mission's men and goods were likely henceforth to be passing regularly through Wanyamwesi country; Stokes's own depot at Uyui was on their territory. He therefore proposed that he himself should organise a regular annual caravan to Buganda by way of Uyui, employing Wanyamwesi porters, by arrangement with their chief. It was a sound idea, but by no means a disinterested one. Stokes proposed that his annual salary for organising the caravan should be £300. O'Flaherty wrote a letter on the same subject, saying that Stokes's idea was worth considering, but that a fair rate for the job would be £120 a year.

Stokes was relieved when his stern superior recovered from his fever and became fit enough to be transported to Buganda. There O'Flaherty (who baptised the first five of Mackay's young pupils, on 18 March 1882) began to improve relations all round. To the surprise, and perhaps the disappointment, of Stokes, he even managed to get on with Mackay and, moreover, to strike up a sensible working relationship with the White Fathers. What he did not do, however, was establish any regular contact with the Kabaka and his ministers. If the CMS needed organisational neatness, O'Flaherty was the man to deliver it. But a neat organisation made no impression on the Africans who were the targets of the Christian endeavour.

The plan was that O'Flaherty and Mackay would remain in Buganda; the Reverend Charles Pearson, who had been Mackay's nominal superior up to now, would leave with Stokes and return to Zanzibar. He was very sick, and deeply demoralised by the almost total indifference to Christ that he had met with in Africa. Stokes was to stop at Uyui, join Copplestone, and run the supply line to Buganda. The one member of the mission's advance guard who still had faith that Buganda could be converted was Mackay, the fervent Scot. He took a dangerous route to conversion, for which many of his followers were soon to pay with martyrdom.

The Buganda regime was far less of an absolute monarchy than it had seemed to the first European visitors. As in a feudal kingdom in medieval Europe, the sovereign's authority depended very largely upon the consent of the provincial rulers who sat on the Kabaka's council, and whose relatives held the great offices of state – the general, the admiral, the master of the kitchens, and so forth. The province chiefs also sent to court the male children of their senior wives: the Europeans, using the analogy with medieval Europe, called them pages. Service in the capital qualified the boys for high office in later life; meanwhile they were in effect hostages for the good behaviour of their families at home. They were subject to the Kabaka's arbitrary will, and to that of the Queen Mother and the Kabaka's senior wives. Everyone ordered them about. If anything went wrong at home they might be killed at once. Their lives were wretched.

It was to them that Mackay had turned his main attention. They were, if they survived, the future ruling generation of the country. He taught them the catechism, encouraged them to read and write, and gave them the attention and respect they were denied by the established system. Inevitably, he also planted among them the seed of disrespect for their elders, and for the whole body of Buganda tradition which had sentenced them to a miserable youth. The Scotsman was saving the young men's souls but he was putting their lives in terrible danger. He knew perfectly well what he was about.

Stokes preferred to deal through established channels. During the week or two that he spent in the capital, the Kabaka called him in for a talk. There was great dissension in the court over the reports brought back by the emissaries to England. They described a culture so immeasurably strange and powerful that the *lukiko*, the Kabaka's council, was unable to digest their words. How could there be such a thing as a row of houses a mile long, with a stone wall higher than a dozen men stretching unbroken each side of it? That was the description given of a London street; the description of the Queen's soldiers, and their great guns, and the ships with their towering sails, was equally untranslatable into any words the Luganda language contained. Some councillors simply said the messengers had been bewitched; others that an alliance with so powerful a people could end only in the subjection of the Baganda; others again, including apparently the Kabaka himself, argued that there was no alternative to accepting the fact of English power, on the best terms that might be offered.

The Kabaka lost the argument: the *lukiko*'s debate lasted many weeks, and ended in deadlock, with no agreement to act in any way as a result of their emissaries' report. But Mutesa wished to behave courteously by sending a letter to his fellow sovereign Queen Victoria to express his thanks for the good reception his people had received in her realm. Stokes was to carry the letter, and it was for this that the Kabaka summoned him.

The king, impressed by what his messengers had reported, vaguely talked about sending one of his young princes to be educated in England. This seemed a suitable subject to mention in a letter to the Queen, who would, he supposed, take an interest in a prince from a friendly royal house. Stokes, ever practical, at once pointed out that it would be expensive to provide for a young man's travel and schooling so far away. He could arrange it, he suggested; payment made, through him, in ivory, would be satisfactory. The Kabaka changed the subject. This was not the sort of matter a king could discuss with a merchant.

Stokes was by now as much interested in his own business as in the mission's. O'Flaherty was later to accuse him of several specific misdemeanours, and the charges cannot simply be dismissed on the grounds of the clergyman's prejudice. The accusations were that Stokes drank too much, that he sold guns and powder to the Baganda, and that he had bought a 'concubine' for forty-eight yards of cloth (a stiff price – the one improbable point in O'Flaherty's report).

But Stokes's conscience – not a powerful organ – was clear. True, his caravan had made slow progress on its journey from the coast. True, a lot of the goods he should have delivered to Buganda were still in store south of Lake Victoria, at Uyui, suffering from rust and damp. True, his personal conduct was not what one would expect from a servant of the Lord. But he had got through, where other caravan leaders had failed, and if his costs were high, his results were good. They were obtained largely by imitating the methods of his Arab predecessors in the caravan trade. He had taken to wearing the long, cool, white robes of an Arab trader, so much healthier than the sturdy worsteds and flannels his British colleagues believed were a necessary protection from the sun – and from the general condition known as 'lowering standards'. It seems much more than likely that he behaved like an Arab in other ways, bartering guns or allowing his followers to barter theirs, and sleeping with native women if he had the chance. That was how things were done in Africa, and Stokes was becoming acclimatised.

Nevertheless, he got the job as regular caravan leader for the CMS; his salary seems to have been the £120 a year proposed by O'Flaherty, rather than the £300 he thought himself worth. He wrote to the CMS asking them to make a separate allowance direct to his old mother in Ireland, 'If you think I am worth an extra £50 a year'. The society did as asked, and on that the old lady survived for years, supporting her daughter too, in the genteel Dublin suburb of Sandymount. Like many wandering people, Stokes had a private vision of himself as a quiet family man. Just at this time came the chance to become one in reality.

The CMS were all too well aware of the sexual temptations that beset its young lay workers in Africa. Sleeping with black women was something the society could not condone, but realised it could not prohibit. As far as possible the senior clergy were married men, whose wives were expected to play a full part in mission life, running sewing classes and teaching domestic hygiene to the converts' women. They were also, as in England, expected to set an example of Christian virtue to the African faithful by steadily increasing their own families. But the mission's young recruits, lay and clergy alike, had left home before reaching marriageable age, and certainly before they had the resources to support a family. The mission's directors therefore decided to ship out some suitable young women, qualified as nurses on the new and relatively scientific lines pioneered by the great Florence Nightingale.

In February 1882, the first missionary nurses had arrived in Zanzibar. The pretty one was called Ellen Sherratt, of a respectable family in Shrewsbury. Charles Stokes, arriving fit and hearty from his long march to the coast, immediately fell for her, and his charm bowled her over. In June he wrote to inform the CMS of their engagement, asking at the same time for a 'run home' on completion of his next assignment. Ellen, for her part, gave a flattering account of Charles's qualities. 'He neither drinks nor smokes,' she assured her mother. 'He is quite a gentleman and has been educated for the Church, only he prefers to be more useful to the Mission as manager of nearly all the affairs out here, in fact he is head over all the money matters.' This, of course, was very far from true. But mothers do need persuading that their daughter's choice has been a prudent one, and men do make themselves out a bit grander than they are to impress pretty girls. Ellen stayed in Frere Town, the settlement for freed slaves, with her two female colleagues, both of whom shortly did what they had been sent out to do and announced their engagements to clergymen. Stokes, the lay worker who thought himself just as much a gentleman as his ordained superiors, had broken the rules again.

But he was indispensable. The task for which he left his new fiancée was intended to bring the Protestant drive for Buganda to fulfilment at last. Mackay had sent messages that the time was ripe, and in March 1882, just under five years after the arrival of the first missionaries, hundreds of young Baganda – or so Mackay reported – were eager to be received into the Anglican Church, and almost fully prepared for baptism. To meet the challenge, five ordained clergymen had been despatched from England. (Mackay, characteristically, made it clear that he thought the most valuable member of the party would be its one lay member, the 'artisan' Charles Wise, who might help him with his practical work.) It was Stokes's duty to escort this large party up to Lake Victoria, and then across the water to their destination in Buganda.

The trip was a disaster. The caravan had been assembled at short notice, and included three disparate elements. There were the usual reliable Wanyamwesi, Stokes's special men; some riff-raff recruited on the mainland coast, who had no caravan experience; and a few Zanzibari ex-slaves, whom the others despised. The Zanzibaris did their best to desert in the first few miles of the journey, taking with them both the advance pay meant to finance their living expenses on the way, and, if possible, their loads for resale back on the island.

This ill-assorted gang of porters had an exceptionally troublesome item to carry. The senior parson, James Hannington, a handsome man and a fine preacher, had given up a fashionable parish in the English resort town of Brighton for the missionary call, on the understanding that he would shortly become the first bishop of the new Anglican province of Buganda. His parishioners had subscribed to equip his team with a fine oak boat, just as Charles Stokes (and Mackay) had recommended. She was the sort of solid craft used for launching off the steep gravel beaches of the south of England, extremely sturdy and extremely heavy. Of course she was completely unscrewed and dismantled, but even so her large timbers could not possibly be reduced to the standard 30-kilogram parcels of a porter's head-load, and some sections had to be slung between two or more men. They hated this constraint on the usual relative freedom of each porter to make his own pace, and there were constant squabbles, for which Stokes seems to have had some sympathy.

The parsons were even more of a nuisance. The elegant Hannington, at thirty-four, was at least a man of some experience, if not of much physical endurance: fever wore him down, dysentery humiliated him. The other four were all just out of university, aged either twenty-three or twenty-four. They were wholly unfit for the rigours of tropical travel, and even if they had been able to speak an African language they would not have known how to manage their untrained servants, or to pick a suitable site for their tent

each night. They could not cook themselves – young gentlemen were never allowed into their servants' kitchens – so
were unable to supervise the preparation of their meals.
When the food appeared, half raw and revolting, they could
not eat it.

Stokes was far too busy managing his awkward caravan
to nurse the young gentlemen along – anyway, he despised
them. They in turn criticised his arrangements and thought
he was too hard on his men. The Reverend Robert Ashe,
a truly devout young man, complained in a letter that
Stokes had threatened to put one of his brethren in chains,
after an especially irritating piece of interference. Hannington, on the other hand, sent a glowing first report on Stokes:
'The men love him, his own boys seem devoted to him, and
everybody out here we have met speaks in the highest terms
of him.' Only later did he realise that Stokes, determined
to add interest to a dull sort of adventure, could be a less
than reassuring companion.

On one occasion, the villagers whose land they were passing through set fire to the grassland, either to delay or
maybe to attack the caravan. Stokes's men began to rush
aggressively around, and Hannington's pious biographer
attributes to Stokes himself these words (note the rendering
of a bog-Irish accent): 'Write it down in ye diaries, gintle-
min; me min have gone to burn the village and I can't stop
them.' Another time, Stokes faked an attack on the caravan
by *rugaruga*, or bandits, simply to create a bit of excitement
on a boring day. He said his men worked better if there was
something going on.

Meanwhile he was playing off one local chief against another, and finally got an exceptionally favourable trade
agreement from his ally Mirambo, of the Wanyamwesi,
allowing him to build his own depot and port at Msalala on
Lake Victoria. The disadvantage was that no other trader
used it, so the trading canoes from Buganda that regularly
plied for hire at the main Arab lake port of Kagei did not
usually trouble to call in there. At Msalala Stokes dumped
the new oaken boat, leaving her timbers scattered carelessly
around in the sun. It soon became evident that oak was not,
after all, immune to termites. But Stokes did not care. He

left as soon as he could, heartily glad to be rid of the snobbish and sickly English parsons.

Unwell and quarrelling, helpless without their much resented guide, they waited about for their transport to Buganda, the boats they expected from Mackay. But instead of transport Mackay sent strong advice that they should not come at all. The old Kabaka Mutesa was growing feeble, and his courtiers were preparing for a terrible struggle to choose his successor. Mackay was surviving on a knife-edge, bravely continuing with the conversion of the court pages, risking all the time the enmity of the court establishment. He considered the arrival of a strong party of inexperienced missionaries could only make things worse: any imprudence or excess of zeal by the newcomers would put in danger not only the Protestant mission, but also the toehold that had been established in the kingdom by the French Catholic priests. In face of mortal danger, the white men were hanging together.

Deeply disappointed, Hannington and his colleagues made their way back to Zanzibar, stringing along with an Arab caravan, which made them pay heavily for protection. Hannington held Stokes to blame for the debacle, and the rift between the two men had tragic consequences two years later. For now, Stokes could not care less. He was confident of his own abilities, which were clearly superior to those of the mission's more orthodox servants. Anyway, he intended to join up with Ellen again, for good.

Chapter 4

Love and Marriage

I hope by the time this reaches you the knot will be hopelessly tied.

Stokes to CMS, on his first, unauthorised, marriage
(December 1882)

My wife is at heart a faithful, respectable woman and an
example to those around. She is also a person of position in
her own part of the country.

Stokes to CMS, on his second marriage (February 1886)

The lovers in Zanzibar were not going to let anything stand
in the way of their happiness. Ellen wrote to her best friend
at home: 'I must tell you the arrangements for my wedding.
I am going to have quite a novel one. I shall have 12 little
black bridesmaids dressed in white native costume trimmed
with red ...' Charles had written to the CMS, to ask for
approval of the marriage. No answer came back, so he wrote
again to say the ceremony was going ahead whether they
approved or no. Next day he received the letter he was
hoping for, but with a most unwelcome message: he was to
cancel his wedding plans and spend the next six months
preparing to lead another caravan inland.

But nothing could stop them. Ellen even made a sentimental little cameo out of a passing tragedy. Mr Ramshaw,
a Methodist missionary, had joined the tiny European community in the town, with his pregnant wife. Mrs Ramshaw
gave birth, and died. Ellen wrote: 'She has left the tiny mite
to be brought up and nursed by a black woman and perhaps

they are going to let me take care of it and bring it to England to its grandmother, won't that be nice, Charlie says I shall!' Thus, unknowing, she foreshadowed her own child's fate.

The wedding of Charles Stokes and Ellen Sherratt took place on 13 January 1883, in the new cathedral, which was still being built, on the site of the former slave-market of Zanzibar. It was followed by a fine party. By April the newly-weds were sailing homeward, aboard the steamer *Simla*, of Mackinnon's British India line.

The Stokeses had no money, but they were happy. They went to Dublin to visit Charles's mother, brothers, sister and various cousins, all hard-up but sustained by their Irish Protestant status. It looks very much as though he was seeking a job but failed to find anything to suit. Despite his disregard of the CMS order not to marry, he had been careful to give them no pretext for sacking him, assuring the mission before he left Zanzibar that his presence was not immediately necessary, since a Hindu merchant – one of the *banyans* from Bombay, who were doing very good business in Zanzibar – could make arrangements for the next caravan, and that anyway his health required a trip home, 'much against my will'.

From Ireland he wrote again, insisting that 'I will not resign my post as caravan leader and agent for the interior until I see how the new agent in Zanzibar understands the difficulty of the store supply.' He assured the committee also that 'I will not involve them in any way with regard to my wife', thus waiving the customary allowance paid to mission wives. By November, after six months in Britain and Ireland, the couple were back again in Zanzibar, and promptly set off up country.

By February 1884, they were living at the little mission station at Kisokwe, in the heart of Unyamwesi. For Charles, life was full of interest. He arranged with Mackay to patch up the damaged timbers of Hannington's oak boat, and launched her as the *Eleanor*. He also did some business with the great chief Mirambo, who had won a battle against some wandering invaders from the south, and was opening up new trade routes for ivory, with high hopes of profit.

Ellen's life in the shared mission house, cooped up under thatch crawling with insects, was dreary, uncomfortable and, amid the permanent crowd of Africans who found everything strange about the lives of these mysterious visitors, wholly lacking in privacy. She did her duty, teaching women who barely owned one piece of cloth how to stitch two together. Just before her wedding Ellen had written to her bosom friend: 'I wish you could come and have a peep at us. All these dear little Blackies are looking in great astonishment at me writing a letter to England, but I have just given them a strict injunction that they are to do their writing and sums just as if I was looking at them.' Now that sweet fantasy was wearing thin. Ellen was expecting a baby.

It is impossible to tell, from the devout and formal letters that survive, whether the inevitability of what followed was as apparent to the actors as it is now to us, the retrospective observers. Of the three young women sent out together as missionary nurses, the other two had done as they were meant to do, and become engaged to clergymen. The CMS gave prompt agreement to their marriages. Equally promptly, the brides conceived. Mrs J.T. Last, at Mamboia, died in March 1883 of complications during pregnancy. Mrs H. Cole, at Kisokwe, died in July 1883, giving birth to a dead child, which was why the Stokeses were at Kisokwe mission, filling in while poor Cole sorted out his affairs.

On 19 March 1884 Ellen Stokes gave birth to a healthy girl. Exactly a week later Ellen died. There was nothing anyone could do. Dr Baxter, the mission's medical man, was away on leave in England to recuperate from his own fever, but the Reverend J.C. Price hurried over from Mpwapwa when news of Ellen's sickness reached him. He recorded that she died peacefully, with great trust in God. He could hardly have made any other report. Easy as it is to point out the follies of these people who went to Africa to bring the love of Jesus to the people, their resignation to their Saviour's will must remain a source of respect and wonder.

The motherless baby, Ellen Louisa, was christened on

Easter Sunday, 1884. Charles took her down to the coast and handed her into the care of the Reverend E. Shaw, who was leaving for home with his wife. That was the last he ever saw of his daughter. Baby Nellie was conveyed at the mission's expense to her grandmother, Mrs Walter Sherratt, in her home town of Shrewsbury. Stokes often spoke of the child at emotional moments, when he was drunk or writing home, but the only financial provision he made for her was in his heavily contested will.

So he went back to his employment. The committee-men of the CMS offered no favours to its bereaved servants: God's work must continue. But they changed Stokes's part in it, without any consultation. He was simply informed that the firm of Boustead and Ridley, merchants of Westminster and Zanzibar, were confirmed in their appointment as caravan agents and managers of business for the interior. The arrangement was logical enough; with one partner working in London and one in Africa, the firm could order its supplies direct from British sources and convey them all the way to their destination. But the way the job was taken away from Stokes was harsh.

When he protested, the CMS told him off for extravagance. He replied that others wasted much more, implying that Boustead and Ridley were among those to blame. Then the mission instructed him to take charge of one last caravan to his old base at Uyui, where he was to settle down. He did the trip and travelled on to the lake, where he met Mackay and the patched-up *Eleanor*, to deliver the goods for transport onwards to Buganda. Then he went back to Uyui, to look after the new resident man there, the Reverend Joseph Blackburn, who was constantly sick, and whose teaching duties were mainly being done by Stokes's clerk, the disgraced schoolmaster Moses Willing. Charles was desolate, longing for his dead wife and his departed daughter. He began a sentimental correspondence with Ellen's sister Polly, and sent flowers from the grave at Uyui as a keepsake for the little girl. For a while he dreamed of persuading Polly to fill the gap in his life; on 22 May 1885, he wrote suggesting that he should fix her up with a job with the CMS, so that she could bring Nellie out to Africa and

marry him there. It was a hopeless notion, and inevitably
came to nothing.

Mackay's position in Buganda was more dangerous than
ever. The old Kabaka Mutesa was evidently dying, and in
all the nations of Bantu Africa the succession to a great
chiefship was accompanied by killing. The deciding influence on which of the possible heirs should follow his father
was that of the Queen Mother, her choice made amid private rites and plottings. In Buganda it was clear that the
favourite of the old lady and her companions in the
women's house was Prince Mwanga, brought up under
their exclusive influence. His mother was, indeed, quite a
junior wife, and he was only just eighteen in 1884, when he
inherited the stool of sovereignty. The only men who had
meant much in his life were the Muslim teachers from
Egypt who had taught him to read and write in the Arabic
script. He would certainly have adopted Islam had his
female protectors not feared that circumcision would disqualify him from the physical integrity required of a Kabaka.

In October 1884 the old Kabaka Mutesa died, and
Mwanga succeeded him after the statutory period of
mourning. The missionaries feared, and affected to despise,
the elegant young man with his great wide eyes, showing in
his beauty the traces of his ancestry among the cattle-rear-
ing Hima people, who centuries before had migrated from
the north and combined with the settled Bantu of the lakeside to form the ruling house of Buganda. The parsons
vigorously accused him of homosexual conduct with his
pages, saying of course that he could have learned about
unnatural practices only through his association with Muslim teachers. In fact he seems to have had the bisexual
preferences that one might expect of a young man cosseted
by an exclusively female household. Political uncertainty
rather than sexual predilection – and no doubt the anxiety
of following his all-powerful and arbitrary father – seems to
have turned him into a tyrant with a propensity to have
people suddenly murdered.

But Mwanga was probably not responsible for the killing

that most sorely affected his country's destiny. Hannington,
the rash and stubborn clergyman whom Stokes had uncer-
emoniously dumped on the shore at Msalala with his flock
of young parsons and his oaken boat, was back in Africa.
After his initial failure to reach Buganda, he had travelled
home to be consecrated as Bishop of Buganda, for which he
had given up his comfortable Brighton vicarage. Stokes was
no longer in charge of caravans travelling from Zanzibar
towards the interior, so Hannington had to make his way
unescorted as far as Lake Victoria. But he could not safely
travel across the lake to arrive in his new see without an
introduction to its ruler, and Stokes was detailed off to meet
him on the lakeside and take him over the water.

Hannington missed the rendezvous: either his map was
inaccurate, or he failed to read it correctly, or he went to
another place of the same name. Stokes waited several
weeks for the bishop, then gave up to go back to his usual
business at Uyui. Hannington, when he did arrive, was furious at what he regarded as a further betrayal by Stokes, and
was determined not to be again frustrated in his intention
of reaching Buganda. He led his party determinedly up the
lake-shore, and attempted to cross the land frontier into
Buganda near the lake's north-eastern corner.

The bishop knew nothing about the country he was ar-
rogantly seeking to enter. He did not know that the old
Kabaka was dead, that the heir, Mwanga, was desperately
trying to snuff out the dissent over his succession among
his provincial barons - or that a prophecy had foretold that
Buganda would be overthrown by white men crossing the
land frontier to the east. At that frontier, the local chieftain
arrested the strangers. On 29 October 1885, without reference to the Kabaka, Bishop Hannington, his Portuguese
cook Pinto and forty-five African porters and guides were
brutally put to death.

The bishop was blinded by piety - and perhaps by ambition - to the realities of life in the continent where his
missionary calling lay. He had hoped for martyrdom, and
martyrdom was his reward, commemorated in many devo-
tional writings. His death was a calamity for Buganda, leading to a new outcry in Britain for military protection to be

extended to the missionaries of the Anglican church, and a
boon to the commercial imperialists who followed the cross.
Had he been a better navigator, or a more prudent traveller,
Hannington would have met Charles Stokes according to
plan, and the Irishman's well-informed advice could have
averted the tragedy.

Stokes, however, had other and more pressing concerns,
arising partly from his bereavement and partly from the
dynastic problem that had arisen at the south end of Lake
Victoria. In December 1884, two months after the death of
Kabaka Mutesa, the supreme chief of the Wanyamwesi also
died. Mirambo had been a great man, and had established
by his personal force the independence of his people. But
the Wanyamwesi had no great court to satisfy, and no ancient traditions to observe on the death of their leader; they
were a confederation of small tribes and villages, not a politically organised nation. Stokes had made many alliances
with junior chiefs within the confederacy: in particular, he
was on excellent terms with Mitinginya, Mirambo's son and
heir, who stepped smoothly into his father's place.

On 25 September 1885, eighteen months after the death
of his first wife, Stokes was married by the rites of the
Wanyamwesi people to Mitinginya's kinswoman, Limi. Her
exact relationship to the great chief is not clear: African
languages often do not make much distinction between
members of a close family. Either she was a daughter of the
old chief, Mirambo, by a junior wife, or she was Mirambo's
niece - either way, she was an honoured member of Mitinginya's household. The marriage was, no doubt, a business
transaction; African chieftains, like great men in Europe,
often gave their female relations in marriage to cement a
useful alliance, and the Arab traders of East Africa often
married chiefs' relations as junior wives. But Stokes was
not ashamed of his wife. She was a woman of good family,
and he wanted everyone to know that.

Stokes was already an undisciplined servant of the mission. Now he had really gone too far. That lay missionaries
slept with native women was well known, but mentioned as
rarely as possible. That such a relationship should be
proudly proclaimed was beyond the bounds of the accept-

able. Three days after the wedding – the hangover was given time to wear off – Stokes informed the CMS that it had taken place. He offered to resign, but asked to retain his duties as caravan organiser for the inland missions. The reply was a stern letter of dismissal: if he had really had to marry a native, wrote the officials in London, he should have chosen a baptised Christian woman from Zanzibar or Mombasa, not a heathen.

Stokes took the insult with dignity, answering in terms that can only have increased the fury of his employers. He knew a lot about native Christians, and did not like what he knew. His wife was respectable and well-connected. 'My marriage means your disfavour, but I trust not of God,' he insisted, and, aiming a shrewd blow at the men who sat in London offices while others toiled in the field, 'May you never pass through such temptations as I have done'.

The marriage of Charles and Limi Stokes was much more than a mere arrangement of convenience. She never bore him a child; but she took care as far as she was able of the children he was to have by other women. He never suggested abandoning her, or promoting any of his other women to equal status as a wife. When he came to launch his own sailing boat on Lake Victoria, as the foundation of his later prosperity, he paid his wife the compliment of naming the craft the *Limi*. After his death, it was Limi who led the scattered remnants of his caravan to safety.

It may seem curious that not one of the many Europeans who met Stokes and recorded picturesque anecdotes about him troubled to mention the wife who was his constant companion. Nor, for that matter, did they refer to his boat as anything but 'Stokes's yawl'. Limi was no doubt unobtrusive, keeping well in the background, and not fluent in English. If her appearance was typical of her Wanyamwesi fellow-countryfolk she was probably no great beauty – medium-brown, flat-faced, stocky. (The old lady claiming to be her, whose photograph, taken in 1950, appears between pages 192 and 193, fits the description well enough.) Yet it takes something else to explain the silence that covers her traces. Sir Harry Johnston, the great colonial adventurer and administrator, probably put his finger on the point in his own memoirs. Of the British pioneers he said: 'Their lapses from continence in Africa, if they occurred, were furtive.'

Then Charles Stokes broke the rules again, by making as much of a show of his marriage as he could. With the help of his new relations-in-law he organised a monster trading caravan of 1,000 porters and travelled down to Zanzibar. There, before the British vice-consul, he registered the marriage under his own country's laws – for Limi, understandably after her treatment by the CMS, refused baptism. One of the witnesses was Edward Muxworthy, who later became Stokes's business partner. The other was a far more important person – General Lloyd Mathews, the former Royal Navy lieutenant who had risen to become commander of the army of the Sultan of Zanzibar. Both Muxworthy and Mathews had long-standing and open relationships with local women (although they had not formalised them by marriage). They had, in the offensive phrase, 'gone native', thereby earning the contempt and ridicule of their fellow Europeans.

With the new chief of the main porterage clan as his family protector, and with the Sultan's military commander as witness to his marriage, Stokes was now in the best possible position to put into practice his intention of running the transport business out of Zanzibar into the interior. The Christian missions were important potential customers, since there was bound to be a regular flow of goods and parsons to be conveyed to the outposts of Christianity, whether in Buganda or outside it. The inland kingdom, though, was still more important.

Buganda was overflowing with ivory. Wild elephants were of course kept well away from the fertile banana groves and well-tended maize-fields of the Buganda heartland. But the Kabakas had for centuries levied ivory in tribute from their outlying provinces, and from the less powerful principalities in the wild country to the west. Their palaces and storehouses were packed with giant tusks, old and new. Arab traders had begun the export trade, but the stock was still largely intact, and had been constantly replenished under the astute and aggressive regime of Mutesa. The country could pay with ivory for imports, and was greedy for them. The traditional bark-cloth, of which the people made their elegant and flowing robes by beating flat the stringy bark of certain trees, is fragile and hard to stitch. Cotton cloth was eagerly snapped up, imported through Zanzibar from India and from the Englands, old and New. The people made beautiful ornaments of wood and brass, but preferred Venice glass beads. The king and all his barons, and the elephant hunters along the borders, would exchange almost anything for guns.

Stokes looked forward to a steadily expanding business, with full loads for the porters in both directions. The white men at the coast were cutting out the Arab traders, and Stokes might profit from their absence. His domestic life was now peaceful. In the heart of Africa he had no means of anticipating the upheaval of the continent being prepared by a group of people practically none of whom had ever been there, or cared a scrap about it – the delegates to the Berlin conference on the Congo and Niger river-basins, which convened in November 1884.

II

BUILDING
the
EMPIRES

Chapter 5

Berlin Rules

The Belgians do not exploit the world. They must be taught to acquire that taste.

King Leopold II of the Belgians (1863)

This whole colonies business is completely bogus, but we need it for the elections.

Otto, Prince von Bismarck, Chancellor of the German Empire (19 September 1884)

Terribly have I been puzzled and perplexed on finding a group of the soberest men among us to have concocted a scheme touching the mountain country behind Zanzibar with the unrememberable name.

William Gladstone, Prime Minister, on the proposal for British annexations in the Kilimanjaro region (14 December 1884)

On Saturday, 15 November 1884, punctually at two in the afternoon, in the great ballroom of the Imperial Chancellor's residence on the Wilhelmstrasse in Berlin, the world's most powerful statesman declared open a conference at which were represented all the nations that mattered in the world. On the wall behind Bismarck's back was hung a vast map of Africa. Accurate enough around the coastline and at its northern and southern extremities, it was vaguely hatched across the centre with putative lakes, rivers and mountain ranges.

Nobody present really knew what might be there, and nobody cared at all what the inhabitants thought. By the

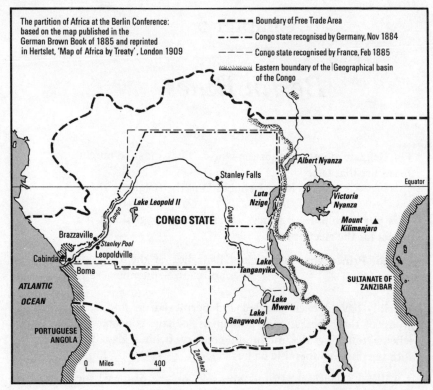

The partition of Africa at the Berlin Conference:
based on the map published in the
German Brown Book of 1885 and reprinted
in Hertslet, 'Map of Africa by Treaty', London 1909

▬ ▬ ▬ Boundary of Free Trade Area

▬ · ▬ · ▬ Congo state recognised by Germany, Nov 1884

▬ ▬ ▬ Congo state recognised by France, Feb 1885

▨▨▨▨▨ Eastern boundary of the Geographical basin of the Congo

Nile

Albert Nyanza

Stanley Falls

Equator

Luta Nzige

Victoria Nyanza

Lake Leopold II

CONGO STATE

Congo

Mount Kilimanjaro ▲

Brazzaville

Stanley Pool

Cabinda

Leopoldville

Boma

Lake Tanganyika

SULTANATE OF ZANZIBAR

ATLANTIC

OCEAN

Lake Mweru

Lake Bangweolo

PORTUGUESE ANGOLA

0   Miles   400

Zambezi

At the Berlin conference of 1884–5 the European powers intended to agree upon rules for sharing tropical Africa peaceably among themselves. On the west coast, French claims northwards of the Congo river, and Portuguese claims to southwards of it, were recognised. The vast unclaimed area between, along the Equator, was described as a Free Trade Area, open to European conquest. The Sultan of Zanzibar was overlord of most of it; his claims were acknowledged, but disregarded, along a ten-mile-wide strip of the east coast. The International Associ-ation of the Congo, a front organisation for King Leopold II of the Belgians, was allocated the entire Congo river basin. But nobody knew where the Congo basin ended. Delegates assumed that it included the lake Luta Nzige, which does not exist: its area is in reality (see Map 3, page 130) occupied by Lake Kivu, which drains to the Congo through Lake Tanganyika; and by Lake Edward, which drains through Lake Albert to the Nile. So the Berlin conference accidentally awarded King Leopold's Congo State a foothold on the source of the Nile.

end of the proceedings, on 26 February 1885, a heavy black line had been drawn around the uncharted area of darkness. Within that line the rules were sketched out for the conduct of capitalist enterprise, and for the recognition by the European powers of each others' claims to sovereignty. The scramble for African colonies was officially open.

The fourteen governments represented, from the United States to Russia, ruled an area considerably larger than that of the present-day Nato and Warsaw pacts combined. To decide the fate of black Africa, every single person present was white. (The delegation of the Ottoman Empire might have counted as brownish, but characteristically arrived late, having lingered *en route* from Constantinople at the smart German gambling resort of Baden-Baden.) Some of the states had claims, of varying antiquity, to existing African possessions and outposts: Britain, France, Portugal and Spain. Denmark and the Netherlands had only quite recently given up small African possessions, by sale to Britain. Germany and Italy were actively starting to make territorial claims. Others had vague historical or commercial links with Africa: Austria–Hungary, Russia, Sweden-and-Norway.

Belgium had a special interest in that its King was actively planning to become, in person, the largest of all African landlords. The United States had a tenuous relationship with Africa through its patronage of the puppet state of Liberia, But its delegation to the conference had much closer links to the continent. Its effective leader was the American diplomatic representative in Brussels, the smart 'General' Sanford of Florida, who was personally employed by King Leopold to further his commercial interests. The King also employed the American delegation's chief adviser, who in addition gave technical assistance to the British delegation. He was H. M. Stanley, who had the advantage over everybody else present of actually having been to the places under discussion.

The formal business of the conference was to ensure freedom of trade and navigation, along with the recognition of 'valid' European claims to colonies, on the two great and newly-mapped rivers Niger and Congo. Along their courses, as European penetration began, European rivalries had at once followed. At the mouth of the Congo, ancient Portuguese claims to sovereignty would, if respected by the other powers, have blocked all access to the river with customs posts and barriers to trade. On the Niger the French, having traced the upper waters, had found when they approached the river mouth that the British were already installed there.

Wherever European travellers and traders had entered, they tried to exclude travellers and traders from other European nations. There was a real danger that these rivalries in Africa would cause antagonism, even war, among the European powers. Already in Egypt the contest to dominate the feeble regime of the Khedive – a sovereign nominally subject to Ottoman authority – had led to British, French, German and even Russian warships manoeuvring off the Nile delta against each other, as well as against the native people. Bismarck, the master of continental Europe since his country's victories over both France and Austria in the early 1870s, was determined to keep the European peace, which was proving so beneficial to German trade and German power.

In 1876, as H. M. Stanley had correctly observed, 'there was not a single white man in possession of any portion of the equatorial belt [of Africa], except at the mouth of the Congo where a few traders had gathered'. But the missionaries, the doses of quinine and the breech-loading rifles were at work, and Stanley himself had completed his miraculous 999-day journey across the continent in 1877. By 1896, the American puppet state of Liberia and the mountain fastness of Ethiopia, from which the Italians had been driven back, were the only parts of the continent to retain even a nominal independence.

Tropical Africa was only a small and unprofitable part of the world scene upon which the manufacturers and traders of late Victorian capitalism were seeking new supplies of raw materials and new customers for their rising production. The French and British were moving in on south-east Asia. China seemed a promising field for exploitation. In the Americas and the Pacific the last bits were falling off

the old Spanish colonial empire; the Americans had
grabbed Texas, lined up Cuba and the Philippines for conquest, and were eying Mexico. On Africa's Mediterranean
coast, Egypt, with command of the new route to the Indies
through the Suez Canal, was the scene of European competition which left the French free to get their hands on the
Maghreb further to the west. In southern Africa, prospec-
tors were discovering undreamed-of riches in gold and diamonds, and Britain's ambitions were threatened by the
descendants of the prior settlers from Holland. Stretching
up towards the Equator on both coasts of Africa were the
weak fragments of Portugal's long-established empire,
which seemed to be following Spain's into oblivion.

Everywhere, the traders of the industrial powers were
seeking to do business, meeting competition from their rivals, and turning to their home governments to support
their right to fleece the natives. The two greatest industrial
powers were governed by people who had done their best
not to get involved in these matters of trade. The British
and German governments were both led by members of the
old land-owning class. The Marquis of Salisbury controlled
British foreign policy from 1878 to 1892, and again from
1895 to 1902; he frankly despised the rising tide of democracy, and the grubby tradespeople who were acquiring
votes as the franchise widened. Bismarck, who came to
power in Prussia in 1862, and ruled the new Germany until
1890, was if anything even more of a country gentleman in
his attitudes. He supported colonial ventures only in order
to placate the German merchant class whose new prosperity
was based upon his own political achievements, and found
it distasteful that quarrels between coconut buyers in the
South Pacific threatened to upset the delicate balance of his
diplomacy with Britain, France and Russia.

Neither of these great gentlefolk acknowledged that the
common people had any right to determine their own destiny. Salisbury's government ruled the alien Irish as though
by divine right. Most of Bismarck's tenants spoke Polish.
It could not possibly have occurred to them that the African
continent, if subjected to the benefit of civilised rule, should
be divided up in accordance with the wishes of its peoples,

or with regard to their linguistic or tribal traditions.

The British, and to a lesser extent the Germans, believed in free trade. Being the most efficient industrial powers, they knew that in a straight fight for markets they would win. The bourgeois democracy of France had the much more straightforward notion that grabbing territory meant grabbing the exclusive right to trade there. France wanted colonies where tariff preferences in favour of French merchants would keep foreigners out. But equally the French wanted other people's colonies to have the lowest possible tariffs, so that the French could get in there if the opportunity offered.

In practical terms, at Berlin, the French wanted to be able to keep other countries' traders off the waters of the upper Niger – but to get access for their own traders to the Congo, which nobody yet controlled. Rather to their disappointment, the British and Germans at once agreed to free trade and equal access for all on both rivers. The main overt purpose of the conference was easily settled. The terms and conditions of the international agreement for free trade and navigation on the river Danube, established after the Congress of Vienna in 1815, were transcribed for use on the two great international waterways of tropical Africa. Granted, the results were absurd, with careful clauses covering wharves, tributary canals, ship repair establishments and such facilities as yet undreamed of – and for that matter still non-existent a century later – on the tropical rivers. Still, it was important to set a legal framework for settling any disagreements that might arise, and this was quickly and easily done.

But this was not what the conference was really about. The key chapter of the Berlin Act is its shortest, and specifies merely that any power acquiring possessions or protectorates on the African coast shall inform all the other signatories that it has done so. There is no mention of inland possessions, no specified method for resolving disputes where two powers might be claiming the same colony. On that brief statement was based a complex unwritten framework for the colonisation of all tropical Africa. The underlying concept was that of *Hinterland*, which in German means the territory in back of a coastal establishment: the word thus passed into English too. The presumption was that a colonial power had rights of occupation anywhere within the hinterland of the coastal places claimed under the Berlin rules, which rights would be acknowledged on three conditions. There must be a treaty with a local chief, handing over sovereignty to or claiming the protection of a European power (both were taken as meaning that the native chief renounced all rights to act on his own). There must be actual possession of the place – that is to say, the European power must have some of its citizens physically present. And there must be effective occupation, meaning that the Europeans had the power to stay even if the native people tried to expel them.

This was a fragile basis upon which to build a set of rival empires, and of course the process went ahead without much regard for matters of principle. Portugal in particular had ancient and valid claims to the sorts of coastal right that the Berlin Act specifically acknowledged. They were swept aside at the mouth of the river Congo; but the Portuguese got the coast and hinterland of Angola southwards of the river-mouth, plus a tiny coastal enclave to the north of it. (Angola was lucky: the Cabinda enclave is where its oil-fields are today.) The river-mouth itself was shared out between two new claimants. One was France, which did indeed have coastal claims, treaties with local chiefs, and the rest of the paraphernalia. But the biggest chunk of Congo land, the largest and potentially the richest imperial possession in all of tropical Africa, came under a regime that had no coastal claims, and was not even a recognised state signatory to the Berlin Act. The Independent Congo State, later the Congo Free State, is now the Republic of Zaire, the most deeply corrupt of all the states on the continent. It began in corruption. Its absolute master was King Leopold II of the Belgians. Since he could not get his parliament to approve the acquisition of a new colony, he himself became the sovereign of his new creation.

King Leopold II was an insecure and deeply unpleasant monarch, ruling a nation invented by the British in 1830 to

keep the French and Dutch apart, and inhabited half by
Frenchmen, half by Dutchmen. The 1830 constitution was
devised in order to keep the country weak: the King, in
particular, was given extraordinarily little power, and a
spare German uncle of Queen Victoria was found to fill
this unattractive post as Leopold I. His son was from his
youngest days presented with examples of the accidents
that could befall crowned heads.

Leopold II's mother was a daughter of the man who
became King Louis Philippe of France, and was summarily
kicked off his throne. Leopold II's younger sister was married off to Maximilian, a silly Habsburg prince from Austria
whom the French employed as Emperor of Mexico, and
who was executed for his pains. On inheriting the Belgian
throne, Leopold II was coolly told by Bismarck that Germany was thinking of splitting up his kingdom again. From
his early youth the King had kept an eye open for ways of
becoming more secure, more powerful and much richer
than he could be in Belgium itself. He had inherited a huge
pile of wealth from his father – but if he lost his throne he
would probably lose his fortune too, and life as an ex-King
looked no brighter then than it does now. Becoming King
of somewhere else did seem a possible solution.

Among the places Leopold at various times thought of
ruling were Crete, part of Texas, the Faeroe Islands, Gua-
temala and the Philippines. Reading Livingstone's travels
turned his mind to tropical Africa – and reading H. M.
Stanley's more exciting adventures made him think Stanley
was the man to get it for him. In 1876 Leopold organised
a grand international geographical conference in Brussels,
and on the basis of its findings set up a series of charitable
and Christian foundations for the exploration of Africa and
the 'protection' of Africans ('rather like the International
Committee of the Red Cross', said *The Times* of London,
in an article secretly commissioned by the King himself).

On 7 August 1877 Stanley emerged at the mouth of the
Congo after his spectacular and gallant 999-day journey
across Africa by way of that river. He travelled home to
England via Marseilles, and there was met by two emissaries of King Leopold, Baron Greindl of the royal household

and – a less likely servant of the monarch – the former
United States minister in Brussels, Henry Sanford. Stanley
was concerned lest an involvement with Leopold might en-
danger his hopes of advancement in Britain, and especially
of the knighthood that he correctly anticipated. But on his
return home he was encouraged to go to Brussels by two
great men, Leopold's main financial partners in his African
investments. One was the great Liberal cotton merchant
from Liverpool, James Hutton. The other was Sir William
Mackinnon, the British India steamship magnate, who was
at the same time contributing to the Anglican mission to
Buganda and bidding to take over from the Sultan the financial administration of Zanzibar. Flattered by Leopold's
attention, and assured of lots of money, Stanley in due
course visited Brussels and accepted service under the
King.

By August 1879, Stanley was back on the Congo in the
service, as he described it, of 'a small body of philanthrop-
ists of which the King of the Belgians is the head'. His own
discoveries had made it plain that commerce could not pass
the 300 miles of falls and rapids that lie between the navigable upper Congo and its tidal lower reaches. His job now
was to map out a possible line of rail past the rapids, and
to break a rough road for use meanwhile. The King wanted
him to rush ahead and ensure political control of the great
inland pool – called Stanley Pool, of course – at the head of
the rapids, above which the river runs clear for 1,000 miles
into the interior. But Stanley refused to make a race of it.
He knew the country and its dangers. He had fever. And
anyway he had come to regard this frightful stretch of country as his own.

But while Stanley declined to race, someone else was
rushing up on his flank. Count Giuseppe Savorgnan de
Brazza was an impoverished Italian gentleman serving in
the French navy. He realised the route up the lower Congo
valley was appallingly difficult, and decided instead to cut
across through the forest land to the north, and thus strike
the river at the Pool, where its navigable course begins. He
started from the tiny settlement called Libreville, in what
is now Gabon, where the French used to dump the slaves

liberated at sea from ships bound for the Americas. Travelling light, with only a couple of dozen black Senegalese marines and as many Gabonese porters, he made his way through the dense rain-forest, visited the Pool, and returned to the coast by way of the river valley. There he met Stanley, slowly surveying his way inland. Stanley gave Brazza a meal, but the two men barely talked: Stanley spoke poor French, and Brazza's thick Italian accent made him very hard to understand.

When Stanley at last worked his way up to the Pool, on 27 July 1881, he was met by a surprising sight. 'We saw ... a French tricoloured flag approaching, preceded by a dashing-looking Europeanised negro (as I supposed him to be, though he had a superior type of face), in sailor costume, with the stripes of a non-commissioned officer on his arm. This was Malameen, the Senegalese sergeant left by M. de Brazza.' With skill and courtesy, Malamine informed Stanley that Brazza had made treaties with the local chiefs on both banks of the Stanley Pool. The place was now under the protection of France, and Stanley's employer had no rights there.

The King was furious at the news. After long bargaining the French abandoned their claim to the left bank of the Congo – Stanley had easily found a rival 'chief' to sign a treaty as bogus as those Brazza had made – but retained the north bank and a huge swathe of country upstream and along the main tributaries. So two capital cities were founded facing each other across the Pool – Leopoldville (now Kinshasa) on the Belgian bank, and Brazzaville on the French. Of all the European conquerors of Africa, Brazza is the only one whose name survives as that of a capital city – a fit tribute to an extraordinary man.

During the course of the Berlin proceedings (the fact is not recorded in the conclusions of the conference) the assembled powers assented to the King's vast land-grab. The whole centre of tropical Africa was marked out as the preserve of Leopold's 'philanthropic' International Association of the Congo, which in reality did not exist. Stanley, the chief adviser to the American delegation and the only man present who had actually been on the river, assured everyone that the association was practically a charity, under royal patronage. Leopold's other employee, Sanford, had prepared the ground well. Early in 1884 he had been over to Washington and persuaded President Chester Arthur and the Senate to afford formal recognition to the flag of the Association, on equal terms with the flags of all nations. So the United States, by the bribery of one of its public officials, became on 10 April 1884 the official sponsor of Leopold's tyranny.

By mid-1885 the non-existent International Association was wound up. Its territory was placed under the administration of a new regime, as the Independent State of the Congo. Leopold in February of that year had persuaded the Belgian government to recognise a new title for himself – *Roi-souverain*, 'sovereign King', of the place he had invented. There was no constitution to limit his power. He was absolute master there.

This amazing piece of political bravura was recognised for what it was by the statesmen of Europe. The chief clerk of the British Foreign Office noted in the margin of a paper on its way to the Foreign Secretary, Lord Salisbury, 'The King of the Belgians' Co. is a gigantic commercial monopoly.' The Berlin Act had specifically banned the establishment of monopolies within the area it covered. Salisbury did nothing. Bismarck was sent a document explaining that Leopold's main motive in Africa was to eradicate slavery. The Chancellor wrote in the margin one word, *Schwindel*, which needs no translation. The great powers acquiesced in the fraud: they were ready to do likewise if they got the chance.

Perhaps the most extraordinary conclusion of the Berlin conference was the extent of the area within which the signatories agreed its rules should apply. Bismarck's map (see page 62) finally showed three overlapping regions. The smallest showed King Leopold's acknowledged claims. A larger region was described as the 'geographical basin of the Congo', corresponding as far as anyone knew to the limits of that river's watershed. (It was significantly inaccurate at one crucial point, which is where Stokes was killed ten years later.) A vaster region yet was included within the

so-called Collective Conventional Free Trade Area; it
stretched right across Africa, far beyond the remotest connection with the Congo, and included the entire Indian
Ocean coastline from the Zambezi mouth, 18° south of the
Equator, to a point in what is now Somalia, at 5° north. All
East Africa had become embroiled in an arrangement meant
to regulate trade on the Congo, which flows out on the west
coast.

The principal established ruler within this new area was
the Sultan of Zanzibar, whose rights were well known, and
whom the British government was committed by treaty to
protect. He was simply flung aside. Travellers, official and
semi-official, from the great powers were already prepared
with blank 'treaty forms', to be filled in and presented for
signature to amenable petty chieftains, who would thereby
hand over rights amounting to sovereignty. The first main
target area lay just inland of Zanzibar itself, across the
established caravan route from the coast to the great lakes
and the far interior.

The British thought they had it sewn up. A tiny, hyper-
active man called Harry Johnston, with the rank of vice-
consul, had met several self-styled local rulers in a tract of
land to southward of the great mountain Kilimanjaro, and
had persuaded them to put their marks upon treaty forms
which purported to request British protection over the districts they claimed to control. (The treaties formally stated
that the people in question had never been subject to the
jurisdiction of the Sultan of Zanzibar: if they were indeed
rulers, this was certainly untrue.) Johnston let it be understood that his journey was a considerable feat of daring, a
venture into unknown country to deal with possibly hostile
natives. At the end of his life, when he had grown out of
that sort of pretence, he admitted that his trip had been
conveniently organised by the most experienced of East
African safari leaders, Charles Stokes. Johnston professed
a liking for his eccentric guide, and did not blame him for
the fiasco that followed.

There was a rival claimant to the slopes of Kilimanjaro
– a name Mr Gladstone pretended to be unable to remem-
ber. A German adventurer had made similar deals with

another set of individuals calling themselves chief, chief-tainess, and even 'sultan', whose claims to sovereignty over-lapped with those of Johnston's friends. This German was a very tough party indeed, by the name of Dr Carl Peters. He was backed by a group of Hamburg merchants with large interests in the gin and arms trades, and Peters used both products freely to persuade his pliable 'rulers' to put their names to bits of paper that they could not, of course, understand.

The Berlin conference ended on 26 February 1886. The very next day, while Bismarck's servants were eating up the cold remains of the final banquet, the Chancellor issued in the name of his Kaiser an imperial *Schutzbrief*, or declara-tion of protection, over the lands covered by Peters's claims. The British could not complain that Bismarck had been quickest off the mark. Neither could they challenge the Peters treaties by producing Johnston's, since both sets were equally phoney, and anyway a legal dispute would only reveal that the Sultan of Zanzibar had better, and prior, rights. The Sultan protested: the Germans sent a warship to aim its guns at his palace. Sir John Kirk, the Sultan's British adviser and supposed friend, was deeply unhappy. But he acquiesced in the theft of the Zanzibari lands, and advised Sultan Bargash to offer no resistance.

The civil servants in the Foreign Office were frantic. The head of the office, Sir Villiers Lister, sent a memo to Lord Salisbury, in which he declared that the Germans were 'de-liberately working to ruin the Sultan, to drive out the British Indian traders, and to provoke anarchy with a view to some gigantic robbery'. Salisbury squashed the agitated diplomat, minuting in the margin of Lister's note, 'I doubt it very much. There is not enough to rob.' The opposition, led by Mr Gladstone, made fun of the whole affair. The Germans had got away with it. They played exactly the same trick in Kamerun (the Cameroons), on the west coast of Africa, managing even to persuade the British govern-ment to agree to the removal of the British Baptist mission long established there. The Baptists were mostly black clergymen from the West Indies, so the Foreign Office made no attempt to support them.

For true German nationalists, the swift seizure of the slopes of Kilimanjaro and the Kamerun coastline was a triumph, a symbol of the resurgence of the German people to its ancestral greatness. The idea of a German empire stretching from east to west across the African continent took root, just as the idea of a north-to-south all-British empire took shape in the minds of the new millionaires then seeking their fortunes in the gold-mines of South Africa. Of course both could not exist: rivalry was implicit in the whole idea of African imperialism. But Bismarck and Salisbury were not going to let rivalry in Africa get in the way of their diplomacy elsewhere, which was at this moment mainly friendly to each other, and directed against the French.

Nor did either of the old aristocrats intend to put their own governments to extra expense in support of their traders in Africa. King Leopold's Congo was to be run by a monopoly operated by the King himself, with no taxpayers' funds – and, for that matter, with no share of the profits, if any, for the people of Belgium. The British and German governments also resolved to privatise the business of imperialism, handing over their new territories to private firms that would in effect become sovereign governments. The trade association of German firms with East African interests was encouraged to form the Deutsche Ostafrika Gesellschaft: its leading spirit was the same Dr Carl Peters who had signed the Kilimanjaro treaties. British commercial interests in the area combined to form the Imperial British East Africa Company, formally constituted in 1888 with a grand board of directors including one field-marshal, three generals, the treasurer of the Church Missionary Society and an Earl who was godson to the Queen. It also included one really useful man, Sir John Kirk, ex-consul-general in Zanzibar (and former friend of Dr Livingstone), whose payment this was for his betrayal of the Sultan he had for so long advised. The leading spirit of the IBEA company was Sir William Mackinnon, the Glasgow shipping millionaire and secret backer of King Leopold.

Thus the British revived, and the Germans copied, an old formula for breaking new imperial ground, that of the chartered company. The Hudson's Bay Company, for Canada, and the East India Company were the prime examples: both had collapsed amid financial scandals and accusations of brutality towards native peoples, but that did not seem to matter. The idea was that a private company set up under royal charter should enjoy the prerogatives of a *de facto* government, and pay for its own administrative and military costs out of trading revenue. To Bismarck and Salisbury, faced with the difficulty of raising taxes through parliaments dominated by merchants, it seemed the only way to acquire new territory without paying for it.

The experiment was a disaster. The German East Africa Company proved unable to raise even a fraction of the capital it would have needed to develop the lands it claimed, and its first attempts to raise revenue in Africa led at once to bitter native resistance. After only four years it was wound up and replaced by an ordinary colonial government paid for unwillingly and inadequately out of the German national treasury. The British company lingered on a little longer, until 1893, when it collapsed, dumping its debts onto a reluctant British government after a long and fraudulent public relations campaign.

But at the start, in 1885, the two companies agreed to respect a demarcation of their territories along a line that was formally ratified in 1890, and which now marks the frontier between Kenya and Tanzania from the coast to Lake Victoria (see page 4). The Sultan of Zanzibar was, for a token few years, allowed to keep his sovereignty over a ten-mile-wide strip of coastline; even this was removed from him, without consultation, in 1890.

The British got the worst of the deal, with the vast area of barren desert that they transformed into what is now the nation of Kenya. The Germans, in what is now Tanzania, got the best land, and command of the only feasible caravan route to the interior. There was indeed, as Lord Salisbury had rightly remarked, no money to be made from either territory until the slow, expensive and laborious business of transporting goods on people's heads could be replaced. That meant building railways, and railways demanded huge sums in capital investment. But still, once there was a cheap

and efficient means of transport inland, it seemed that great
fortunes might be won from the heart of the continent,
where lay the as yet unclaimed lands of the kingdom of
Buganda, with its rich soil and ingenious people.

Both the British and the Germans wanted Buganda, and
began at once to advance towards it in the wake of the
missionary outriders. So, from the east coast, two rival commercial monopolies were headed for the far interior. From
the west, too, through the forbidding terrain of the Congo
rain-forests, King Leopold's even more single-minded commercial monopoly was also heading for Buganda and the
source of the Nile. In the unoccupied lands between these
three forces Charles Stokes was the sole independent white
trader already operating, and he was beginning to prosper.

Chapter 6

✥

The Grab for Equatoria

Stokes is the only person, so far, who has won the hearts of the people. He has great influence with them.

The Reverend H. Cole, letter to the CMS (March 1887)

If Germany becomes a colonising power, all I can say is 'God speed her'.

William Gladstone, Liberal Prime Minister (12 March 1885)

While the white-gloved diplomats were drawing their lines across the uncertain map of Africa, Stokes was building up his business around Lake Victoria, at the centre of the continent. His marriage to Limi ensured that he could muster her Wanyamwesi clansmen as porters to the coast and back. Travel across the limitless landscapes became his life's routine: up at dawn, the night's fires relit with dry grass to boil the morning porridge; the men grumbling and squabbling as they hoisted the loads on to their heads; the journey of ten or a dozen miles on to the next well-known camp-site, there to fall asleep by midday; the heat building to a peak as the men sprawled unprotected, sweating, under the vertical rays of the equatorial sun. The evenings were better: time for a joke, or a bout of drumming, until the light went out as the sun dropped suddenly over the horizon, and the fires were built again to keep off the wild beasts and ghosts that wandered in the scrubland.

It was boring. The caravan boss, most of the time, had as little to do as the captain of a ship sailing with a well-

trained crew across a familiar, empty ocean. The ports of
these inland odysseys were the occasional villages and inhabited strips of land that interrupted the plain: there some
trade might be found, and provisions bought, after the usual
long haggle with the chief and his many advisers, wives and
casual friends. And at journey's end came the excitement of
buying and selling, the delicate transactions in which
neither side declared his hand without a show of bluff and
protestations that times were hard. After that, if things went
well, came the drinking.

For those who did not fall sick it was sometimes a good
life, always a free one. Stokes began to plan ahead. He had
finally parted from the Anglican mission after his marriage
to Limi, at the end of 1885. It was a low point for the
caravan trade. Until then a single large annual caravan had
taken care of all the goods for import and export into Buganda and Unyamwesi. With the effective closing of the
Buganda border after the death of the Kabaka Mutesa, in
1884, the volume of business dropped. Mackay and a single
French priest maintained a tenuous presence there, at the
risk of their lives. South of Lake Victoria there was no
significant quantity of ivory to trade. Several small mission
stations were scattered around the region, and the Africans
had not the least objection to white men settling among
them. But with nothing to sell, they had not the means to
buy imports, and they found the new religion of no special
interest.

The first result of the Berlin conference was an end to
the old freedom to travel at will, and the drawing of the
first frontier across the open land, between British and German territory. But the coming of the Imperial companies
meant the start of organised business in East Africa. In the
relatively prosperous communities on the German side of
the line trade began to grow, as the Deutsche Ostafrika
Gesellschaft set promptly to work. On the British side
things went more slowly. The Imperial British East Africa
Company had trouble attracting capital in the City of London. Along the stretch of coast to seaward of the British
possessions there was only one safe harbour, at Mombasa,
offering little trade. Between Mombasa and the habitable

parts of the interior lay a cruel semi-desert, and behind that the hills were inhabited by the warlike Masai people, who resisted any outside incursions onto the vast ranges where they wandered with their cattle.

Zanzibar, still nominally an independent sultanate, remained the chief port and financial centre for the whole East African coastline. The small harbours of Bagamoyo and Saadani, on the mainland facing the island, were the jumping-off points for all caravans to the interior; although the Sultan was theoretically allowed to retain sovereignty over a ten-mile-wide strip of mainland coast, the Germans were in control. Stokes knew how to run a caravan business. His wife's family supplied the porters. He saw the need to make a deal with the Germans, and the Germans, for their part, desperately short of men with relevant African experience, wanted to employ him as a transport contractor. Both sides were happy with the arrangement that made the Germans Stokes's best customers.

The Germans and the British in East Africa generally got along very well together, being much the same sort of people. The German administrators had great respect for the work done by their British predecessors, especially in collecting and writing down the many local languages. British Protestant missionaries, especially in Unyamwesi, had laid the groundwork for the German occupation – and the missionaries, for their part, found their new German masters most co-operative. As far as Stokes was concerned, the British and German officials, and the Christian missionaries, were all working together to pacify and make prosperous the region where he operated. That, anyway, was how it seemed at the start.

On the Swahili coast, however, the Germans had a very different reception. The established traders there were Muslims, mostly of part-Arab ancestry; some of the larger businesses were run by Indian Muslims from Bombay. The Germans told them to close down and get out, saying that the whites would no longer allow the exploitation of blacks by brown-skinned usurers. In reality the Germans were trying to make room for their own people – company officials recruited mainly from the ambitious and unsuc-

cessful of the North Sea and Baltic cities, and private traders encouraged to think that they would make quick fortunes in Africa. Most of them were very inefficient: their
prices were high, their supplies irregular, their behaviour
often brutal; they were, of course, constantly sick.

A further, accidental, calamity struck the Swahili trading
community. Most African purchases were for very small
amounts, and the currencies in circulation – Indian rupees,
Austrian dollars, pounds sterling – included no coins of
very low value. The traditional currency for small payments,
for matches, salt and such necessities, was cowrie shells,
tiny grooved objects found along the Indian Ocean beaches,
whose value depended on their rarity. An enterprising
Frenchman discovered that cowries could be picked up in
shovelfuls on the beaches of the remote Maldive Islands,
far off to the south of India. He loaded up a schooner and
delivered hundreds of thousands of cowries, at a huge
profit, to East Africa. The supply of small money was increased several hundredfold, and the inevitable result was
massive inflation and the destruction of the petty currency.
Small traders were ruined as their hoarded bags of cowries
became worthless.

On top of all that, the native Africans found themselves
facing demands for small taxes, payable in cash. The people
did not use or own money: the Germans punished them for
not paying, tried to force them to work and used excessive
violence. The protests of traders and village chiefs were
crudely dismissed, and in 1886, very soon after the German
company had opened its doors for trade, chaos broke out,
and full-scale resistance began. The Germans, however
illogically, described it as a 'rebellion', and named it after
the most effective resistance leader, a Swahili fighting man
called Bushiri. The Germans were few, and not at all
equipped for their own defence. They panicked, and the
company fell into confusion at the unexpected prospect of
running a small war. Their brutality was unlimited. In one
famous massacre at Pagani, they set up a machine gun out
of musket range of the town's defenders, and indiscrimi-
nately mowed down at least 100 men, women and children.

Troops and warships were ordered out from Germany,

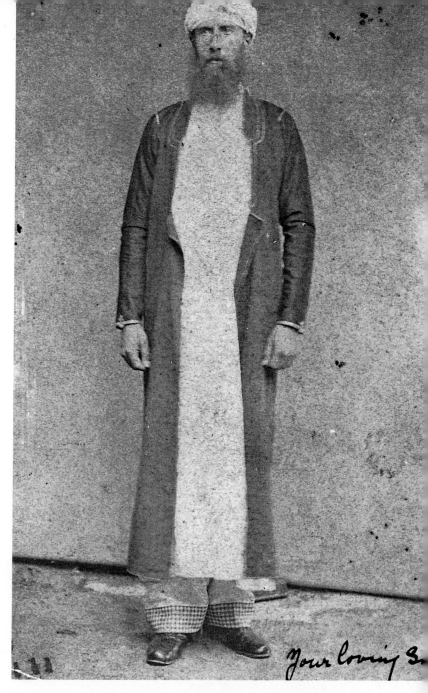

1 Charles Stokes in his Arab travelling dress – a photograph
sent home to his mother in Dublin, from 'your loving son', in 1881.

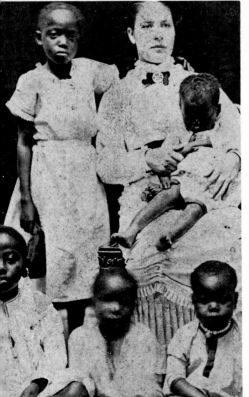

2-5 On their honeymoon in 1883, Charles and Ellen Stokes sat for their formal portraits by a London commercial photographer. In Africa they had been photographed by a friend in their more usual settings – Ellen surrounded by the pupils she called 'my little Blackies' and Charles resting on a leopard-skin on the verandah.

6 Charles Stokes was an unreliable correspondent. In 1888, four years after the death in childbirth of his wife Ellen, he briefly tried to persuade her sister Polly Sherratt to join the mission, bring his little daughter Nellie back to Africa and presumably marry him there. But she was not keen, and his enthusiasm faded. This letter from Zanzibar consists mainly of apologies for not writing more. Three years later, in May 1891, it was to Polly that he sent flowers for little Nellie, gathered from her mother's grave at Kisokwe mission.

and help was requested from Britain. There was no trouble on the British side of the demarcation line, and the officials there felt, fairly enough, that the Germans' problems were entirely of their own making. But because the general policy of the government in London was to co-operate with the Germans, in order to spite the French, Royal Navy ships were sent to terrorise the coastal settlements of the German zone, and vessels of both navies worked together to impose a blockade of all non-European shipping along the entire East African coast. In particular the import through East African harbours of weapons, of any kind, was prohibited. The sale of guns to 'natives' was banned. As a result of this imposed shortage, the price of guns already in East Africa soared. Anyone who could get his hands on arms or powder stood to make a fortune.

The ingenious Charles Stokes stumbled across one source of muskets that did not involve their import by sea. Down south, on Lake Malawi, the Scottish missionaries who had followed the call of their countryman, Dr Livingstone, were making very few converts – and their missionaries were dying like flies of disease, those who survived spending most of their time fighting Arab slave-traders bound for Portuguese Mozambique, where slavery was still tolerated. Congregations at home in Scotland were glad to subscribe funds for the conversion of the heathen, but not to support fighting men. Money ran short, and it was decided to wind up the missionaries' trading organisation, known as the African Lakes Company.

A valuable part of the Lakes Company's stock-in-trade was muskets. Given the embargo on arms sales to natives, it seemed likely that the company would find no buyers for them, and would suffer a heavy loss. The problem was solved by selling them to the one non-native trader in East Africa who was happy to buy surplus guns, and whose former missionary connections made him seem a respectable customer. So Charles Stokes went into business as an arms wholesaler.

There is no record of how many weapons he bought from the African Lakes Company. There were certainly several hundred muskets, British army surplus, identifiable by the

mark of the Tower of London armoury; their old flint-lock
mechanism had been modified to accept the far more efficient cap-firing method. There were also some much more
formidable breech-loading rifles.

In April 1888 it was widely reported that Stokes had
transported 100 breech-loaders to the south end of Lake
Victoria, where he was offering them in exchange for ivory
to the young Kabaka Mwanga of Buganda. Stokes made no
attempt to deny it, and the Anglican missionaries, who regarded Mwanga as the prime obstacle to their progress in
Buganda, were furious. Alexander Mackay wrote an angry
letter of protest, which Stokes disregarded. The new Anglican Bishop of Buganda, Henry Parker, had not yet visited
his new diocese (and was to die before getting there); he
wrote a more moderate protest, which Stokes also ignored.

The German authorities knew what was going on: the
rest of the goods in Stokes's caravan were mostly for their
use. But they made no attempt to interfere with his arms
deal. It is possible that they actually favoured it, as a way
of building up the power of Mwanga. Stokes was now, for
good or ill, involved in the international intrigues that the
Berlin conference had formally unleashed upon Africa.

A central focus of these intrigues was the vast region then
known as Equatoria, lying across what is now the wild frontier between Uganda and the Sudan. In the 1880s it seemed
hugely significant. It borders the upper reaches of the
White Nile, where the great river debouches from Lake
Albert to flow north towards the Sahara desert and offers
the only practicable route for human traffic between the
Mediterranean coast of Africa and the southern lands where
the black people live. This was the territory the Europeans
hoped to open to commerce, but to close to the Islamic
influence of Egypt.

The allure of the Nile's headwaters had more than mere
reason behind it. It seemed the destiny of Egypt itself was
at stake. The river, as everyone knows, provides the annual
flood that enriches the lands along its course. (Most of the
flood-water arrives from Ethiopia, by way of the Blue Nile,
but this was not understood at the time.) It was therefore

assumed that control of the headwaters would give the country holding Equatoria the ability to grant or to withhold the flood: a Frenchman had published a celebrated scientific paper in the 1870s, showing how a dam could do the job. This was, of course, pure pseudo-engineering. Such a dam would have to stretch for hundreds of miles across the Sudd, the immense marsh through which the Nile winds and steams on its upper course. (The Sudd is still not dammed or drained – a team of French engineers making the latest attempt to do so was chased off in a local civil war in 1984.)

However useless Equatoria might be, it was firmly in the sights of the leading imperialists of the day – the British, French and German governments, and King Leopold of the Belgians. Their interest was increased when the region fell into a political vacuum. Nominally, it was a province under the Khedive of Egypt. But in 1884 all contact between Equatoria and Cairo was cut off by the growing power of the Islamic revolutionary regime of the Mahdi in the Sudan; the following year, Mahdist forces captured Khartoum, capital of the Sudan, and killed the governor-general, Charles Gordon Pasha, in the residency there. Also in 1884, the Kabaka Mutesa of Buganda died, and communications southwards out of Equatoria were cut off by the civil war in that country.

Meanwhile the government of Equatoria continued in isolation, under the leadership of one of the most improbable of all the great African pioneers, once famous throughout the world by the name and title of Emin Pasha. He was born Eduard Schnitzer, of Jewish origin, in Austria, qualified as a medical doctor in Berlin, and gained real distinction as a student and collector of African flora and fauna, which he diligently sent off as circumstances permitted to the great museums of Europe. The Natural History Museum in London lists eleven mammalian species whose original scientific appellation commemorated the name of their discoverer, Emin.

He had wandered across Europe into Turkey, where he developed a fascination with eastern language, culture and religion, adopting the powerful Islamic name of Mohammed el Amin, the beloved of God. From there, he drifted on through the Holy Land and into Egypt, then up the Nile into the Sudan where he found at work the team of European mercenaries employed by the Khedive of Egypt to incorporate and extend the wild southern frontier lands firmly within his kingdom. General Gordon was desperately short of men and of money. He employed Emin as medical officer in the remotest of all the Sudanese provinces, Equatoria. In 1878, there being no other candidate, Emin was promoted governor of the province.

For four years he ruled as competently as circumstances permitted. He had a small group of friends - a Tunisian Jewish secretary, a few explorers and fortune-seekers - and a beautiful Ethiopian wife, who gave him a daughter, Ferida. From canny dealings with local chiefs he amassed a considerable stock of ivory, which would make him a rich man if he could ever get it down to the coast for sale. For protection he had two battalions of black soldiers, recruited from the slave peoples of the southern Sudan, under officers drawn mostly from Egypt proper: all were devout Muslims, and passionately loyal to the Khedive of Egypt.

In the early 1880s the rise of the Mahdi in the lands to his north, and the dynastic struggles in Buganda to his south, cut Emin off from the outside world. Physically, he was safe. He had plenty of ammunition for his soldiers, and plenty of food, supplied by efficient farms operated by his soldiers' local womenfolk. Two small but sturdy steamboats, hauled up the Nile rapids on Gordon's orders, gave his little army mobility on Lake Albert and about sixty miles downstream as far as the first rapids on the river. Emin did not want to leave. But he longed for companionship, and for recognition of his growing scientific achievement as a collector of wild plants and animals. Moreover, his spectacles were broken: always dreadfully short-sighted, he was finding it increasingly hard to examine specimens or make notes on them, and this was an acute frustration.

After two years of isolation, Emin found a way at last to communicate with the outside world. The Scottish missionary, Alexander Mackay, had moved clear of turbulent Buganda and established a tiny base across Lake Victoria, maintaining meanwhile by way of Stokes's messenger service his contacts with Zanzibar and the east coast. In November 1884, Emin got a letter through to Mackay, who reported to his friends in Britain the survival of this last outpost of the former British-dominated provinces of the Sudan. On 31 December 1885, Emin wrote and sent off to Mackay a whole bundle of correspondence for friends and missionary leaders in Britain and Germany. They were clearly written in a fit of year-end depression, and complained bitterly of the world's indifference to the writer's long, lonely stand in the middle of Africa. Two of them in particular had dramatic effects. One was to Robert Felkin, the former missionary, now working as a doctor in Edinburgh. The other was to Charles Allen, secretary of the Anti-Slavery Society in London – the main pressure group for beating back Islam and its Arab propagators.

In late October 1886, Felkin and Allen received their letters, realised their value, and arranged for them to be published in *The Times*, which had lately become the principal mouthpiece of British imperialism. The timing was perfect. The killing of General Gordon by the Mahdi's soldiers in Khartoum, and the unleashing of imperial ambitions after the Berlin conference, had made the upper Nile the fashionable topic for Britain's armchair explorers, missionaries and conquerors. *The Times* backed up Emin's letters with excited editorials pleading for public action to revenge Gordon, and to rescue the last survivor of his regime in the Sudan.

Stanley's appeal for the Christianisation of Buganda, published in the *Daily Telegraph* in 1875, had launched the British drive for that country. Now *The Times* had the chance to rival its competitor's coup. This newspaper stunt involved many of the same cast of characters as the earlier episode. In particular the Glasgow shipping tycoon William Mackinnon – now Sir William, and a most respectable pillar of imperialism – saw a way to advance his own interests and those of his eminent business associate, King Leopold II of the Belgians. The main front for the campaign was the Scottish Geographical Society, backed by Mackinnon and with Felkin as its main African expert. The society sent a pressing plea for action to the Foreign Office, who were obliged to respond to the campaign, especially since it had the backing of *The Times*.

The problem was that Emin made plain that he did not want to leave Equatoria, or to remove it from the sovereignty of Egypt, in whose name he and his soldiers were there. 'Believe me that I am in no hurry to break away from here,' he said in a letter to Mackay, on 6 July 1886. But the same letter added: 'It would be most desirable that some commissioner came here from Europe ... in order that my people may actually see that there is some interest taken in them. I would defray with ivory all expenses of such a commission.' The word Emin actually used, in the original German text of his letter to Mackay, was *Kommissar*, which can mean an official messenger rather than an agent with authority. But Mackinnon and King Leopold – an avid reader of *The Times* – saw in the phrase the chance to achieve their ambitions for the upper Nile.

Mackinnon's ambitions matched Leopold's. He had for some years been trying to take over the financial management of Zanzibar, by agreement with the Sultan; the Foreign Office had thwarted him. For some years, too, he had been seeking to arrange for the British government to lease to Leopold its dubious claim to Equatoria: this too the Foreign Office vetoed, not so much because Egypt had a better claim to the province than Britain, but because the French were against the deal. Emin's appeal allowed the two greedy men to join forces and send a 'humanitarian' expedition to his rescue. Mackinnon organised a public campaign, like the one he had backed on the Buganda issue, in support of such an expedition, and Leopold seconded two of his hired British officials to organise it. General Sir Francis de Winton, a former administrator of the Congo State, was appointed secretary of the 'Emin Pasha Relief Committee', to raise funds for and administer the expedition. As leader of the expedition itself, Leopold offered the services of the greatest African explorer of all, the real founder of the Congo State, H. M. Stanley, whom Mackinnon recruited in November 1886, and who visited the King in Brussels on 14 January 1887.

The claim that Emin's rescue was the real object of the scheme fooled nobody. The purpose was to get armed men into Equatoria, and thus to persuade the governor to put his province under the 'protection' of a European power, which would then claim sovereignty over Equatoria and the source of the Nile. The charitable public was not keen to subscribe to that bare-faced end. Nor was the British government. Since the previous year the argument had raged to and fro about whether, and how, to avenge the killing of that peculiar hero General Gordon Pasha. The Liberals wanted to leave Africa alone. The Conservatives hankered for revenge and a wider empire. But neither party was prepared to increase taxes to pay for what might well turn out to be an expensive failure. It was not the anti-imperialist Gladstone but the Tory Lord Salisbury who brushed the agitation aside: 'It really is their business, if Emin is a German,' he said.

The British government found a brilliant solution to its financial difficulty. Equatoria nominally belonged to Egypt; Egypt was in effect a British puppet. The Foreign Office thought Egypt might as well put up half the money. Stanley had reckoned the cost of his expedition at £20,000, and reminded everyone that Emin had promised to repay it out of his ivory hoard. Sir Evelyn Baring, the British representative in Cairo, was told to 'advise' the Khedive's ministers to make a voluntary contribution of £10,000 to de Winton's committee. Thus the Egyptian taxpayer subscribed to take a province away from Egypt's own empire, in order to add it to the empire either of Queen Victoria or of King Leopold. Most of the rest of the money was put up by Mackinnon, who hoped to make a profit on the venture.

The British and Belgian plotters appear not to have reflected that Emin was also writing to his missionary friends in Germany, and that Germans, too, could read the newspapers and get up agitations in favour of acquiring colonies. Emin was a Jew who had perhaps turned Muslim. But for imperial purposes he could conveniently be presented as a gallant member of the *Volk* who needed rescuing. Dr Carl Peters, the Kilimanjaro land-grabber, saw the opportunity. He had lost his job in East Africa as a result of the Bushiri

'rebellion', which had largely been caused by his own brutality. Under his aegis, a German Emin Pasha committee
was set up in Hamburg, financed by trading houses, and
with discreet but not secret backing from Count Herbert
von Bismarck, the nephew whom the old Chancellor sometimes used for unscrupulous semi-official business. The
committee raised only about half as much as its British
counterpart – the Germans had no way of raiding the Egyptian Treasury, as the British had done – but with that backing Peters led off his own Emin Pasha expedition.

The supreme absurdity was that Emin did not want to be
rescued at all. Had he wanted to leave Equatoria, he could
have skirted southwards around turbulent Buganda, thus
reaching Lake Victoria and making his way to Zanzibar by
the long-established caravan route through German territory. By that route, in the reverse direction, Stanley's
expedition could conveniently have found its way to Equatoria. But Stanley was the servant of Leopold and Mackinnon: the King, in particular, wished to demonstrate that
the best route to the source of the Nile was by way of his
own Congo State, so that he could claim Equatoria as part
of the Congo's hinterland.

Stanley sailed from Europe to Zanzibar, where he hired
many of the experienced long-range porters who had
worked for him on previous safaris. One of Mackinnon's
ships took him and his followers right round the south of
Africa, and up the west coast to the Congo mouth. Once at
Stanley Pool he took over all the steamers available on the
river (simply hijacking the one belonging to the Baptist
mission, which strongly disapproved of his aggressive expedition). The caravan marched behind a flag chosen to
underline its independent character – not that of Britain,
Stanley's home; nor of the United States, whose citizen he
was; nor of the Congo Free State, where he was operating.
It was the flag of the New York Yacht Club, lent by Stanley's newspaper patron, Gordon Bennett of the *Herald*. The
officers' mess was fully, even luxuriously equipped: Stanley
recorded that 'Messrs Fortnum and Mason of Piccadilly
packed up 40 carrier loads of choicest provisions. Every
article was superb.'

The river-boats carried Stanley's people as far as possible
up the Congo and its tributary, the Aruwimi. Then they
started to walk through the uncharted rain-forest, beset by
strange sicknesses and stranger tribesfolk. The horrors of
the journey and the heroic incompetence of its leader are
recounted in several rival best-selling books of the period.
Stanley's white companions behaved atrociously under the
terrible hardships to which they and their black followers
were subjected. James S. Jameson, a whiskey heir from
Dublin, had paid £1,000 to go on the trip. Just before his
death, on 17 August 1888, he had written, 'I would rather
a thousand times go through all sorts of hardship than lead
this miserable existence – doing nothing and living upon
what we can get in ransom for the few native women we
can catch.' Jameson's death was from the natural cause of
fever. His colleague Major Bartelott was shot dead by a
porter who was due to be flogged for drumming in a way
that annoyed the major. Episodes of cannibalism, brutality,
murder and desperation were very much to the Victorian
taste, whether taken as vindicating the imperial cause or as
discrediting it.

Had they taken the rational route across East Africa,
Emin's would-be rescuers might have done the journey in
under six months. (Emin's letters, travelling in the opposite direction by way of Stokes's messenger service, had
taken three months from Equatoria to Zanzibar.) The
politically-motivated journey through the Congo forest cost
them seventeen months, and many lives. At last, on 29 April
1888, the destitute and fever-stricken Stanley stood on the
shore of Lake Albert, while Emin steamed calmly in aboard
his gunboat. Stanley handed over the supplies intended to
relieve what had been presented as the dire plight of Emin
and his battalions of sturdy Sudanese. Practically everything useful or eatable had been consumed on the frightful
journey, and delivery to Emin consisted of thirty-one cases
of ammunition for the soldiers' Remington rifles, plus
a mouldy pack containing clothes, copies of eighteen-
month-old German newspapers and letters, and some old
and inaccurate maps of the area.

Stanley also handed over a letter of commendation to

Emin from the Khedive of Egypt, and a parchment confer-
ring on the governor the exalted title of Pasha. In exchange,
the new and supposedly forlorn Pasha supplied Stanley and
his followers with hot baths, clothes and shoes to replace
their tattered outfits, honey, fresh fruit and vegetables,
cows, sheep, goats, chickens and a month's supply of sound
grain. All this was the produce of the farms that Emin had
organised to make his little army self-sufficient. He was, he
said, grateful for the ammunition, but had no pressing need
of it.

After much debate, delay and confusion, Stanley was reinforced by the European officers of his rearguard, and
more porters. Their arrival disrupted the already delicate
relations between Emin and his Sudanese soldiers, who had
trusted the governor only in so far as they could be sure
that, like themselves, he was absolutely faithful to the Khedive. The Sudanese officers detested the English, and suspected that Stanley had come to bring orders from England
for Emin. They were right. Against his will, Emin was
forced to march away from his beloved province – this time,
the Congo point having been disastrously made, by the
logical route through East Africa to Zanzibar. Only 60 of
the Sudanese soldiers went with him. Well over 1,000
stayed put, under their own officers and commanded by the
senior Sudanese, Major Selim Bey.

Stanley, with Emin in quasi-captivity, now led a vast
concourse of people slowly to the south. Stanley's own soldiers and porters numbered 230; along the way they had
accumulated 700 followers of their own. Emin's 60 Sudanese
soldiers had in tow 600 women, children and slaves. The
travellers were beset by the smallpox they had brought with
them from the west coast. Many died, many more dropped
out along the way. Stanley's discipline was fierce. A Sudanese, Rehan, was ordered to be hanged. The rope broke.
Stanley had him hanged again on a stronger one, which
took the strain. (The Irish doctor, Thomas Parke, took the
opportunity to study the feelings of a man facing his second
execution: he found Rehan indifferent to his fate.)

The porters could not bear their loads. Almost all Emin's
ivory, which Stanley had hoped would make the trip pro-

fitable, was abandoned in villages along the way, to be collected by petty chiefs and buried beneath their huts. Finally, the weary survivors passed into the territory newly taken over by the German Imperial government from the bankrupt Ostafrika Gesellschaft.

There, relief was waiting. Charles Stokes had brought up a large stock of food, trade goods and comforts for them in his last caravan out of Zanzibar – the same caravan that had transported, with evident German approval, the first big consignment of rifles for Mwanga. The supplies were stored at Usambiro, near the expanding German port of Mwanza, at the south end of Lake Victoria. There, the White Fathers and the Church Missionary Society had both set up houses and chapels, for the use of missionaries who had been forced to take temporary refuge from the troubles in Buganda. The ganda. The Catholic mission was at this time vacant: it was the tireless Alexander Mackay who welcomed Stanley and Emin, at the CMS post, on 28 August 1889.

Mackay greeted Emin warmly: the two old Africa hands had long been in correspondence, and had much local knowledge to swap. The missionary commented afterwards on Stanley's authoritarian style of leadership. In fact there was very nearly a nasty row. Mackay and Emin had been exchanging letters in German, and naturally now spoke it to each other. Stanley found himself excluded from conversations that he deeply wished to share – there might be a fragment of intelligence for his political master, Leopold, or a sensational nugget for his next blockbusting best-seller. He suspected that Mackay and Emin were plotting on behalf of Germany against British – or, for that matter, Belgian – interests; they did indeed discuss plans for bringing German Protestant missionaries into East Africa. Stanley's fears began to seem justified when the weary travellers, refreshed by Stokes's supplies, made their way at last, after three more months of steady marching, to the coast.

There the full extent of Stanley's failure became apparent. His overbearing rudeness, and the patronising behaviour of his officers, had inspired in Emin a new hatred of everything British. Stanley repeated his offer of protection to Emin, on behalf of King Leopold or of the British government. (Either way, Mackinnon would have gained effective control of Equatoria – that was the real objective.) Emin prevaricated. He was frightened of Stanley, and virtually his prisoner. But he was now resolved, if protection was needed, to seek it from his German-speaking friends.

On 4 December 1889, at the port of Bagamoyo on the mainland opposite Zanzibar, a great dinner of welcome for the two heroes was held in the German officers' mess. There was wine to drink, and schnapps, and lots of brandy. Emin was not used to spirits, or to two-storey houses. He wandered off to relieve himself, opened a full-length window that he took for a door, and fell to the ground from the upper floor of the house, fracturing his skull in the fall. (That at least is the official version – something more sinister may have happened, or maybe the 'accident' was a put-up job designed to get Emin out of Stanley's clutches.) The Germans took the Pasha for treatment aboard one of their warships offshore, together with his darling daughter Ferida. It was several months before he was fit to plan his next expedition, as an officer in the service of the German imperial government.

Emin's detestation of the British was reciprocated, with contempt. The German commissioner, Hermann von Wissmann, formally notified Stanley that Emin was now in the German service. Stanley's deputy, A. J. Mounteney-Jephson, noted: 'This is the best thing that could possibly happen for the English company, for the Pasha is bound to make a mess of anything he puts a hand to.' This was true; it was also sour grapes. Stanley's terrible journey to 'rescue' Emin had been a disaster. It began with 700 men, who left the Congo mouth luxuriously equipped. By its end, 550 of them were dead, by disease, murder and accidents. Equatoria, the target of Stanley's venture, was not won either for his British or his Belgian patrons: Emin was driven into the arms of their German rivals. But great publicists never allow failure to obscure their reputations. Stanley's book on the journey made him another small fortune, and marked the end of his African career. He was elected to Parliament (as an imperialist, of course) in 1895, knighted in 1899, and when he died in London, in 1904, he was given a hero's funeral in Westminster Abbey.

Charles Stokes, whose name is recorded only in footnotes and casual asides by the historians of the episode, was the man who had carried to the coast the letters from Emin which provided the pretext for the operation. He had, moreover, delivered the supplies that made possible the return of the expedition to the coast of Zanzibar. He was a disreputable figure, a pawn in the schemes of the great – but without him they could not have conducted the manoeuvres that were supposed to lay the foundations of great empires. He knew he was indispensable. Now he resolved to turn that position to his own advantage.

Chapter 7

The Master of the Lake

Stokes means to be well paid for his services . . .

> The Reverend Robert Walker to Consul-General Euan-Smith (October 1889)

I have been too long in Africa not to know how useless precise orders are, when the changing events of each moment may make them entirely unworkable: 'masterly inactivity' would be your best counsel.

> Emin Pasha to Lieutenant Stuhlmann (1892)

Stokes had one asset to bargain with. He was the only European with reliable contacts in Buganda, which was regarded by the colonising powers as the jewel of Africa, and which became, as soon as they had asserted their power along the East African coast, the target of their greedy rivalry. The Kabaka Mwanga longed for weapons, both to reinforce his shaky internal position as heir to a disputed throne and, if need be, to repel foreign invaders. Stokes had supplied some guns, and held out the prospect of more, including the breech-loading rifles that could transform the might of the royal army.

The British authorities in East Africa were backed by their country's long experience of fighting native tribesmen all over the world. They recognised the danger of arming indigenous peoples, and were prepared to implement the various agreements banning the arms trade. The Germans took a more relaxed view. If guns could buy the friendship of a native ruler, then guns he should have, and the consequences could be faced later. They were prepared to tolerate, and even to encourage, Stokes in his dealings. His co-operation might give them a start in the race for Buganda over the British, and for that matter over the Belgians, who could approach its western border by way of the Congo.

Quite apart from their willingness to tolerate his trade in arms, Stokes had good reasons for working with the Germans. The Anglo-German frontier was drawn so as to include his whole caravan route, from the coast to Lake Victoria, in German territory. His home at Uyui was in German East Africa; his own people, the Wanyamwesi, were German subjects – although, to be sure, they did not yet know it. There were profitable contracts in prospect for transporting supplies inland to the Germans' expanding military outposts. He did not particularly care who formed the government, so long as they left him alone to do business with his great ally, the Kabaka.

Mwanga was badly in need of friends. At the death of his stern father, in 1885, he was just nineteen years old, and his kingdom was divided by the normal turmoil of succession. That same year, the Baganda had seen the European powers combine to strip of his sovereign powers the greatest ruler of their small universe, the Sultan of Zanzibar. Their court, for centuries given stability by the unquestioned authority of their ancestral tradition, was divided by the presence of teachers proclaiming three rival new religions, none of which had a place for the semi-divine authority of the Kabaka.

The first open breach between Mwanga and the Christians at his court was almost certainly not his fault. The killing of Bishop Hannington, as he blundered across Buganda's eastern frontier in October 1885, was the act of an over-zealous provincial chief (although in Europe it was taken as justification for an all-out drive to make Buganda safe for Christians). But at the same time Mwanga was creating his own martyrs, among the well-born pages of his court.

Both the Anglican and the Catholic missions had been concentrating their efforts at conversion upon the young men who would become the next generation of national leaders. The pages began to question authority – to deny the religion in which the Kabaka played a central role, even to refuse direct orders. The missionaries claimed that the pages' disobedience arose when they refused to satisfy the Kabaka's 'unnatural desires' – which, they had always insisted, he must have learned from his Muslim teachers. That may well have been a slander. But it is certain that the Kabaka, backed by the majority of his council, the *lukiko*, decided that the pages must be taught a severe lesson.

The membership of the *lukiko*, reflecting the general disarray of the nation, was split. Since the arrival of the alien religions, their followers had formed factions which soon became, in effect, political parties within the court. The Protestants were known as the waIngerezi, or people of England; the waFransi, Roman Catholics, followed the French missionaries; the Muslims were called the waIslami; the supporters of the traditional beliefs of the Baganda were known to their critics as the Futabanghi, the marijuana smokers. The Kabaka, desperate to have power on his side, aligned himself with whichever party seemed to have the temporary ascendancy.

Under the influence of the Futabanghi, the Kabaka determined once and for all to settle the problem of the insubordinate pages. The young people of the court were offered the choice of renouncing their new faith, or facing a horrible death. On 3 June 1886, thirteen Roman Catholic and thirteen Protestant pages were publicly burned alive, having preferred that fate to apostasy. (Twin shrines, at which Pope Paul VI said an ecumenical prayer for their souls in 1969, stand side by side at Namugongo, just outside Kampala.) The story of the martyrs caused an outcry throughout Europe, and gave new strength to the clamour for an invasion of Buganda, to which activists both in Britain and in Germany were eager to respond.

The twenty-six Christian martyrs were by no means the only people to die in what was as much a political as a religious purge. The records of the churches in Uganda commemorate the killing of twenty-three Anglicans and twenty-one Roman Catholics in 1885 and 1886. Islam does not publicly commemorate its martyrs, but near the Christian shrines of Namugongo stands an unobtrusive mosque, at which the unrecorded Muslim dead of a century ago are quietly remembered.

The three monotheist parties – Protestant, Catholic, Muslim – had united in opposition to the traditionalists and the Kabaka. They formed militias, and bought themselves guns (mostly from the stock previously imported by Charles Stokes). The Futabanghi chiefs learned of their preparations, and on 10 September 1888, when they discovered that their plot was no longer secret, the monotheists launched a pre-emptive attack on the palace, overwhelmed the guards and held the Kabaka at their mercy. But they dared not shed his blood, and allowed Mwanga, with a few of his leading chiefs, to escape. They were paddled in two canoes across the lake to Magu, at its southern end. Some Arab chiefs took the fugitives in, possibly not knowing what had happened in the capital of Buganda; but when they too let Mwanga go, it was without his escort's weapons (which included about thirty French Snider rifles, obtained from the Catholic mission). Destitute and defenceless, Mwanga managed to get to the small mission at Bukumbi, near Mwanza, where a small team of White Fathers was awaiting the opening-up of Buganda. The priests received him hospitably and with respect. They well understood the advantage of being in possession of the king's person.

The unity of Muslims and both kinds of Christians had deprived the Kabaka of his throne. But it did not last. The three factions were each heavily influenced by their foreign religious leaders, and the Arab merchants who led the waIslami had no intention of making terms with the Europeans of the waFransi and waIngerezi. The Christians, fewer and less well-armed than the Muslims, were thrown out only a month after the coup against the king. The Arabs first installed Prince Kiwewa, of the royal line, as pretender in Mwanga's place. Then, again, arose the problem of circumcision: Kiwewa refused to have his genitals tampered with. His brother Kalema accepted the small operation, and was installed as Kabaka for his reward.

The French Catholics, at the south end of Lake Victoria, held the lawful king. Appalled at the collapse of his ordered world of power, Mwanga seems to have done whatever the priests told him. But with neither strong boat nor guns, there was little the Frenchmen could do to reinstate the puppet they had so luckily acquired. The Protestants had both. Alexander Mackay, in the *Eleanor*, had got clear of Buganda, taking with him the French priest, Father Lourdel; their doctrinal hatred was suppressed for the emergency. The *Eleanor* also carried a few selected Christian chiefs, and fifteen Baganda orphans thought sure material for a Christian upbringing.

Now, in the nick of time, Charles Stokes came on the scene. Early in 1888 he had led the caravan from Zanzibar to dump supplies in German territory for Stanley's Emin Pasha expedition; this caravan also carried a consignment of muskets ordered by Mwanga before his deposition. These Stokes put into his store for later delivery. Then he returned to Zanzibar, where he found the old order of things much changed, and new officials in charge of British interests there.

Old Sir John Kirk had retired from his job as consul-general, to collect his reward as a director of the new Imperial British East Africa Company. Kirk had always despised Stokes, and refused to have more than the necessary minimum of dealings with him as a British subject. His successor was Colonel Euan-Smith, with the triple job of 'advising' the Sultan, supporting the imperial company's work, and reporting on all East African affairs for the Foreign Office. Euan-Smith thought Stokes might be useful, both for his general knowledge of the area and as a source of information about the German authorities who employed him. The new consul-general wrote a despatch to Lord Salisbury, promising a rich harvest of intelligence from his forthcoming interview with the trader.

In fact, Stokes proved useless as a spy: the promised report on the consul-general's interview was never written. But he remained the only reliable means for getting messages up-country. Late in 1888 he left Zanzibar once more, carrying a personal message to Mwanga from Euan-Smith, who evidently did not yet know that the monarch was in exile and living on the charity of the French priests. The message stated that the British in general, and the CMS missionaries in particular, were friendly and disinterested observers of the benign rule of the Kabaka. It was a typical piece of deception, designed to persuade Mwanga that the new consul-general was not committed to support of the acquisitive Imperial British East Africa Company.

Stokes was on his way to the lake when he heard of Mwanga's exile. The news was in one sense a set-back: obviously Stokes would have preferred simply to do business with the reigning monarch. But in another way it offered him an unrivalled opportunity. He had ordered from England, and his porters were now carrying, the timbers and fittings for a sailing craft which, once assembled, would give him both commercial and political power all around the 1,000 miles of its shoreline. The trader was about to become the master of the lake.

In his dealings with Buganda, Stokes's journeys had had to be made in two distinct parts. From the Indian Ocean harbours to the south end of Lake Victoria, his Wanyamwesi porters could be relied upon for all deliveries. For transport on the lake itself he was dependent on the Baganda, who dominated the water with their hundreds of fishing canoes and their formidable war-fleet, organised and disciplined under the admiral, who was the most important of the Kabaka's great chiefs. But the Baganda had no craft suitable for carrying heavy loads. There were almost no great trees near the waterside, so they could not make ordinary African dug-out canoes. Instead they used long, slim, tree-trunks to make a sort of keel, to the sides of which they stitched planks to form a hull. (They had, of course, no nails and no accurate wood-working tools to join timbers by means of dowels.)

The Buganda canoes were fragile; they were propelled inefficiently by kneeling men wielding paddles; and they could not sail – indeed, the Baganda had no cloth for making sails, except the light cottons sold by traders which were unsuitable. The journey along the lake took at least two weeks; the canoes were dangerous in high waves, which can blow up quickly, so they were forced to hug the shore.

All early visitors to Lake Victoria had seen at once that a sound boat could transform travel, and put an end to the isolation of Buganda. The Arabs had built a few small dhows, but were limited by the lack of suitable timber and of any craftsmen. The first CMS missionaries had the timbers and engine for the *Daisy* carried up from the coast, but the engine was never installed, and she was soon wrecked when used under makeshift sails. Hannington's oak boat was next: she was damaged before she could be assembled, then patched up and launched as the *Eleanor* by Mackay. She was heavy and unhandy in the water. Mackay, a genius with engines, knew little about rigging sails, and anyway had no suitable canvas or sailmakers. He taught a crew of Baganda to row European-style, sitting down, and by this means the *Eleanor* became the most efficient craft so far known on Lake Victoria. (It is curious that Africans, who well understood the principle of the lever, did not spot that it can be applied to moving a boat through water by means of oars.)

Mackay had allowed Stokes to use the *Eleanor* a few times, to convey mission supplies to Buganda. But he absolutely refused to allow guns in the mission boat, so Stokes's first consignment of arms for Buganda had to be transported dangerously in canoes. In March 1889, when his porters arrived at the lake-shore carrying the sections of the large and sturdy sailing-boat specially ordered to match his requirements, he took care to keep her away from his Arab rivals at the usual lake harbours, finding instead a suitable launching-place at the fishing village of Urima. Mackay, who loved mechanical work, came over to put her together. The timbers were undamaged, and none of the gear and rigging was missing. Triumphantly, the Wanyamwesi shoved her into the water, where she was named the *Limi*, after Mrs Stokes.

Now all sorts of things became possible. By one account the *Limi* could carry up to sixty people: even if that is an exaggeration, she could certainly take over three tonnes of cargo - more than the loads of a hundred porters. She was yawl-rigged on two masts; on the steady south-east wind she could make the journey of 180 miles from north to south of Lake Victoria in two days. With Stokes as their ally, Mwanga and the leaders of the two Christian factions now had both guns and transport for a reinvasion of Buganda.

First the boat was to be tried out, and a crew trained. Stokes was not going to help Mwanga until he had collected his existing debts. His first voyage in the *Limi* was to the Arab trading-post at Magu, whose inhabitants had first helped and then robbed Mwanga and his party. Among the goods taken had been a consignment of ivory, intended for Stokes in payment for firearms. The Arabs were astonished at the appearance among them of this white Christian. But they were businessmen too, and a debt was a debt. They handed the ivory over, and Stokes sailed back to Bukumbi to meet up with Mwanga and the combined leaders of the Christian factions.

The waFransi and waIngerezi exiles were starting to get organised. In Ankole, on Buganda's western border, they had assembled a small army of around 2,000 men, with some firearms, for the reinvasion of Buganda. Skirmishes had started on the lake between Christian and Muslim canoe parties. At Bukumbi, the arrival of Stokes in the *Limi* was greeted as the turning-point in the Christians' plan to reinstate Mwanga under their protection.

The White Fathers were keen to fight. The founder of their order, the celebrated Cardinal Lavigerie of Algiers, had long been preaching fervently for the revival of the spirit of the Crusades, and of the armed struggle of St Louis against the Muslims. The Fathers belonged to the church militant: so, in his Calvinistic way, did Mackay. The Christian missions did not formally control the militias of their supporting parties; but they assured Stokes that they would give full support to military action by Mwanga's people.

Stokes saw a profit ahead. In exchange for a promise of payment in ivory after victory, he agreed to add his own rifles to the Christian armoury. On 29 April 1889 he set sail in the *Limi* for Buganda, with the Kabaka aboard. The party was armed, Stokes wrote, with 'about forty guns, mainly Le Gras and Sniders, and 500 to 600 rounds of ammunition'. These were French carbines and rifles, from the White Fathers' armoury: Stokes does not state how many of his own weapons were involved.

At Buddu, within a day's march of the capital, they made their rendezvous: 'Many thousands of fighting men joined Mwanga's standard, and after ten days the Christians, about 800 strong, joined us.' Mwanga's army had one great advantage. The people of the Sesse islands, scattered about Lake Victoria within a day's paddling from the Buganda coast, had remained faithful to the rightful king throughout all the changes on the mainland. With Stokes's boat and the islanders' canoes, the royalists could strike where they wished along the shoreline, and retreat to a safe haven if the opposition ashore got too strong.

Whatever his inclination to caution, Stokes was now admiral of the Kabaka's fleet. It was not easy to hold the fighting men together. The Protestants and Catholics kept squabbling: 'Very strong and bitter feelings are held by both parties.' Stokes claimed to belong to neither faction, and urged a swift attack while the waIslami and their Arab organisers were still unprepared. But nobody on Mwanga's side wanted to take the initiative. After several days of indecision, the Arabs came by land and attacked the Christian camp; the invasion force took to their boats and sailed ingloriously off into the lake. They landed further along the shore and set light to the vegetation upwind of the capital, in order to force the Muslims to retreat towards it and fight the blaze. Mwanga then settled down in safety on Bulingugwe island, about 800 yards offshore facing the site of his late father's former palace. The Arabs could not get at him, nor he at the Arabs. It was stalemate.

Stokes was clearly fed up with the reluctance of his Christian allies to do any serious fighting – and besides, the delay was costing him money. He rushed off to the south end of the lake, saying he needed to fetch more powder for the muskets and ammunition for the rifles. But he did not hurry back. Instead he hung about his base camp at Uyui, looking after his business. In answer to queries he said his boat needed fixing, and that anyway he was sick.

In fact he was doing his best to make peace on the lake. He approached his Arab fellow-merchants, offering (on

what authority is not clear – probably his own say-so)
safe-conduct to all their colleagues still in Buganda. He
wanted as little fighting as possible, and all the credit he
could get from all parties. But the Arabs did not accept his
mediation. Their dhows, sailing slowly north, were am-
bushed from the rear as they neared the Buganda mainland
at Entebbe, by a flotilla of war-canoes loyal to Mwanga,
based on the Sesse islands. The dhows were burned, and
that was the end of the Arabs as a trading force on the lake.

Stokes followed them north aboard the *Limi*. His passengers were Monsignor Lourdel, the acting bishop and the
most vociferously anti-Protestant of the White Fathers, and
Father Denoît; they shared the boat with a cargo of guns,
powder and shot. Since the Protestant clergy preferred not
to travel in the company of the priests or the firearms, Cyril
Gordon and Robert Walker, both ordained parsons, made
the journey up the lake in canoes. It took them over two
weeks of acute discomfort to reach Bulingugwe island,
where they found the Kabaka surrounded by squabbling
factions of Protestants and Catholics, united only in their
opposition to the Muslims.

Robert Walker watched Stokes with interest and disap-
proval, noting especially his reluctance to call for outside
help from the Imperial British East Africa Company:
'Stokes doubtless thinks that if we take the country there
will not be sufficient to pay the two parties,' he wrote home.
He sourly reckoned the price that the trader had already
established for his help to Mwanga: 'Stokes ... claims 1,000
frasilahs of ivory.' One *frasilah*, the standard Swahili
measure of ivory, weighed 35 pounds, and the price was
£17 for top-quality tusks, less for lower-quality pieces. The
charge for restoring the Kabaka to his kingdom was therefore about £15,000 – equivalent in terms of 1985 to just
under £500,000. It was a stiff price, but perhaps not unrea-
sonable in the circumstances.

Stokes wanted an agreed settlement, as well as his money.
He liked peace for itself; probably he also reckoned that a
peaceful Buganda would be more likely to pay its foreign
debts. But the conflict ended bloodily. On 5 October 1889,
the combined Christian forces stormed the capital, Rubaga,

and burned it to the ground. There was a terrible massacre
of the Arab traders and teachers, and of anyone who had
taken their side. So the Christians, with fire and slaughter
of the infidel, restored their champion Mwanga to his
throne.

Stokes, his boat and his guns had won the war. Now he
had to make his profit from the peace. He brought off one
coup, ensuring that if the Arabs had a blood-feud with
anyone on the Christian side it would not be him, by locat-
ing and protecting two Arab traders with whom he had
previously done business, Hamadi and Khalfan. Khalfan
was a rich man, and promised to pay Mwanga a ransom –
sixty guns, plenty of powder and some cloth – in return for
his life. Two weeks later, Stokes transported the men under
safe-conduct to rejoin their colleagues at Magu, thus winning friends on both sides.

In Buganda itself, with the Arabs defeated and the pagan
traditionalists keeping quiet while the conflict raged, the
rivalries between the Christian sects at once broke out
again, and the national affiliations of the French and British
missions came fully into play. The Anglican clergymen acknowledged that Mwanga was unlikely ever to accept their
faith without coercion. They needed an official British presence to enforce Protestantism. Mwanga's prime minister,
Apolo Kagwa, was of their party and accepted their view.
(Later, Kagwa became Uganda's first Knight of the British
Empire, to which his services had indeed been signal.) The
Anglican missionaries, and Kagwa as leader of the waIngerezi party, wanted to bring the Imperial British East
Africa Company in to guide the nation's destiny. Obviously
the Kabaka did not want such a foreign take-over. Nor did
Stokes: the company was a state-backed monopoly, able to
set its own rules for trade – and he was an independent
entrepreneur.

But the British company, and other European interests too,
was moving in. Emin Pasha and his cry for help had provided the excuse: two expeditions claiming to support his
cause were at this very moment approaching Buganda. First
was that sent by the IBEA company itself, under a rather

dim gentleman-adventurer called Frederick Jackson (whose
later reward was to be made governor of British Uganda).

Jackson had advanced across the arid highlands of what
is now Kenya, on the pretext of seeking news of Stanley's
Emin Pasha relief expedition (although, since it was well
known that Stanley intended to skirt round Buganda to the
west, there was not the remotest chance of encountering
him). Having successfully found his way across the country
of the Masai tribesmen, Jackson was by the middle of 1889
known to be nearing Buganda's eastern border. Stokes
foresaw trouble, on two counts.

The IBEA expedition would, if it continued as it was
heading, cross the Buganda border near where Bishop Hannington had been killed, and where it too would probably
meet resistance. Stokes wanted to avoid all fighting, if possible. Moreover, if Jackson did enter Buganda he stood a
good chance of obtaining from Mwanga, or from one of his
rivals, a trading concession that would put the IBEA company in just the position of advantage Stokes himself was
hoping to obtain. In an effort to dissuade Jackson from
advancing into Buganda, Stokes wrote him a letter explaining that things were at a very delicate stage in Buganda,
with civil war in full swing and the Kabaka on the point of
reasserting his authority. Reinforcements and ammunition
were on their way in Stokes's boat. The intervention of
another European at this stage might upset everything, and
lead to a victory by the Arabs, instead of Mwanga and his
Christians.

This letter was entrusted to Mwanga's officials in their
headquarters on Bulingugwe island, to be sent by them to
Mumia's village just outside Buganda's border, where Jackson was bound to pass. Mwanga knew it was designed to
deter Jackson from coming to his help, in order to preserve
Stokes's unique position in Buganda. But the king was no
fool, and he wanted support, wherever it came from. So he
dictated a letter himself, and had it delivered together with
Stokes's. It was written, in quite good English, by the Kabaka's Christian secretary, Henry Wright Duta (later ordained as an Anglican clergyman), and specifically asked
Jackson for help from the 'White men English men'. It

included the crucial promise: 'I will give you plenty of ivory
and you may do any trade in Uganda, and all you like in
the country under me.'

Duta would of course not have written to this effect without the assent of the white Protestant clergymen to whose
party he belonged. They were growing increasingly uneasy
about Stokes's role. Instead of working for British interests
he was working for his own, and actually trying to keep
out the IBEA company. The shrewd Cyril Gordon saw a
way round the problem, by exploiting Stokes's desire to
safeguard his position as chief intermediary between the
Kabaka and the outside world. The trader was making extravagant claims for his own importance: 'Whether Stokes
did right to promise Mwanga help in the name of the Consul and the English, as he did before us in court the other
day, we do not know ...' So Gordon decided to take Stokes
at his word, and persuaded him that it was his duty to go
in person to the British consul-general and the company
officials in Zanzibar, to state the case on behalf of Mwanga.
The Catholic priests agreed to this course.

Stokes set out on his way across the lake with a mixed
boatload. For the Protestant party he had Henry Wright
Duta, representing the waIngerezi; for the waFransi he had
a senior Catholic prince, Cyprian Kawuta. For himself, he
transported two delightful presents from Mwanga, pretty
little girls of noble birth from the royal harem, Nanjala and
Zaria. (Both, when of age, were to become Stokes's mis-
tresses, and Nanjala was the mother of his posthumous son.)
The girls were descendants of the family of the Kamu-
swaga, or prince, of Koki, a territory to the west of Buganda
proper; that royal family was of pure descent from the
cattle-raising Hima people whose physical splendour is
famous. The girls had been brought to safety under the old
Kabaka's protection during some dynastic disturbances in
their homeland, and their rank and beauty made them
splendid gifts. The photograph of Nanjala, taken in 1958
when she was about eighty, shows she was a fine woman to
the last.

Power, sex and money were the preoccupations signified
by the passengers aboard the *Limi* in October 1889. But

Stokes's schemes, like his girls, were not yet mature. He decided, as usual, to do nothing hasty, staying put at the south end of the lake and sending off messages to the appropriate destinations. To Zanzibar, for Colonel Euan-Smith, the consul-general, he despatched Duta and Kawuta to present the united view of the Protestant and Catholic parties in Buganda on the Kabaka's need for British help: Stokes made sure they carried a letter explaining that he alone had brought about this unity within the Kabaka's court, and that he therefore deserved a favoured place in any settlement the British might help to bring about. To the Arab merchant community on the lake he sent the *Limi*, to collect on Mwanga's behalf the ransom agreed for the businessman Khalfan, as negotiated by himself. The ransom consisted of cloth, guns and powder. With this cargo the *Limi* sailed back to Buganda.

The ammunition arrived in the nick of time. In Stokes's absence the Buganda Muslims had gathered their forces for one last onslaught; they had driven Mwanga, with his Christian allies and the leading Christian chiefs, back once more to the safety of the offshore islands. Rearmed, the Kabaka's forces counterattacked and drove the Muslims out for good, to take refuge in the outlying provinces of the realm. That was on 11 February 1890.

Mwanga had defeated his domestic enemies. But the white men were still prowling around his frontiers, awaiting the restoration of order in the kingdom before they began their predatory moves against it. Stanley, escorting Emin Pasha as a virtual prisoner of war out of Equatoria, had skirted clear of Buganda on his journey south in 1889, because he had been warned that entering the country was dangerous. In December the two travellers had reached the coast, and Emin had joined up with the Germans to try to win over the Kabaka.

And on 23 February 1890, just twelve days after Mwanga had finally regained control of his capital, an entirely unexpected element appeared on the scene. Dr Carl Peters, at the head of a small but heavily-armed German expedition 'to relieve Emin Pasha', burst into Buganda. Peters had passed through Mumia's village on the frontier, and had

opened the letters left there for Jackson from Mwanga and
Stokes. The Kabaka's message revealed that he was ready
to hand over his kingdom to anyone, even to the greedy
Imperial British East Africa Company, in order to save
himself from his domestic rebels. Peters saw no reason why,
if a British commercial monopoly stood a chance of acquiring Buganda, the German emperor should not have the
country instead.

Chapter 8

Buganda is German

Germany will, since I have the distinction to work for German interests, be 'indignant' at me. I have 'contrived' to make myself 'unpopular' in wide circles there.

Dr Carl Peters, *New Light on Dark Africa* (Berlin, 1891)

How sad the fate of our poor Uganda! A little more and it would have become a Catholic kingdom.

Monsignor Hirth, Vicar-Apostolic of the Nyanza (1890)

Dr Carl Peters was the sort of German modern Germany would like to forget – brave, humourless, stubborn, brutal, fanatically patriotic. He believed that the 'Nordic races' were destined to rule the world. Britain, he thought, had shown the way: the Indian empire, where a few thousand whites ruled over millions of 'inferior' stock, was the model for his racist vision. (His father, a Lutheran pastor, so admired Britain that the boy was christened with an English-style C to his name, rather than the authentically German K.) With German unity accomplished in the 1870s, the young man believed the time had come for the new great power to acquire its own place in the sun. The last unconquered continent was Africa, and there Peters determined that Germany would become a worthy rival to Britain.

He read with youthful passion the accounts of the early explorers of the interior – Livingstone and Stanley, of course, and also the German missionaries Krapf and Rebmann, and the more scientific travellers Schweinfurth and

Junker. From them he devised a dream of German rule over the sources of the Nile. Buganda became his target. The German government brushed his ideas aside, Bismarck believing Germany must consolidate at home before seeking colonies abroad. But in the early 1880s Peters found merchants in Hamburg and financiers in Berlin who saw in his African vision the answer to their worries about supplies of raw materials, and of new customers for their industrial wares.

From such men he raised the funds to start his Society for German Colonisation, and set off under its auspices for East Africa. In the society's name he secured phoney treaties with the African 'chiefs' of the Kilimanjaro districts, and his sponsors' influence was sufficient to convert those treaties into letters bringing the districts under the effective sovereignty of the Kaiser. The newly-acquired territory was handed over, under the rules agreed at the Berlin conference, to be administered by the Colonisation Society's legal heir, the Deutsche Ostafrika Gesellschaft.

In 1886, the ignorant brutality of the company's officials provoked the so-called 'Bushiri rebellion', which was put down only with the help of the neighbouring British colonial authorities, using ships of the Royal Navy. This humiliation sharpened Peters's ambition to get even with the British in the business of conquest. The agitation for the relief of Emin Pasha gave him the pretext for his next African adventure. In Britain the Pasha's appeal for support had been brushed aside by the government, but taken up by private interests (with King Leopold's backing, and under H. M. Stanley's leadership). In Germany too the government was lukewarm, but Peters provided the impulse for private action.

Emin had written to his friends in Germany, as well as in Britain. Peters ensured that the letters got wide publicity, reminding his fellow-countrymen that Emin was, after all, a German. He got up a committee of super-patriots – merchants, members of parliament, pastors, prominent men – and secured private assurances of support from Bismarck's influential relatives. A subscription was raised in Germany with objectives identical to those professed by the British

Emin Pasha committee. Despite Peters's reminders that Emin had promised to reimburse all expenses out of his hoard of ivory, the German fund was only half the size of that raised in Britain and in Egypt. With this money behind him, Peters set off for Africa.

The problem for the German force was that there seemed no way it could get to Equatoria without trespassing on territory already claimed by Britain, Belgium or France. Peters identified one route that might just not be illegal. Towards the northern extremity of the coastline of British East Africa, where the Tana river runs to the sea, lay the tiny Sultanate of Witu, whose Arab ruler claimed independence of the Sultan of Zanzibar. There an insignificant German trading post had been established. (Its main import, said a British consular report, was bottled beer, its main export empty beer bottles.) At Witu, therefore, Germany had a sort of claim to the right of colonial acquisition defined in the Berlin agreement of 1885. Under the Berlin rules, if Germany had rights on the coast, it also had rights in the hinterland. Peters decided to penetrate if he could up the almost untravelled valley of the Tana river, and to attempt to march from its headwaters across the mountains into Buganda, and from Buganda into Equatoria. Only a hero or a lunatic could have contemplated such a journey, against such odds. Peters was a bit of both.

From Germany he had brought an ample supply of Mauser rifles and ammunition, and one prize piece – an experimental machine-gun, mounted on wheels, donated by the firm of Krupp, who wanted a report on how it worked against live targets. At Aden the British allowed him to hire a rag-tag collection of Sudanese and Zanzibari mercenaries to carry these weapons. The British did not take his project seriously, and carelessly allowed his force to pass unhindered through Zanzibar. So he landed in the surf of Witu, marched up the desolate Tana valley, turned across the highlands behind Mount Kenya and the great Rift Valley, and emerged on the frontier of Buganda, where the Kabaka Mwanga had just been restored to his throne for the third time, thanks to Stokes's supply of guns.

Peters's account of his journey, told in inimitably brutal

prose, is both ferocious and comic. The Krupp gun was a useless impediment: he dumped it, naming a nearby moun-tain peak after the firm in gratitude for its contribution. Under attack by the fierce Masai who controlled the Kenya uplands, he held his men steady on a hill-top, ordered fire at the last moment, repulsed the gallant tribesmen, and discouraged a further assault by cutting off the heads of his dead enemies and bowling them down to the survivors. On Christmas Day, 1889, his second-in-command, Lieutenant von Tiedemann, was very sick and depressed, suffering from fever and dysentery. Peters read him Schopenhauer's philosophical discussion of the theory that 'there is no true pleasure without true need', and thought poor Tiedemann felt better as a result.

The British considered Peters a bounder. He proved it on arrival at the Buganda frontier when, in Chief Mumia's village, he found the letters sent from the Kabaka's capital to await Frederick Jackson and told Mumia that, as a white man, he had a right to see the other white man's mail. The letter from Stokes aroused Peters's interest: he had heard of the Irish trader as a useful man whose services were for sale. The other letter, from the Kabaka himself, was even more significant. It asked Jackson for help, and offered trade concessions and a treaty of friendship. Peters correctly concluded that the Kabaka was desperate, and was willing to sell his sovereignty in exchange for safety.

Peters had already made plans to offer Mwanga the pro-tection and patronage of the German emperor. In that hope he pressed on into Buganda and entered the poor huts of Rubaga, hastily built to replace the splendid reed palaces that had been burnt to the ground in the recurring civil wars. There, as planned, he found allies at the court of the Kabaka – the White Fathers of the French Roman Catholic mission, in the persons of their outgoing Superior, Monsig-nor Siméon Lourdel, and his assistant, Father Denoît.

The British had no idea of the alliance prepared between the French Catholics and the German Lutheran. It was in fact logical enough: England was a solely Protestant coun-try, and its missionaries seemed to the Frenchman to be agents of the national Anglican Church. Bismarck's new

7-9 Tippu Tib (left), the overlord of the Swahili traders in the interior, owed allegiance to Said Bargash, Sultan of Zanzibar (right). The basis of the Zanzibar economy was slavery; Dr Livingstone's campaign against the slave trade included imaginative illustrations, like this engraving of shackled slaves on the march under their Swahili captors.

10 Eduard Schnitzer, the Austrian doctor appointed by the British General Charles Gordon as Governor of the Equatoria province of the Sudan, took the name Mohammed el Amin and became famous under his Egyptian title, Emin Pasha. He was photographed in about 1884, probably by the Russian explorer Dr Junker.

11 At Mpwapwa in June 1890, the officers of the German military expedition advancing towards Buganda. Left to right: Lt von Tiedemann, Lt Janke, Emin Pasha, Capt. Dr Stuhlmann, Dr Carl Peters, Lt Langheld, Lt von Bülow.

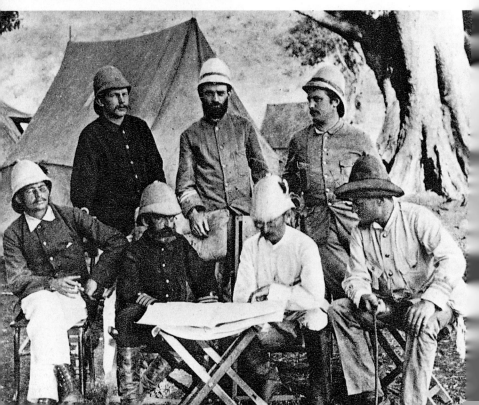

12 Dr Carl Peters, founder of the German Colonisation Society and chief creator of Germany's East Africa empire – here on the Kilimanjaro expedition of 1891.

13 Lt von Tiedemann, Carl Peters's assistant on the drive for Buganda, was pictured at home in Germany in his African get-up.

14 Father Auguste Achte, of the Society of Missionaries of Algiers (the White Fathers), was described by his British Protestant rivals as a Frenchman, but was in fact a patriotic citizen of the newly acquired German province of Alsace.

15 The party of White Fathers that headed for Buganda in 1878 to forestall a Protestant take-over of the country. In front, centre, is their first Vicar-General, Monsignor Livinhac; to his right is Father Siméon Lourdel.

Germany, containing vast Catholic regions, was far more likely than Britain to favour all churches equally. There was another good reason for the White Fathers to favour the German cause. Their new chief, waiting at the south end of Lake Victoria to take over from Monsignor Lourdel as Vicar-Apostolic of the Nyanza, was Monsignor Hirth. He had been born a Frenchman – but in the village of Nieder-spechbach, in Alsace. Following the French defeat in the Franco-Prussian war of 1871, German-speaking Alsace had been absorbed into Germany. Hirth's letters, written in a crabbed Gothic hand, show by their style that they were not written by a native speaker of French, and it is clear that he positively hoped that Buganda would be included within Germany's new African empire, as a Catholic province. He had advised his colleagues to co-operate in every possible way with Peters. They were glad to do so, if only to frustrate the Anglicans.

Lourdel knew the original purpose of Peters's expedition had been frustrated. In August 1889 a letter from Stanley, sent from Mackay's homestead, had told how Emin was a captive in British hands, Equatoria abandoned, and the pretext for the adventure nullified. But if Peters could get Buganda, that would more than compensate for the loss of Equatoria. Peters and Lourdel prepared a treaty, in Luganda, Swahili and French, promising Mwanga 'friendly relations with the German emperor'. There was no mention of sovereignty, or of trading rights, such as Peters had imposed upon less grand and more pliable African chieftains. On 1 March 1890, Mwanga signed the apparently innocuous document, and committed his country to the German sphere of influence. Even without a text in German, Peters seemed to have won for his Kaiser the jewel of tropical Africa. It was an amazing triumph.

The pro-British party was sure to fight back once its chiefs understood what had happened. It was up to the Catholics to get guns first. On the advice of Monsignor Lourdel, Mwanga therefore ordered an arsenal from his usual supplier, Charles Stokes. Payment for muskets, rifles and powder would be made in ivory, from the Kabaka's store. Since Stokes was now at his home in German territory, Peters agreed to convey the order to him there. Peters was anyway in a hurry to leave. He needed to inform his government of the Buganda treaty signed on its behalf, so that the imperial Foreign Office might formally register its claim to this new bit of dubious hinterland. Moreover, Fred Jackson was on his way with his armed party.

Messages, once again, were moving more slowly than events. Before Peters had even arrived in Buganda, the Kabaka had written a second invitation to Jackson. It was countersigned by Monsignor Lourdel for the Catholic mission, and by Cyril Gordon for the Anglicans; both men were apprehensive that Mwanga, if he did not get Christian help, would revert to the traditional faith of the Baganda, at the head of the Futabanghi party. Jackson found this letter awaiting him at the contact point in Mumia's village on the border. He also found the previous batch of letters left there for him, and realised that the cad Peters had opened them. Angry at this ungentlemanly conduct, and hoping to take revenge for it, Jackson entered Buganda at the head of a strong party of Sudanese riflemen, superior both in numbers and in training to Peters's small scratch force.

Peters was gone. He had marched off southwards into German East Africa, pausing only to make contact with the missionaries expelled from Buganda. He had messages for, and high hopes of, Mackay, the pro-German Scotsman – but Mackay died just before Peters arrived. Hirth, the Alsatian White Father, enthusiastically supported the German aims. Peters's raiding party was exhausted, and short of food and ammunition, but Peters used up his bullets on the tribesmen along the way, to whom he refused to pay the customary *hongo*: 'It would have been reversing the natural order of things for the masters of the country to pay tribute to their subjects', he explained.

At Mpwapwa, on 20 June 1890, Peters met at last the man he had come to Africa to rescue. Emin Pasha, far from being a lost hero, was now at the head of a heavily-armed German raiding force, heading inland with Stokes as transport officer. Peters urged Emin to press ahead to Buganda, and establish Germany's claim there, encouraging Emin with the news that Mwanga had ordered a supply of guns and ammunition to bolster the Kabaka's resistance to the British.

Emin and his colleagues had good news to give in exchange. Bismarck, they said, was gone from the Chancery, sacked by the young Kaiser Wilhelm II, who had appointed in his place General von Caprivi, a Prussian gentleman of no strong political views. Caprivi was to carry through the programme of social and political reforms that Bismarck had been unwilling to complete. At last, the weary travellers agreed, there was a chance that imperialism would be pursued as a methodical part of German foreign policy, not, as under Bismarck, reluctantly and almost by accident.

On their way to the coast, Peters and Tiedemann passed through a region of settled farms and villages, whose chiefs greeted the travellers by hoisting the little German flags that signified their new allegiance. All the Germans' patriotic sentimentality was aroused. As they neared the coast, a party of disciplined African soldiers marched up to greet them, under German officers. Proudly, Peters prepared to tell them of his great coup in Buganda. But their news was more interesting than his. Caprivi had signed away all possibility of a German claim to Buganda. Peters had made his terrible journey in vain.

Caprivi had been instructed by the Emperor to sort out Germany's international rights and obligations, and so to prepare the consolidation of a world-wide Reich. This meant reaching a series of compromises with the greatest existing empire, which was Britain's. It also meant confining the ambitions of France in Africa to an area that Lord Salisbury described in the House of Lords (on 5 August 1890) as 'what agriculturists would call "very light land"; that is to say, it is the desert of the Sahara.' (That is why the nations of the drought-stricken Sahel of the early 1980s all use French as their official language.)

The territorial settlements of 1890 were global. They recognised certain German trading rights in the South Pacific: the resulting German colonies there passed at the end of the first Great War to Australia and the United States,

which still rule large parts of Micronesia. The oddest
arrangement gave Germany access to a strip of desert 20
miles wide and 225 miles long in the desert hinterland of
the German colony of South-West Africa – a ridiculous
appendage meant to give the Germans a route to the upper
waters of the Zambezi river, on which a joint steamship
service was to be run by the British, Germans and Portuguese. (Nobody realised that the Zambezi's falls and rapids make it impassable by any vessel.) South Africa acquired
the Caprivi Strip after 1918, and has illegally held on to it,
as part of Namibia. The strip has enabled the South Africans for over twenty years to terrorise and subvert the
black-ruled nations to its north. Such careless accidents by
the European powers in Victoria's day have determined
Africa's future for long after the original colonial powers
left the continent.

In this global chess-game Buganda was a mere pawn.
Caprivi's government now acknowledged that it lay within
the British sphere of influence in East Africa. In direct
exchange, Britain handed over to Germany its least profitable overseas possession – the barely inhabited North Sea
sandbank of Heligoland. If the British fortified the island,
they could block the movement of Germany's Grand Fleet
towards the Atlantic. So the Germans swapped it. It was,
said Peters, 'the exchange of a fly-button for a piece of stout
cloth'.

Under Caprivi's settlement, the treaty Peters had signed
with the Kabaka was dishonoured before it had even been
registered with the German government. Peters had promised the Kabaka protection: the German government had
refused to provide it. The adventurer had to accept that
decision, taking it as yet another proof of the decadence and
liberalism at home against which he and all true Germans
were bound to struggle. For the Kabaka, when he found
out, it provided new evidence that Europeans were
heavily-armed liars.

It was only a matter of time before the British subdued
Mwanga, as they had subdued so many recalcitrant little
monarchs around the world. But the White Fathers,
although frustrated in their immediate hope of German pro-

tection, still thought it worth encouraging resistance to the British. They explained to the Kabaka the nature of the threat, which would involve a take-over of his kingdom by the commercial monopoly of the Imperial British East Africa Company, and the forced conversion of the people to a heretical version of Christianity.

The Germans had formally withdrawn their claim to the country. It was excessively unlikely that France, racked at this time by successive constitutional crises at home, would step in. But in Britain the Liberal Party had declared that, if it won power, the government would refuse to accept any colonial responsibilities, even as gifts from adventurous fighting men. From his base in Algiers, Cardinal Lavigerie, the founder of the White Fathers, was manoeuvring to have Buganda declared an international protectorate. In Rome itself the Pope's advisers, with French backing, were scheming to set up a force called the 'Papal Zouaves' to acquire colonies for the Church. ('The crusades offer a precedent, but not an encouraging one', minuted Lord Salisbury drily.) The White Fathers at Mwanga's court knew of these international manoeuvres only in outline, and by occasional messengers. But with Jackson's raiding-party on the spot, and the British closing in fast, there was no time to lose. Stokes's arms would, if they arrived in time, strengthen the delaying power of the Catholic faction.

Monsignor Hirth, for a while, held back the tide of British expansion by sheer force of character. Frederick Jackson and his Sudanese mercenaries took control of the Kabaka's capital as soon as Peters left, and Jackson asked Mwanga to sign a new treaty to replace the one he had signed with Peters. Hirth persuaded the king that, having just sworn to establish a special relationship with the German emperor, he could not immediately go back on his word and do the same with the British East Africa Company. Faced with this logic, Jackson could only complain that the 'evil influence' of the French priests had poisoned the Kabaka's mind against the benefits of British protection. After little more than a month he gave up and travelled down to the coast, by the route he had pioneered through British East Africa; it took him three months to reach the new British port of Mombasa, where he took a boat to Zanzibar, arriving in September 1890.

In Mwanga's capital Jackson left his junior assistant, a feeble young man called Ernest Gedge, with thirty-five soldiers, plenty of ammunition and enough cloth to barter for local food and supplies. Gedge existed under the protection of the prime minister, the Katikiro Apolo Kagwa, who led the Protestant WaIngerezi party in the Kabaka's court. The platoon of trained riflemen was reinforced by an organised Protestant militia, led by Kagwa and armed by Gedge.

Down in Zanzibar, Jackson found a new atmosphere of co-operation between the British and German administrations. The Imperial Commissioner, Hermann von Wissmann, and the IBEA company's administrator, George Mackenzie, got along well together, and had agreed in writing to ban the sale within their respective territories of all breech-loading rifles to Arabs and Africans, and to limit the hitherto unrestricted sale of muskets and gunpowder.

Both dutifully accepted the Buganda-for-Heligoland swap. But they knew well that decisions taken in Europe, without consulting them – and, indeed, without any knowledge of local circumstances – could suddenly change the rules under which they were working. Next year's treaty might say something quite different from this year's. Under the still valid – but everywhere flouted – Berlin rules, Buganda would be recognised as a British possession only when the Kabaka had been forced by a soldier, or cajoled by a missionary, to sign his sovereignty away. That had by no means happened yet. Wissmann in particular was not resigned to accept the Caprivi deal as final, and manoeuvred to be ready to take any advantage that shifting policies at home might throw in Germany's way.

The strongest cards in the German hand were the eccentric scholar Emin Pasha and the erratic trader Charles Stokes. German flattery and British arrogance had forced these two entirely dissimilar men into close collaboration. Contact with the vulgar and overbearing H. M. Stanley had given Emin a particularly strong distaste for things British, and through the courteous flattery of Reichskommissar von Wissmann he had easily been won over to the German

cause. He had never wanted to leave Equatoria, and he
longed to return. Nursed back to health after his unhappy
fall in Bagamoyo, Emin agreed to enter the service of the
German empire with the rank of Reichskommissar, on
special duties. At the head of a strong armed force he set
off for the far interior.

Emin had three main objectives. One was to nose around
Buganda with the hope of claiming it for Germany; his
meeting with Peters on 20 June and the news of the treaty
with Mwanga strengthened this hope. The second objective, and Emin's principal personal aim, was to get back to
his old province of Equatoria, and to reassemble there his
remaining Sudanese troops, and as much of his stock of
ivory as had not been lost through Stanley's mismanage-
ment; then he would claim German protection for the province, and rule it for the Reich. Third, Emin was told to
make treaties for Germany with as many amenable local
chiefs as possible: in particular he should push out the frontiers of German Africa westwards from Lake Victoria, towards the territory likely to be claimed by King Leopold's
Congo Free State.

Emin set out on 26 April 1890, assured of the full backing
of the German government. On 1 April, an Imperial governor had at last been named for German East Africa. He
was an aristocratic military man, von Soden; his orders were
to regularise the administration that had hitherto been hap-
hazardly run by von Wissmann, with grossly inadequate
funds and staff. And on 12 May, just after Emin's departure, Chancellor Caprivi requested the German parliament
to vote the large sum of four and a half million marks 'for
the suppression of the slave trade and the protection of
German interests in East Africa'. The Germans had seemed
to be on the warpath. Perhaps this was just bluff, to persuade the British to sort out their problems with Germany
quickly; or perhaps Caprivi's government simply changed
its mind – whatever the reasoning, on 1 July the Heligoland
treaty was signed, and Emin's first objective, which Peters's
coup seemed to have made easily attainable, was snatched
away. Emin had been walking across Africa for almost five
months before the news caught up with him.

It was a bitter blow. But Emin still kept his eye on Equatoria. No European power yet had a sound claim to the province. No firm demarcation lines had been drawn to the west of Lake Victoria, since nobody really knew how the land lay there, where the Congo watershed actually was, or where King Leopold's claim to territory began. If Emin could make enough treaties, and establish a practicable route through that unclaimed landscape, he might grab a strip of land linking German East Africa with Equatoria, and thus cut off British East Africa from the Congo State. He pursued German aggrandisement in a way that was ambitious, but vague. Emin himself was both those things, and Reichskommissar von Wissmann knew it. He had therefore, while giving Emin the honour of commanding the expedition, put its military arm under the authority of a much junior but much more reliable officer.

Lieutenant Friedrich Stuhlmann was probably the best man in the German East African service at the time. He was a medical doctor, and shared Emin's interest in natural history: his main responsibility seems to have been to keep the Pasha in order – a task beyond even his abilities. The party also included two priests, Father Achte and Father Schynse of the French missionary order of the White Fathers. But neither, now, was a Frenchman. Both were from Alsace, like their superior. Both, like Hirth, were stout German patriots.

The purely military arm of the expedition was commanded by the able but rather unimaginative Lieutenant Langheld, a professional soldier of great administrative ability. He was supported by a *Feldwebel*, or warrant officer, Mr Kühne, and two competent sergeants, Kay and Hoffmann, one of whom was specifically responsible for a Krupp 35mm machine-gun, mounted on wheels. All the white men were armed with Remington magazine rifles, and the 150 locally-recruited black riflemen with light hunting carbines or single-shot Mausers. Supplies and ammunition were carried by 400 porters. The only problem as they went along was to stop the soldiers making a nuisance of themselves with the women of the villages, or smoking too much of the excellent marijuana grown by the Wanyamwesi farmers whose lands they passed through.

The German armed party was backed up by Charles Stokes, in charge of supplies and communications, with the rank of assistant Reichskommissar, and a fine blue uniform. He was on a year's contract, for which he was paid £1,000: ten years before, the CMS had employed him for £120 a year, so this was good money. Moreover, provided he did his job satisfactorily for the Germans, Stokes was free to do his own business on the side. It was agreed that he would use his influence with local chiefs to persuade them to sign treaties of protection with the Germans.

Apart from the money and the dignity, Stokes stood to gain in several ways from this arrangement. Like it or not, the territory within which he mostly operated, and from which he drew his Wanyamwesi porters, was now definitely under German sovereignty. If he wanted to carry on business, he must make friends with the new masters. It suited the Germans to employ him as treaty-maker, since his contacts were unsurpassed. It suited him too, setting him up in African eyes as a peace-maker and go-between with the new lot of powerful white men. His family-by-marriage would certainly benefit from the new connection. Stokes made much of this, and wrote to Mackenzie, the IBEA company administrator: 'I have not joined [the Germans] for money, but to secure the best interests of my people.' This was partly true.

He also assured the British authorities that he would co-operate in their attempt to control the arms trade. In February 1890 he had informed Consul-General Euan-Smith, in Zanzibar, 'I have written to Mwanga that I cannot send ammunition to Buganda without the consent of the Imperial British East Africa Company.' This was not true at all. He was perfectly placed to move weapons through German territory, and then by boat across Lake Victoria, without stepping on to the IBEA company's lands. That he fully intended to do, if the Germans would let him.

In other respects, although now an official in German service, he continued to work for British interests. The Church Missionary Society had lost two Bishops-designate of Buganda before either could reach the new see, with James Hannington killed and Henry Parker dead of sickness. Early in 1890 the third, Alfred Tucker, had arrived in Zanzibar with a party of seven newly-recruited clergy. Stokes had agreed to escort them to the lake, delaying the departure of his caravan until they were ready. Neither the delay nor the advantage to Britain of having a stronger mission in Buganda can have pleased the Germans. But there was no possible replacement for Stokes, so they had to put up with him.

What the Germans surely did not know was that Stokes, their assistant commissioner, had also accepted a political commission from Consul-General Euan-Smith and Administrator Mackenzie. They had handed him a stock of British flags, and a box of the forms printed by the Foreign Office for making treaties with native rulers. (These came in several nicely-graded variations of wording, for important chiefs, subordinate chiefs, Muslims, pagans, and so on.) The British officials impressed upon Stokes that any chiefs he could sign up on their side of the Anglo-German demarcation line would be gratefully received. If he could do a deal for Britain with the Kabaka Mwanga, their gratitude would be suitably expressed in the form of trading concessions.

The Germans had given Stokes solid proof of the benefits of co-operation with the colonial powers. On his arrival in May 1890 at the coastal port of Saadani to collect the weapons ordered by the Kabaka Mwanga, he brought with him a huge caravan of 2,500 porters – almost all of them Wanyamwesi, his own people. He had the princely sum of $40,000 (about £6,700) in ivory to spend. Being Stokes, he acted as though it all belonged to him, although a lot of it was presumably Mwanga's, in advance payment for the guns. Wissmann, the Imperial Commissioner, laid on a great dinner of welcome, with champagne and toasts to King Mwanga and his distinguished agent. Stokes lapped up the flattery. He was even happier about the trade concessions that the Germans offered. Wissmann authorised free transport over to Zanzibar for the ivory, aboard the German government steamer. Export duty, chargeable on the ivory at 10 per cent, was remitted in exchange for a token pay-

ment. The British had never done such favours for a man
who, after all, was one of their citizens.

Stokes made the point in a letter to the British consul-
general: 'I ask you plainly am I recognised as a British
subject? ... If I am not a British subject, I wish to seek
other protection, but I honestly tell you I will do nothing
in German territory to favour England, and nothing in
English territory to favour Germany.' Euan-Smith asked
Stokes in for a conciliatory talk, at which the Irishman
characteristically apologised for his defiant tone, and swore
he had never meant to give offence.

Now Stokes was backing three horses at once. For the
Germans he was organising Emin's transport and getting
chiefs to sign treaties. For the British he was helping to
deliver Bishop Tucker and obtaining other signatures on
other treaties. For Mwanga he was buying and transporting
guns.

The European powers had promised each other they
would not arm the natives. Stokes had promised the British
he would abide by their prohibition. But the Germans knew
all about his deal with Mwanga. The large volume of powder in his caravan was packed in neat 5-pound waterproof
barrels bearing the seal of the Imperial powder-factory in
Hamburg, Europe's only remaining manufacturer of old-
fashioned 'trade powder' (*Negerpulver*, 'Negro powder', the
Germans called it). This was not contraband, but an authorised supply with which Stokes would reinforce Mwanga
in his resistance to the British and the Protestant party in
his kingdom.

Stokes had too many different errands for too many different customers. He sorted out the finances of Mwanga's
arms deal, working through British–Indian money-lenders
and financiers whose books – if they kept any – would show
no trace of such delicate transactions. There were delays in
assembling Tucker's party of clergymen, and the trade
goods they needed to take with them. Emin, in the advance
party, grew impatient, and travelled around in Wanyamwesi
country making treaties with the chiefs he came across. This
was meant to have been Stokes's job: even Emin's German
colleagues thought it a bit hard when the Pasha obtained a

treaty for Germany with the head of Limi Stokes's own family, the paramount chief Mitinginya of the Wanyamwesi confederation.

It was almost the end of June before Stokes left for the interior. A few days after his departure came the news from Europe of the signing of the Heligoland treaty, which nullified the main purpose of his journey. Stokes was carrying that news, as well as the supplies that could have enabled Emin to complete Peters's acquisition of Buganda. Now that country, and the entire northern half of Lake Victoria, was out of bounds to German claims. But treaties could be unmade, as well as made – and Equatoria lay ahead. Stokes, with his arms and his civilian supplies, pressed ahead to join up with Emin in September, as near as possible to the northern limit of German territory on the western shore of the lake, at Bukoba.

It was a healthy place, with a safe little harbour and a site that was easy to defend. Emin, unable to advance northwards as he had intended, organised things there as he had done for the armed bases that had been the key to survival for himself and his Sudanese troops in Equatoria. First the soldiers built a stockade on the slopes overlooking the harbour. Then they set to work to ensure self-sufficiency in food. They planted small patches of maize and millet that came up well after the November rains, and a small, well-watered salad-garden for the European mess, with sweet peppers, tomatoes and fresh greens.

With an iron pot and a musket-barrel Emin fixed up a simple still, through which a sort of schnapps could be evaporated from the weak but plentiful banana beer brewed by the locals. (This nasty-sounding stuff, now called Uganda *waragi*, is not bad, and can make you drunk if you want.) With rest and good feeding, there was for once no sickness in the camp. The soldiers and porters made friends with women from the nearby villages. Bukoba had the easy air of a military expedition on a summer outing.

Stokes was as happy as the soldiers. Business was going well. He had completed some valuable deals in Buganda. As far as he knew, his main supply of guns and powder, awaiting delivery to Mwanga, was safe in store at Mwanza, the newly-designated port and administrative headquarters at the southern extremity of the lake where Lieutenant Langheld had taken over independent command. The deals with Mwanga looked like producing an even better load of ivory next time. He had a good job at good pay under the Germans; next year, with a bit of luck, he might wangle a long-term trading concession from one or other of the colonial powers. Limi was with him in the Bukoba encampment, and about this time his second woman, Kabula, bore him a daughter: he called the little girl Louisa, after his old mother in Dublin, and he adored her.

Stokes seems to have had no inkling that things had gone badly wrong for his German masters, blocked off now by their British rivals from their ambitions of northward expansion. So far as he was concerned, there was no hurry. He did offer to produce some of the treaties that the Germans had expected of him, suggesting he should sail across to the opposite shore of the lake where he could make contact with the Arab merchants and rulers he was used to doing business with. Pacifying them would indeed have been a coup. But Stuhlmann wryly noted: '*Er hat dies jedoch nie gethan*' ('All the same, he never did it').

The best day of that comfortable time came on the Kaiser's birthday, 27 January 1891. There was banana beer for everyone, and for the white men enough of Emin's raw new schnapps. Above the stockade the imperial standard floated from its brand-new staff; the air turned cool by the lake as the evening sky darkened from blue to blue-black, and the African stars shone down, as bright as buttons on a naval uniform. The Europeans had their benches carried out and ranged against the stockade, beneath the flagstaff. The black people danced for their masters, over a hundred men cavorting and stamping over the dusty ground.

After a while Stokes could sit still no longer. He reached out for the tough, jolly sergeant-major, Feldwebel Kühne, and together the two men jumped and shook their behinds to the rhythms of the drums, while all around the people, black and white, laughed at them, and with them.

This was the last of those good days by the cool lake at Bukoba. Beneath the German flag Emin Pasha, peering painfully through his new pebble glasses, was conjuring up a fantastic scheme to enhance the glory of the Reich. And up north in Buganda the British, under the toughest of their imperial adventurers, were cleaning the Maxim gun that would seal their conquest.

III

DIVIDING
the
SPOILS

Chapter 9

~

Lugard and the Maxim Gun

He is one of the most *cranky* men I have seen.

> H. M. Stanley, reporting to Mackinnon on Lugard (1892)

We regret one thing, not to have been held worthy of the crown of martyrdom; all chance is not yet lost.

> Monsignor Hirth, Vicar Apostolic of the Nyanza, on his dealings with Lugard (1892)

Then the King told someone to sign for him. I would not have this and insisted on his making a mark. He did it with a bad grace, just dashing the pen at the paper and making a blot; but I made him go at it again and on the second copy he behaved himself and made a proper mark.

> Captain Frederick Lugard, on the signature by the Kabaka Mwanga of the treaty giving control over Uganda to Britain (1890)

Frederick Lugard ended his life laden with honours, a peer, creator of the British colony of Nigeria, author of *The Dual Mandate* – the classic work on how to run an empire on the cheap by getting the natives to do the work for you. To the end he remained a terrifying figure, small, handsome, upright, laconic. His forceful charm won the admiration of two of the most remarkable women of his age. Flora Shaw, the colonial correspondent of *The Times* in the 1880s and 1890s, gave him his first reputation as a hero of empire; later she married him and they went off together to govern Nigeria (whose name she invented). His glory was preserved after his death by Dame Margery Perham, the great

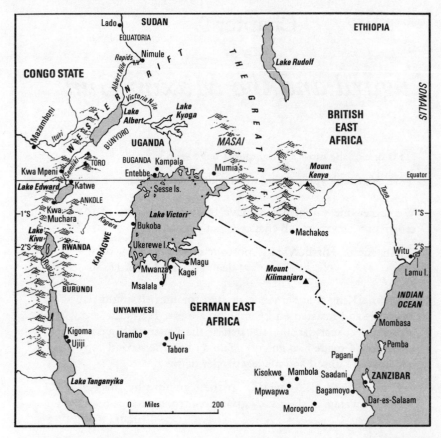

By 1890 Britain and Germany had agreed to share East Africa, along a line running from the Indian Ocean to Lake Victoria at 1° south of the Equator. The interior of German East Africa was well-travelled, and the caravan route from Zanzibar to the south end of Lake Victoria was dotted with Christian mission stations. British East Africa was practically untravelled, partly because its terrain was hostile, partly because its Masai inhabitants were. Buganda remained unconquered, but threatened. Equatoria to the north of it was occupied by Emin Pasha's little army, cut off from their former capital down the Nile at Khartoum, which was in the hands of the Mahdi's Islamic state. Between the ocean and the lake Charles Stokes was the main transport contractor, exporting ivory and importing cloth, metal and guns.

imperialist historian, whom he chose to write his biography. Lugard was a great man; Charles Stokes was a nuisance whom he brushed aside and helped to ruin.

Lugard was a professional fighter, and a brave one. He had served with the army in India and Afghanistan, and been decorated for distinguished service in a campaign against the hill tribesmen of Burma. Then, on leave in Lucknow, he fell in love with a beautiful divorcee, who threw him over and went off to England with a rival, as if in an early Kipling story. Lugard took sick-leave and ventured into Africa with forty-eight sovereigns sewn into his belt - not to shoot the proverbial lion, but to kill or be killed by his fellow-men.

In 1888, aboard a seedy steamer southbound out of Aden, he met by chance a British official on the look-out for promising young frontier-breakers. This was Colonel Charles Euan-Smith, ex-Indian Army, taking up his new post in succession to the famous Sir John Kirk as Her Majesty's consul-general in Zanzibar. Euan-Smith gave Lugard a note to his colleague down south in Mozambique, who employed Lugard to fight the Arab slave-traders on the shores of Lake Malawi. Careless of death, Lugard showed ridiculous courage, leading his black soldiers against Mlozi's stockade, receiving a terrible musket-wound through his arms and chest, and finally defeating the slave-traders. The officials of the Imperial British East Africa Company, alerted by Euan-Smith, rightly thought him a good man for a tough spot. In 1889 he entered their service.

The first assignment was to establish a new route to the great inland lakes, from the new capital of Mombasa on the coast, across the barren country where the warriors of the Masai people put all travellers' lives at risk. Only one Englishman had so far made the journey and described it. He was the charming Joseph Thomson, who did tricks - taking out his false teeth, making water fizz by throwing in Eno's Fruit Salts, claiming to cause an eclipse he had predicted from his calendar - that made the Masai laugh, and not attack him. Lugard had no time for such fun. The Germans had been allocated the traditional caravan-route to the lakes;

the IBEA company had been given Masailand, and now Lugard was told to begin transforming it into the white man's Kenya, where obstructive natives would stand aside before their masters. British East Africa – the name of Kenya had not yet been invented – seemed valuable only as the approach to Uganda.

Early in 1890 Lugard was at work on the route, with his surveying equipment and his rifle. He had firm orders not to cross into Buganda itself, while it remained in its present state of civil war. He had got to Dagoreti, near the as yet undreamed-of city of Nairobi, when orders came to travel on, fast. News had got through to the British authorities of Carl Peters's treaty with the Kabaka, giving Germany a sound claim there. The British also knew that the Germans were planning to send Emin Pasha to back up Peters and make formal arrangements for the take-over with the Kabaka and Germany's allies, the French priests. Lugard's formal orders were to keep the peace in Buganda. His real mission was to cancel Peters's deal, and to forestall Emin's expedition.

A merely brave man would have gone ahead, and would probably have been caught up in some terrible slaughter. Lugard had experience as a transport officer in wild country in India and Burma. He knew that an armed expedition is likely to do more harm than good unless it has assured supplies at its back, a well-defined mission ahead, and a leader with a clear mandate. He had none of these. He knew, too, that the IBEA company was seriously under-financed. The capital it had raised was inadequate to develop the potential – slim as it seemed – of what is now Kenya. To take in Buganda as well was far beyond the company's capacity. Even the cost of Lugard's own voyage of exploration was almost more than the company could afford. He was instructed to shoot every mature elephant he could find, to produce a token revenue in ivory that might keep the nervous share-holders in hope of more.

Lugard disobeyed his first orders to advance. He insisted that his mission must be properly defined and supported. That meant a journey back to Mombasa for an interview with the IBEA company's new resident administrator there. For that job Sir William Mackinnon, the company's chief, had secured a very senior man indeed, Major-General Sir Francis de Winton. Sir Francis was a good friend of the King of the Belgians, and a party to his obscure conspiracies with Mackinnon. He had done two years as administrator of the King's Congo Free State, and had then been seconded as secretary to Stanley's Emin Pasha expedition. The general was used to giving orders, and expected Captain Lugard to obey them. Instead, Lugard insisted on getting sensible orders, and enough resources to have a chance of carrying them out. He got his way, and was put in sole charge, above other army officers of greater seniority.

In June 1890, Lugard was in Zanzibar, explaining his problems to his original patron, consul-general Euan-Smith. He was also hoping to hire Zanzibari porters for the harsh journey to Buganda by the all-British route from Mombasa. But all the available labour was already employed, mostly on work for the German administration. In Zanzibar, Bishop Tucker, the new titular head of the Anglican Church of Uganda, was facing the same difficulty in arranging transport for himself, a new team of clergymen and their baggage up to his new diocese. So the two Britons travelled over to the mainland of German East Africa to meet the one man who could - at a price - organise transport to Buganda. This was Charles Stokes, now wearing a German colonial uniform and in receipt of a German salary.

Stokes was talkative, boastful, drunken, sly, charming if you liked that sort of thing. In his new prosperity he insisted that, although a man of business, he was a gentleman, an Irish gentleman. Lugard, silent, reserved, nervous, controlled, was the very model of an English officer: that he was a gentleman needed no emphasising. The two men detested each other at once.

Stokes was busy organising his Wanyamwesi porters to carry the supplies for Emin's expedition and the guns ordered by the Kabaka Mwanga. But he was never one to turn down extra business, if the price was right. With Tucker, he agreed to escort the parsons and their supplies by the German route to Lake Victoria and up to Buganda by water. With Lugard, he contracted to transport by the same route several tonnes of cloth and other necessary trade goods that the IBEA expedition would need once they got to Buganda. His prices were terrific: Lugard grumbled that he was being charged $40 a load, almost £200 a tonne. But there was no alternative. Lugard agreed to pay, deeply resenting the man who had won the bargain.

By now, after the delays, the political situation had changed, and Lugard's mission had to be redefined. The Anglo-German treaty swapping Buganda for Heligoland had been signed. Lugard's job was no longer to see the Germans off, but to sign up the Kabaka for Britain before any other imperial power got to him. Lugard's father had been an army padre in India, and he no doubt wanted the Protestant cause to win. Mainly, he thought it an honour to bring new territory to the British empire. He returned to Mombasa and set off with a small party by the all-British route that he had pioneered, towards the inland kingdom.

The journey was an ordeal. Lugard started out with three young white men. George Wilson broke down on the journey and had to be left to find his own way home. William Grant got through, but was sick with 'depression' almost all the time. Young Fenwick de Winton, son of the administrator Sir Francis, was useful at first, but was later to die of fever in the back country, alone. Lugard, tough as nails despite his old wound, kept going throughout. His most useful companion was the black Sudanese officer, Shukri Aga, commanding about sixty riflemen, veterans of Emin Pasha's old Equatoria battalions who had followed their leader with Stanley to the coast. They were backed up by about 300 servants and porters, some of them armed, and all recruited in Zanzibar. Lugard somehow managed this team, although neither he nor any of his British juniors spoke a word of any African language, and none of the Africans spoke any English.

Eight Zanzibaris carried Lugard's most persuasive instrument in the struggle to pacify Buganda. This was one of the new 'machine-guns' developed by the American engineer Hiram Maxim (later Sir Hiram, a devoted British subject). The gun could throw 600 bullets a minute well over a mile, accurately, and to devastating effect. Maxim, anxious to have his invention tested on live targets, was literally giving early models away to African explorers. The Maxim Lugard took to Buganda had been dragged all across Africa with Stanley's Emin Pasha expedition, and was apt to jam. Its failures would save many lives.

On 18 December 1890, Lugard, at the head of his armed force, entered the district of abrupt little hills where the Kabaka had established his new capital around a traditional reed palace hastily built on the summit of Mengo hill. Overlooking it from the nearby hilltop of Rubaga stood the

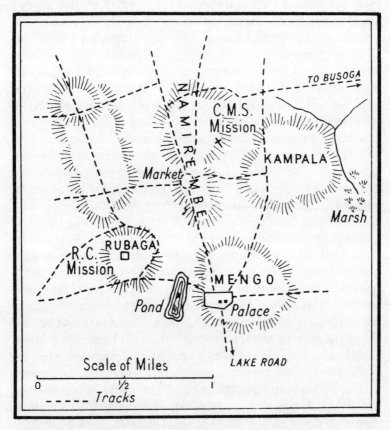

Mengo and environs, as shown on the Reverend R. H. Walker's sketch map, reproduced in Lugard's *The Rise of Our East African Empire* (1893).

strongly entrenched and stockaded headquarters of the French priests, with their simple thatched church inside. On Namirembe hilltop nearby was the smaller fence surrounding the church and huts of the Anglican mission. Lugard at once selected a campsite on yet another eminence, within Maxim range of the three existing strategic points: the hill was called Kampala, the antelope hill, and from it the city that later grew up there takes its name.

The scattered settlement was full of armed men, lounging about in several half-organised factions. Lugard resolved on an instant show of strength. The day after his arrival he marched across with his Sudanese – rifles at the ready, bugles sounding their sharp blasts of alarm – to visit the Kabaka in the Mengo palace. Five days later, on Christmas Eve, he presented to the King the treaty the company wanted signed, stating bluntly that he expected a signature on it within forty-eight hours. Then he went back to prepare for Christmas dinner on Kampala hill. He shared it with an uneasy and ill-assorted company of Europeans, one of whom he had not at all expected to find in Buganda.

The host was the IBEA company's representative, Ernest Gedge, left behind by Jackson almost a year previously. ('Poor fellow, the strain has been too much for him,' wrote Lugard.) There were the two resident Anglican clergymen, Gordon and Walker, nervous but devout. The French Catholic mission was represented by a gentle fellow called Father Brard, with whom Lugard shared no common language except a few catch-phrases in Swahili – 'Pole pole', 'gently, gently', was the priest's constant advice. The unexpected guest was a German, Doctor Stuhlmann. Lugard contemptuously described him as a 'Lieutenant of something', with two stripes on his sleeve. But everyone knew Stuhlmann was Emin Pasha's second-in-command. He emphasised that his presence was purely unofficial, as a guest of the Kabaka and an observer at the court. This did not fool Lugard, nor was it meant to. If the Kabaka refused to sign a treaty with the British, the Germans would feel free to make their own approach. Stuhlmann was there to take whatever opportunity might offer itself.

The morning after this uneasy Christmas feast, Lugard

marched across again to Mengo hill, to extract the vital
signature from the Kabaka. Mwanga was scared of Lugard.
With his flashing blue eyes, his smart Sudanese soldiers and
his well-sited Maxim, the British officer was formidable.
Only a year before the Kabaka had signed a treaty promising the protection of the German emperor which had been
revoked without explanation or notice. The white men were
clearly liars – so it seemed best to do what they asked with
threats. On 26 December 1890, the Kabaka Mwanga sulkily
put his mark at the foot of a document granting 'suzerainty'
over Buganda to the Imperial British East Africa Company,
for two years. Just what suzerainty is, and how it can be
translated into Luganda, is a matter for scholars.

The Baganda were too well-informed to accept that the
new treaty settled anything. The Kabaka was advised by
the French priests, whose new Vicar-General – acting
bishop – had arrived in the country in Stokes's boat, along
with Stuhlmann: he was the German-speaking Alsatian,
Monsignor Hirth. He explained to Mwanga that the IBEA
company was desperately short of funds, and that the
British were likely to pull out just as the Germans had done.
France might step in, or the Pope might succeed in winning
international guarantees for the sovereign independence of
the country. Mwanga decided to hedge his bets. To keep
the Germans happy, he summoned Stuhlmann and went
through an elaborate ceremony of blood-brotherhood with
him. Monsignor Hirth looked on benignly while this pagan
ceremony took place. It was not only the Catholics who
mistrusted the intentions of the British and insisted on
keeping alive their ties to the Germans. The Katikiro Apolo
Kagwa, the prime minister and Protestant leader, wrote to
Emin Pasha asking him to come and make peace in Buganda.

This message was carried away by Stuhlmann to Emin's
base at Bukoba, the nearest point on the shore of Lake
Victoria within German territory. Stokes came up in the
Limi to fetch Stuhlmann back, and was granted the honour
of an interview with the king. His news was best of all. The
weapons from the coast, he said, were on their way, awaiting transport up the lake from the store at Mwanza, where
they were safe under German guard. Stokes persuaded the

Kabaka that, while the other Europeans might be up to any amount of scheming, he at least was faithful, and could see to it that the Baganda were not left defenceless. Perhaps he meant it: he does not seem to have understood that he too was a pawn in the imperial game.

The next arrival was the Anglican Bishop, Alfred Tucker, on 27 December. Stokes, having escorted him and his party as far as the southern end of Lake Victoria, had declined to take them further. The parsons had been delayed, and had finally got hold of the slow-moving *Eleanor* to row them up, in a foully uncomfortable three-week voyage. Tucker had left the coast with seven British clergymen. Three had died on the way, and on arrival only one was fit to walk from the boat to the mission-station. Bravely, the survivors recovered and began the work of evangelism. Tucker was appalled to see that the men of his congregation came to church armed with muskets, loaded and primed. During his second Sunday service they suddenly rushed out with their weapons, gleefully preparing for a scrap with the Catholics gathered outside their own thatched church across the valley. There was no fighting that day, but the menace always hung in the air. Tucker could not take the strain for long. After a few weeks he left for home, where he discreetly reported on Lugard's abrasive behaviour.

Lugard was as tough as nails. He acted as though he had no doubts about the future of Buganda, and described any scepticism about the permanence of the British presence there as rebellion, or even treason. With his tiny force of disciplined soldiers he was just able to impose order on the capital. But he could not bring peace.

In January, just after Lugard's thirty-third birthday, re-inforcements began to come in by the all-British route that he had pioneered, from Mombasa on the coast. Captain Williams, of the Royal Artillery, came up with seventy-five more trained Sudanese soldiers from Emin's Equatoria battalions, and a Maxim gun less battered than Lugard's. (The first task was to deal with a Sudanese sergeant-major who had disobeyed orders: Williams wanted to hold a court-martial and shoot him; Lugard succeeded in imposing the lighter sentence of fifty lashes, the chain gang and dismissal without pay.) Williams spoke Arabic, so was able to give orders direct to his soldiers. The British military position was immensely strengthened.

Politically, though, Lugard was by no means secure in Buganda. The Kabaka was loudly complaining that, although he had signed the Englishman's treaty, he had received no 'present' in exchange. Without payment, Mwanga hinted, the deal might be off. But Lugard had nothing to give. Stokes had not delivered the cloth and other trade goods ordered by Lugard, which were in store at the German customs post at Mwanza, at the south end of the lake. The Mwanza store also contained the guns and powder ordered by Mwanga. Lugard needed to get the cloth and stop the guns. Stokes, in possession of both, was the main threat to British power in Buganda. If he sided with Mwanga, the imperial game might be up.

The Irishman's importance was underlined in March, with the arrival of the big supply caravan from Mombasa that had been meant to follow close on Lugard's heels. The only man the company had been able to find to lead it was a Maltese seaman known as James Martin, who was working as a quartermaster with the Sultan of Zanzibar's army. Martin's brutality and incompetence had caused many of his porters to desert, dumping their loads as they ran. The loads that remained were in a dreadful muddle because, being illiterate, Martin could not read the lists of contents. (Later he was found to have been stealing the company's property, and was quietly sacked to hush the scandal up.) This was the standard of efficiency the British company could expect from its employees in Africa. Stokes, unpredictable and independent as he was, could at least be relied upon to deliver goods if he chose to do so. And the British had much to fear from him as an antagonist, with his African alliances. Personally, Lugard might despise the Irishman; politically, he was a force to be reckoned with and treated with respect.

Stokes had returned to his German employers, south of the demarcation line. They knew that Britain's hold on Buganda was tenuous: Emin had letters from both the Kabaka

and his prime minister to prove it. Equally, Emin had strict
orders not to move northwards into British territory. If
circumstances changed the Germans might be able to move
across and try their luck; for now they had to stick to their
own side of the border and wait. There was plenty of work
to be done in their own share of East Africa – setting up
border posts, studying languages, classifying tribes, drawing maps, pacifying and imposing German order and German taxation on the huge territory that is now mainland
Tanzania. Lieutenant Langheld, the professional soldier,
turned with a will to these tasks.

Neither Emin nor Stokes was content with that. Stokes
did not want a settled frontier; he wanted plenty of ivory,
the freedom to go as he pleased in search of it, and no
taxation. Emin wanted to get back home to Equatoria and
his curious studies of natural history: his imperial commission gave him authority over the other German officers, and
wide powers provided he kept to the limits – vague enough
– of the Kaiser's treaty obligations with other European
powers. But, unlike their white colleagues, Stokes and Emin
both believed that Africa mattered as much as Europe. Both
men had, in the contemptuous phrase, 'gone native'.

Emin had lived long years in Equatoria as the head of
what was in effect an autonomous African tribe, made up
of his black Sudanese Muslim soldiers, and their local
wives, children and slaves. His own dead Ethiopian wife
had left him Ferida, the beautiful brown daughter he
adored; he acknowledged at least one other little girl as his
own. He spoke several African languages, as well as Arabic
and Turkish and English and French on top of his native
German. He was in his conduct, if not necessarily by faith,
a Muslim. (A Koran was found beside him at his death –
his Christian apologists said it had no religious significance,
being merely an elegant copy presented to the former governor by his old chief, Governor-General Charles Gordon.)
Whatever Emin's religion, if any, it was surely not Christianity. He was born a Jew, and had never been allowed to
forget it at home in Austria, or during his medical studies
at Berlin University.

Stokes too had in his very different way broken out of the

limits of European culture. His family was African. His
business as a caravan boss was modelled upon that of the
Arabs, whose style of dress he had adopted in place of the
worsted suit and revolver belt of the conventional European
traveller. In his long, cool, white cotton robe he fitted into
the African landscape. When he or his men needed a rest
they would settle down in camp on the outskirts of a village,
and the people would drift in to exchange pieces of ivory
for cloth, beads or brass wire. Sometimes these casual trading posts would grow into permanent stations, to which he
returned on his later travels to collect the profits made in
his absence. He knew, as the Arab merchants knew, that
the safest place for valuables is under the bed with a comfortable woman in it. Yet none of his occasional liaisons
threatened the affectionate, though childless, marriage with
Limi, by which he had joined the family of the supreme
chief of the tribal confederation of the Wanyamwesi.

But now, after fourteen years in Africa, Stokes was growing tired and slightly crazy. He wanted to go home to see
his old mother in Ireland – like many Irish exiles he became
a bore about that. He wanted to return rich and respected,
as the gentleman he claimed to be but had never quite
become. A gentleman would eat with the officers, as an
equal with Lugard and Williams, or Stuhlmann and Langheld, not tucked away in the no doubt greater comfort of the
German sergeants' mess. A gentleman's wife and daughters
would be respected, be they brown or white – and Stokes
had both. The white men found him comic and disreputable, as indeed he was. He believed one last coup in the ivory
trade would change all that. With Emin on the upper Nile,
and in alliance with the Arab and African rulers of the last
empty space in Africa, there was a chance to make a fortune,
and to that end the remainder of his life was devoted.

Chapter 10

~~~

Emin Pasha Plays the Arab Card

Just above the Falls the as yet unbroken power of the Congo Arabs slumbered uneasily.

> Joseph Conrad, diary entry, on arrival at Stanley Falls
> (21 September 1890)

Even the common soldiers slept on silk and satin mattresses, in carved beds with silken mosquito curtains ... Here we found many European luxuries, the use of which we had almost forgotten: candles, sugar, matches, silver and glass decanters were in profusion. We also took about twenty-five tons of ivory; ten or eleven tons of powder; millions of caps; cartridges for every kind of rifle, gun and revolver perhaps ever made; some shells; and a German flag, taken by the Arabs in East Africa ... I have ridden through a single rice-field for an hour and a half.

> Dr Sydney Hinde, on the capture by his Belgian expedi-
> tion of Kasongo, Haut-Congo (1892)

Stokes and Emin, pioneers of the first, freebooting incursions into tropical Africa, had no place in the new colonies being established by the soldiers and officials now moving in from the coasts. But in the middle of the continent, between the British and the Germans advancing from the east, and the Belgians moving up the river Congo from the west, lay a vast area in which European claims to sovereignty were still vague or non-existent. The western frontier of British Uganda was still undefined. Equatoria was wide open. In the trackless forests of the Congo basin, King Leopold's regime had so far failed to make good by possession the sovereignty so carelessly allocated him by the other European powers. There the only authority was held by people owing nothing to Europe – the Congo Arab warlords. Emin saw them as rulers of an area where political advantage might be gained. Stokes knew that the ivory of their domains had hardly been exploited. To them, the two men now turned.

In February 1891, they set off separately on their fatal gamble. Stokes moved towards the coast, by way of Buganda, to sort out the supplies and commercial arrangements for the expedition. Emin marched off into the mountain country to the west, leaving the lakeside camp at Bukoba on 12 February. His ostensible purpose was to beat the bounds of German East Africa, and to establish a German presence in the wild, untravelled country of Rwanda. But the size and strength of his expedition indicates that much more was at stake. The Pasha was accompanied by Lieutenant Stuhlmann, fresh back from witnessing Lugard's masterful Christmas coup in Buganda. Their escort was a company of Swahili riflemen, a Krupp machine-gun, and about 200 porters to carry supplies.

After a week's march this formidable military force turned north, into the unmapped terrain where German, British and Belgian claims to sovereignty met in geographical confusion. The German Imperial Commissioner, von Wissmann, had written warning Emin not to move across the agreed Anglo-German demarcation line, at 1° south of the Equator. But Emin was still in possession of papers given him before that line had been definitively established by the Caprivi treaty. They were signed by Wissmann, and included letters and guarantees of safe-conduct for certain Arab chiefs known to be living north of the line. Emin now prepared to make use of them. He was playing the old German game. Carl Peters had 'unofficially' acquired Buganda – however briefly – for Germany. Now Emin was attempting more unofficial acquisitions. If the scheme went wrong Wissmann, and the whole official apparatus of German power, could disown him.

Emin's target was his own former province of Equatoria, and the little army of Sudanese troops left behind there when Stanley had hijacked him down to Zanzibar, back in 1889. In Equatoria were two battalions of aging bŭt well-trained men with serviceable Remington rifles, under their own black officers, based upon their own self-sufficient forts, and backed by two small steamboats able to travel at will along the 100-mile stretch of Lake Albert, and for another 60 miles downstream as far as the first rapids on the White Nile. Whoever controlled this force would be master of the heart of Africa. Emin meant to take command of them again.

Emin and Stuhlmann pressed on northwards. They were clearly outside the area where German claims were recognised; but it was not certain whether the country they were passing through would be taken over by Britain or by Belgium, since there was no accurate map on which to draw a frontier. The place was a political vacuum and a geographical mystery.

From the open plains and scrublands of East Africa, the travellers moved into the chaos of the Western Rift Valley, beyond which the immense Congo forest begins. The rift is lined with great mountains that divide two climates – the east side parched and bare in the dry season, the west tree-covered, dripping in the steamy winds that sweep up from the far Atlantic coast. The earth is cracked and twisted into strange shapes by volcanoes, not quite extinct, that puff their everlasting fumes into the air. Even the human beings of the region were at odds with nature, and with each other.

Quite separate peoples lived in Rwanda side by side. The immensely tall Tutsi, wandering with their cattle, kept in subjection the tiny, thick-set Hutu who lived by slash-and-burn farming on the edges of the forest; in the forest itself, secretly, were pigmies who did not farm at all, but lived by hunting and gathering wild fruit and insects. Even deeper in the woods were gorillas, their echoing humanoid yells striking terror into mankind. The indigenous peoples were not clear where the line lay between men and apes. The gorillas, they said, would from time to time rip away a hut and take off food and women to their lairs. From that belief arose the legend of the *soko*, half man, half ape, strong as its wild parent and cunning as its human one. H. M. Stanley, travelling not far to the south, had seen skulls set up at the entrance to a village, and was told they were the remains of *soko*. He took some to England for examination. They were found to be the crania of *homo sapiens*, and they seemed to have been cooked.

The East Africans – Swahili and Wanyamwesi – of Emin's escort and baggage-party held in horror the eaters of human flesh; the Muslims among them thought it an abomination that the pastoral people should drink blood warm from the cow. The diet of the settled farming people was strange enough. Some ate plantains, boiled fresh, or dried and pounded to an anaemic paste. Others subsisted mainly on cassava, whose bulky roots are poisonous unless painstakingly washed, dried and pounded. The porters were used to regular meals of maize porridge, in vast quantities, easily transported and quickly cooked. But the expedition was travelling light, trying to live off the land as it went along. The strange provisions made the men feeble, liable to sickness.

Weakening but persistent, Emin's war-party moved in quest of the Sudanese soldiery, north up the shores of Lake Edward, and north again along the fever-ridden valley of the Semliki river that runs across the Equator to Lake Albert. There they picked up rumours of fighting beside the lake, between the local chieftains and the waTurki, the Turkish people. The Sudanese soldiers were still marching under the red crescent flag of the Ottoman Empire, since their sovereign, the Khedive of Egypt, was in name a vassal of the Turks.

Far inside Congo territory, on 19 July 1891, Emin caught up with his former troops. Their base-camp was at the settlement controlled by the old chief Mazamboni, on the upper Ituri river, where the rain-forest thins out into the savannah that little by little becomes sparser as it spreads towards the Sahara desert. Major Selim Bey was still in command – the man who had previously rejected Emin's orders, on the suspicion that the Pasha was collaborating with the Christian Europeans. The military discipline that Emin had instilled ruled the men's lives. They had clerks, and parades, and regimental orders, and an efficient message system linking their scattered posts. They regularly sent their women out to tend the crops of maize and cotton that kept them fed and clothed. The old Remington rifles were clean and oiled, and the soldiers' loyalty to the Khedive was undimmed.

That loyalty was Emin's problem. The officers welcomed him cautiously, hoping that since he had held their sovereign's commission he would have remained as loyal as they, and that he had returned to lead them once more in the service of Egypt – from which they had received no orders, and no pay, for at least eight years, since the Mahdi's soldiers had cut them off from Egypt. But Emin made it clear that he was now in the service of the German emperor, who would pay them, renew their uniforms and their rights as disciplined troops, and set them up once more as an effective fighting force.

This invitation they proudly rejected. They would never serve a Christian monarch – and they had long experience of Emin's promises, and of his indecisiveness when he could not fulfil them. Of the original 2,000 men in the two Equatoria battalions of the Egyptian army, death, desertion and the defection of a substantial party with Emin and Stanley had removed half. And of the men assembled at Mazamboni's village, only twenty-nine, including three officers, now agreed to accept Emin's authority. They brought with them about 100 camp-followers – women, children and slaves. With this feeble addition to its strength, the party led by Emin and Stuhlmann set off on the march again, due west this time, deep into the equatorial rain-forest of the upper Congo basin.

The true scale of Emin's ambition was becoming clear. His notes begin to refer to Equatoria as the 'hinterland of the Cameroons', a phrase dismissed as senseless by most of those who have studied his life. But in terms of the rules agreed at the Berlin conference, the concept of hinterland had acquired a precise meaning. Once a coastal settlement was recognised as permanently under the control of a European power, that power had the right to expand its dominion inland. Germany had grabbed its colony of Kamerun,

on the Atlantic seaboard, in 1885. Now Emin was asserting
that the hinterland of Kamerun extended right to the centre
of the continent. He was asserting a claim to German
sovereignty over some 1,500 miles of unbroken rain-forest,
from the Atlantic to the Nile.

This was certainly an extravagant claim, but by the standards of the time it was not an eccentric one. British imperial visionaries - notably the cheating financier Cecil
Rhodes, backed by his gold and diamond concessions in
South Africa - were seeking to work out an all-British right
of way the whole length of Africa, from Cairo to the Cape.
French interests were trying to work out a similar line from
east to west, from Senegal through Ethiopia to their colony
at Djibouti on the Red Sea. Emin's vision was comparable.
The first stage of his march had blazed a trail from recognised German territory in East Africa to Equatoria. Now he
intended to complete the journey across the continent, as
Stanley had done earlier by the Congo line. He relied for
support on dangerous allies among the rulers of the forest.

The march west was a fiasco. The straggling party
plunged into the rain-forest, downstream along the Ituri
river, a tributary of the Congo. They were openly trespassing on territory to which the King of the Belgians had a
recognised title. But there were no Belgians there. The real
opposition came from the climate and the indigenous
peoples of that strange place. Beneath the high tree-canopy
everything was perpetually damp. There was no dry wood
to burn, no food to be bought, no farms to be raided. The
few permanent forest-dwellers were pigmies, regarded from
the outside as an amusing aberration of nature. Here, on
their home ground, they were formidable, scampering un-
seen amid the tree-trunks, skilled in diverting large strangers from their secret homes.

On the tracks - mere monkey-scrambles, a Belgian officer
called them - they dug pitfalls to catch large animals or
human intruders. A fallen tree might be a cunning trap or
diversion. Sometimes, from the steaming shadows, came a
flutter of tiny poisoned arrows, fired softly from slack bows.
There was no target for the soldiers to aim back at: firing
blind produced only a dense cloud of powder-smoke to

hang in the warm, damp air. Also in the forest were sparse
bands of full-sized Bantu people, who wandered among
and raided their tiny neighbours. Deprived of protein, they
ate what meat they could find: a good catch of locusts was
a luxury to them, and human flesh was a feast. If a group
of strangers passed through the woods, they would lurk
around to pick off the stragglers. Emin's party, with its tail
of heavy-laden women and children, was dreadfully vulnerable to the weird dangers of the forest. The people fell sick,
lost courage, and turned back to reach Mazamboni's place
less than four months after they had left it.

They found everything changed. Lugard, in Kampala,
had got wind of Emin's drive to recruit the Sudanese, and
had set out to prevent it. As an intermediary, he had the
Sudanese officer, Major Shukri Aga. Shukri presented Lugard's terms to his former colleagues, and they agreed to
follow the British officer back to Buganda, accompanied by
their women, children and slaves. Emin, on his return,
found Mazamboni's settlement inhabited only by its native
residents. The Sudanese were gone, every one.

That was a bad enough disaster. Now a worse one struck.
Stanley's expedition in quest of Emin had passed along the
Ituri valley and lingered for some weeks near Mazamboni's
prosperous and well-ordered settlement. Stanley's men had
brought with them from West Africa a range of exotic
diseases and parasites, which spread with frightening viru-
lence among the isolated population of the forest, who had
no immunity to them. Mazamboni's people were ravaged
by sickness, which they now passed on in turn to their latest
visitors.

The maladies that destroyed the people had, for the most
part, been imported to Africa from the New World, in the
course of the Portuguese slave-trade with Brazil: jiggers,
tiny burrowing insects, penetrate the feet and raise great
aching blisters right up the leg; the spirochaetes of yaws
cause terrible swellings that burst and lay open the bones;
gonorrhoea, the army sickness, spread with every sexual
contact between troops and local women. Then the smallpox came. Mazamboni's villagers recognised its symptoms
and fled in terror. Emin's soldiers, porters and camp-

followers were left to their own devices in the deserted
settlement.

Emin responded gallantly to this calamity. He ordered
Stuhlmann and those members of the party who seemed
free of infection to move off southwards, staying on himself
at Mazamboni's with the sick. He signed a written order
commanding Stuhlmann to set up camp in the Semliki valley, and to wait a maximum of one month there. If by then
no news had come, Stuhlmann was to take his people back
to Bukoba. This he did, eventually reaching the coast more
dead than alive. (Of the seven Germans who had originally
set out with Emin, Father Schnyse and Feldwebel Hoffmann died on Lake Victoria, of sickness; Feldwebel Kühne
reached the coast, but died there.) The Pasha was now on
his own.

He stayed six months at Mazamboni's. Somehow he escaped the smallpox and survived the fever. But even before
Stuhlmann left he noted that the Pasha had a bad leg and
a pustulant finger, and that his shortness of sight had de-
generated to near-blindness: 'You could see a great cloud
behind his pupil.' His escort was reduced to three Sudanese
officers and nineteen soldiers, and his entire party consisted
of only thirty-eight people, including the faithful Circassian
clerk, Siver Effendi. Their arms were seven Mauser and six
Remington rifles, and a dozen muzzle-loaders. Nevertheless, Emin, free now of all ties to reality, pursued his great
scheme to walk westwards to Kamerun and the Atlantic
coast. He was entirely at the mercy of the people of the
forest, the Africans and their Arab overlords.

As the Europeans tightened their grip around the coasts of
Africa, a new culture and commerce had sprung up in the
far interior. For centuries the merchants and soldiers of the
Arab settlements on the East African coast had traded with,
and raided, the inland peoples, bringing out slaves and
ivory. But the Swahili settlers were divided by their own
rivalries, weakened by tropical diseases, and dominated by
the sea-borne power of raiders from the Arabian peninsula
to the north. By the mid-nineteenth century their power on
the coast had been broken by the Christians; and by 1880

Zanzibar, their last great coastal emporium, was dominated by Europeans, its Sultan a British puppet. Deprived of access to the coastal trade, the Arabs settled down and established themselves far inland.

The Congo Arab warlords are a forgotten people now, their only surviving legacy the Swahili language that lingers on in the markets of the forest. But to the Africans of the places where they traded and settled they were masters, imposing their will by the power of the guns and the spears of their native mercenaries. They grew crops, cleared and drained the forest land, built towns and markets, and established a network of internal trade routes whose highways were the great lakes and rivers of the equatorial zone – Lake Malawi, Lake Tanganyika, Lake Victoria, and the headwaters of the Congo and the Nile. They also began a process of what we now call economic development, which differed in one crucial aspect from that later brought by the Europeans.

The ethnic Arabs from the coast could not, as Muslims, take their wives with them on their travels; nor, obviously enough, could they get home often. Wherever they went they took local womenfolk, and by deliberate interbreeding sought to establish new generations of Muslims reared in their own traditions. They discouraged the conversion to Islam of ordinary African men and women, for the practical reason that a Muslim may not be enslaved. But they encouraged the conversion of local chiefs, who, once included in Islam, were treated as equals and partners. The distinction between 'Arab' and African was religion, not race.

As the power of the Sultan of Zanzibar declined, it was replaced in the deep interior by that of his most important subject, the merchant prince Hamid bin Mohammed, better known as Tippu Tib (a name that may mimic his curious trick of blinking as he talked, or perhaps the double flash-and-bang of his men's flint-lock muskets). Tippu was already the leading trader of the interior when, in 1867, he first befriended Dr Livingstone, and did his best to help the poor, witless old holy man in his last desolate wanderings. By this connexion Tippu earned the respect of H. M. Stanley, who once told Emin Pasha that he preferred the Arab chieftain to all his European officers put together.

Tippu was fascinated by Stanley, and rather scared of him. This strange white man, with his wonderful repeating rifles and his instruments for navigation in the unknown, was up to something that Tippu respected but could not understand. They met again in 1876, when Stanley was on his great voyage across Africa from east to west. Stanley arrived at Tippu's headquarters at Ujiji, on Lake Tanganyika, and asked for help in reaching the great falls at the head of the Congo's navigable waters. Tippu replied that he dared not venture so far downstream, into savage country full of sickness and guarded by cannibal tribes. But Stanley went ahead. He reached the falls – Stanley Falls – and journeyed on past them to the Atlantic. Tippu saw that the falls could indeed be passed. Below them stretched 1,000 miles of navigable river, and countless more miles of tributaries and forest tracks, along which Tippu and his allies penetrated in search of ivory, which they found aplenty. Stanley had shown the Congo Arabs the way.

Once on the upper Congo, the Arabs transformed it, recruiting – brutally – the indigenous people of the forest to clear it and work the land, and venturing far from the river in search of ivory. Ten years after he had first passed the falls, Stanley returned to the upper river. He was now in the service of the King of the Belgians, travelling to 'rescue' Emin Pasha. Stanley had left Europe under the impression that the settlement of Stanley Falls (now Kisangani), the highest navigable point on the river, was a peaceful little trading post under Belgian control. Far from it. The Belgians had tried to enforce their monopoly of ivory-trading around the place (they called it 'suppressing the slave-trade'), but the Arabs and their locally-recruited militia had fought the white men off, with serious loss of life. Tippu Tib had made his capital at Stanley Falls, with a ragged but determined little army to back him up. Stanley had far too few people to fight the Arabs. Indeed, he could not move away from the river without their help in providing porters, guides and food.

Stanley and Tippu made a deal. Tippu provided some

food for Stanley's men, and a few very inefficient porters for his goods. Much more important, he promised not to impede the expedition's passage. In return, Stanley promised Tippu protection against European interference, and recognition of his authority at Stanley Falls. Tippu was given a salary of £30 a month, and the title of governor of the Belgian province of Stanley Falls, which he ruled anyway. By accepting the office of governor, he also acknowledged the overlordship of the King of the Belgians on what had until then been Arab ground.

King Leopold's more sincerely Christian supporters were appalled. The appointment guaranteed the authority of a man who, as the chief slave-dealer of the region, typified everything the King claimed he wanted to abolish in Africa. They would have been more shocked had they known the full truth: Stanley had authorised Tippu to hold his own slaves, to acquire more from his province, and to buy modern rifles and ammunition from the Belgian armouries for the purpose.

Tippu's Arab followers were just as angry. They saw, as Stanley had seen, that the deal gave the Belgians time to establish themselves at the Falls, and that the Christians would surely betray their new ally as soon as it was convenient. (Sure enough, the old boy was soon shipped off to retirement in Zanzibar.) Tippu's reasoning was probably sound – the alternative was to fight, and muzzle-loaders would in the end always lose against rifles – but the Arabs were split. They had always been a quarrelsome lot. Now they were set against each other, as well as against the Belgians. Even those most opposed to Belgian influence would, to win a tactical advantage, do the Christians' dirty work in exchange for good Christian rifles. Blood-feuds complicated the shifting networks of cynical and temporary alliances.

The Belgians had been taught to despise the Arabs. They soon learned to fear them. In the fever-ridden miasma of the forest the struggle for survival dominated the white men's lives. Next came the struggle for ivory, to meet the new state's enormous expenses, and to win a reward for the finder too. Later there developed a market for the wild rubber of the forest. Belgian officials were empowered to seize any valuable product, without compensation, from the natives. But the people who had ivory were not natives, but Arabs, who fought back with guns and determination.

Stanley's deal with Tippu created further confusion. Some Arabs were now officially classed as 'friendlies'. But the Belgians and their white mercenaries could not tell one Arab from another: the names were confusing, and given the long history of Arab interbreeding with Africans a man's appearance was no guide to his status as friend or foe. A prudent European treated all Arabs as hostile. Each side regarded the other as a pattern of treachery.

The horrors of the war that resulted would be beyond description, had not an eyewitness described them in one of the most terrible stories in the English language. Among the drifters, misfits and adventurers employed by the Congo state was a young Polish ship's officer who had anglicised his name as Joseph Conrad. As probationary mate of the river-steamer *Roi des Belges* he arrived at Stanley Falls, after a tedious journey upstream, in September 1890, and was delayed there, sick with fever, and hearing all the time the tales of his fellow-mercenaries.

Conrad's story *Heart of Darkness* tells of the death on the river of a visionary Belgian official called Kurtz, whose character is closely modelled upon that of a real man called Klein, which means much the same. It describes the reign of random terror imposed by the Belgians, themselves always in fear, upon the wretched people of the forest. The story is often praised, rightly, as a metaphor of the human condition. Conrad's diaries show that it is also a faithful – if not literally accurate – account of the state of affairs that the writer himself observed. His health never fully recovered from the Congo fever, whose hallucinatory presence adds a distorting menace to the dreadful events he describes. It was the Congo, said Conrad, that made him a writer. That is about all the world has to be grateful for in the whole history of King Leopold's colonial venture.

After Conrad left – refused promotion to command of a river-boat, he promptly went back to London – things got even worse. The unexpected resistance of the Arabs and their African allies had incalculably added to the expense of

developing the new state. In the early 1890s there was a
general slump in the European capital markets, making it
impossible for Leopold to finance the investments he
needed to make. In 1891 a royal decree created absolute
monopolies in ivory and rubber. He desperately needed
quick profits. The following year the entire north-east
corner of the state – Wele and Aruwimi provinces, where
the borders with British and German East Africa were
awaiting definition, and where Emin was on the move – was
declared *domaine privé*, the private estate of the King.

Within the royal domain there was no pretence at the rule
of law. The people were subject outright to the orders of
any officer holding the king's commission. A Swedish missionary reported on the system whereby raw rubber was
extorted from the people, by quotas assigned to each village.
The punishment for non-fulfilment of the quota was that
the non-producers lost a hand. The Belgian-officered soldiers were rewarded for efficiency if they made a good hand
collection. To ensure that the severed hands were preserved
for accurate counting, the soldiers were instructed to smoke
them lightly over a slow fire.

The Congo Arabs found their power shaken by people
far more ruthless even than themselves. They grew desperate. In their inland fastnesses they were amassing vast
hoards of ivory, some of it by killing wild elephants, much
more by extortion from the native people, who had hitherto
valued tusks for ornament and prestige, but not for the
market. Whether to kill elephants or to terrorise people, the
Arabs needed imported firearms, which they could pay for
only by exporting ivory. Ringed round by the Europeans,
the Arabs sought an escape route from their trap.

The traditional way to the east coast at Zanzibar was
blocked by the British and the Germans. Westwards, the
Belgians were on the Congo, and the Portuguese commanded the coastline south of the river mouth. For 600
miles to the north, the coast was in the hands of the French.
The next piece of Atlantic shoreline northwards (apart from
the tiny Spanish enclave of Rio Muni, the present-day hell-
hole of Equatorial Guinea) was the unprofitable German
colony of Kamerun, whose acknowledged hinterland ran all

the way inland to Lake Chad and the fringe of the Sahara desert. (The present-day map, on page 4, shows that the same borders still exist.)

The Germans, appalled by the expense of their colonial acquisitions, were anxious to increase their revenue by channelling through them as much trade as possible. If Kamerun could become the route through which Congo ivory was exported, it would be so much gained for Germany and so much lost for Belgium. If Emin, the German with a Muslim name, could work out a deal with the Congo Arab ivory dealers, both might profit – Germany, by the ability to trade through Kamerun and the acquisition of a German-owned strip of land right across Africa; the Arabs, by the chance to sell their ivory and buy modern guns.

Between Emin's Equatoria and the Atlantic coast of Kamerun was a trackless journey of 1,600 miles which nobody – so far as was known – had ever attempted. But the map, however vague its detail, showed the possibility of skirting round the northern fringe of King Leopold's Congo through unclaimed territory (today included in the Sudan and the Central African Republic), and so into Kamerun. The Arabs knew the Europeans had special skills in finding their way through uncharted country: Stanley had shown them the way past the Falls; Brazza had out-navigated Stanley on the lower Congo. Now they hoped Emin could work the trick again.

The scheme had taken shape during Emin's enforced stay in Zanzibar, after the accident that freed him from captivity to Stanley. There, Stokes had introduced him to Tippu Tib's main financial backer, the Indian Muslim Seewa Hadji, and Seewa had been given the main contract for supplying Emin's first expedition in the service of Germany. Lieutenant Stuhlmann disapproved of the connexion between the Pasha and the Hadji, and thought the 18,000 German marks – $6,000 – paid to Seewa was too much.

The plan began to be put into effect when Emin set off from his little lakeside fort at Bukoba to make his covert journey towards Equatoria. He was baulked by the refusal of his Sudanese troops to join the venture, and then by the disease that struck his camp. But Stuhlmann, before he left the Pasha to face the smallpox on his own, had observed mysterious transactions between Emin and some Arab visitors to their forest camp.

The most important visitor was one Said bin Abedi, a part-Arab, part-African chieftain whose father was a senior follower, and probably a relative, of Tippu Tib himself. Said was identified by the Belgians as their most dangerous enemy: he had resisted their ivory raids, and was held responsible for the deaths of several Belgian ivory traders. Unknown to Stuhlmann, Emin was carrying an official letter for Said, promising him safe-conduct through German territory and favourable customs treatment for any ivory he might bring with him. The letter was signed by Imperial Commissioner von Wissmann, and confirms that Emin's venture had been sanctioned by high German authority. But that official sanction had been given before Emin had left Zanzibar – before, that is, the signing in Europe of the Anglo-German agreement of 1890, by which Chancellor Caprivi officially renounced his country's expansionist policy in Africa. Emin, in fact, was implementing the aggressive plan that his political masters had decided to abandon eighteen months previously.

When they got wind of this, the German authorities grew worried about the unpredictable Pasha, who seemed likely to cause them serious embarrassment with the British. In March 1892, Lieutenant Langheld wrote Lugard 'a nice letter' asking him to rescue Emin from Mazamboni's village on the edge of the forest. Lugard had no resources for a rescue, even if he had wanted to oblige. But the Germans had safely dissociated themselves from their errant commissioner.

When Emin had sent Stuhlmann off to get clear of the smallpox epidemic, he had also rid himself of the one man who might have restrained him from carrying on with his far-fetched adventure. He was set on finding his Atlantic escape route, and to that end he made contact with the Arab commanders of the fighting bands that controlled the forest trails. The most formidable was Kilongalonga, an outstandingly aggressive leader who had given infinite trouble to Stanley's Emin Pasha expedition when it passed through this same forest. Theoretically subject to him was Ismaili, who commanded his own fighters and fortified villages. Both these men were nominally under the feudal mastery of Tippu Tib – but they did not accept Tippu's alliance with the Belgians, and were therefore in revolt against the established order of the Arab chieftains.

It was under Ismaili's protection that Emin, in June 1892, started again to try to walk to the Atlantic. He went slowly along at the head of his tiny band of followers, dependent for everything on the hospitality of the Arabs. As he went, he continued his notes and observations of the strange flora and fauna of the forest. By October he had come to the edge of the territory controlled by Ismaili, and was passing into that ruled by yet another of Tippu's feudal warlords, the son of a Zanzibari soldier. His Arabic name was Hamadi bin Ali el Anzagizi, but he was much better known by his African name of Kibonghe. The Belgians, in particular, had learned in battle to fear him. His troops, men of his mother's people, the Manyuema, were reputed to be the best fighters in the forest. With their teeth filed to points and their bodies decorated with crude tattoos, they looked like and were cannibals.

Emin entered Kibonghe's country at a village called Kinene, after its commander, who despatched a messenger to Ismaili to ask whether or not Emin should be allowed to continue on his journey. The messenger returned. Exactly what happened next is a mystery that will never be solved.

The only detailed account was obtained from the subsequent interrogation of Ismaili by an American, R. Dorsey Mohun, a mercenary in the Belgian service. (The story cannot be checked, since Dorsey had Ismaili executed as soon as the questioning was over; Kibonghe, under Belgian interrogation, later denied it, but was himself at once put to death.) According to Dorsey, Kibonghe sent two replies, which arrived within minutes of each other. The first was a note authorising Emin to proceed unharmed, the second an order that he be killed at once. Emin's followers were shown the *laissez-passer*, and put aside their guns. The Pasha was invited by Kinene to take a walk in the bush, in order to observe some interesting natural object worthy of his study. Once away from his own escort he was seized and shown the second letter, authorising his execution: Kinene had to hold it very close to the victim's fading eyes, so that he could read the Arabic writing.

Then Emin was held down on his back while a man called Mamba, on Kinene's orders, cut his throat wide open with one stroke of the knife. The body, headless and stripped of its clothes, was thrown into the bush. The Pasha's personal boxes, containing a few books and papers (including his beautiful Koran) as well as the scientific notebooks that were his main achievement, were sent under safe guard to Kibonghe, in whose possession they were found by his Belgian captor, Captain Lothaire, just over two years later.

Other, less detailed, accounts of the Pasha's killing place the blame not on Kibonghe but on his superior, Said bin Abedi. The Belgian authorities, indeed, took Said's responsibility for the murder as an accepted fact, and the following year they put him on trial for it. But he was acquitted, and in exchange made a formal alliance with the Belgians, for which he was generously rewarded. Only after Said's acquittal was a charge made against Kibonghe, who had refused all invitations to join the Belgian side. Certainly the Belgians had been desperately anxious to frustrate Emin's expedition, of which they were kept fully informed by their existing allies among the Congo Arabs, headed by Tippu Tib himself.

It made no difference to Emin who gave the orders: his throat was cut anyway. But it did make a difference to Charles Stokes. On 23 or 24 November 1892 – even the date of Emin's death is uncertain – he was camped at Mpeni's village on the Semliki river, awaiting news of the Pasha who had gone ahead, and bargaining keenly for ivory with Kibonghe, Kilongalonga, Kinene, Said bin Abedi, and anyone else with a tusk for sale.

Chapter 11

❧

The Congo Gamble

I want to tell you Captain Williams, I am a Britisher though
not an Englishman born, I am Irishman born and bred and
a true and loyal subject of Her Majesty the Queen of Great
Britain and Ireland, and I am not going to give up my rights
of trading in these parts and ruin myself just to advance the
English Company.

Stokes to the officer in command, Kampala (November
1891)

It is time Mr Stokes was shewn that he cannot defy the
Company.

Lugard's report to the IBEA company (January 1892)

When Stokes parted company with Emin, in February
1891, his instructions were to return to Zanzibar and acquire arms and trade goods for the fighting party. But first
he had anxious business to do in Buganda with Lugard,
commander of the precarious British garrison. In store at
Mwanza, under German guard, Stokes had two consign-
ments of valuable goods, both of which were of vital interest
to the British. They were the civilian supplies ordered by
Lugard, and the arms and ammunition ordered by Mwanga.

Lugard's cloth, beads, copper-wire and scientific equipment were contained in 300 headloads – 9 tonnes – of pack-
ages. Possibly Stokes had not delivered them for the reason
he stated, which was that the Germans were making difficulties about the amount of export duty chargeable. Much
more likely, he was holding the consignment hostage, to
persuade Lugard to see reason about the arms for Mwanga.

Lugard had no doubt about the position. Stokes, he believed, was an arms smuggler and an enemy of civilised
white rule. The trader saw it entirely differently. When he
originally obtained the weapons, it was in a perfectly lawful
transaction on behalf of the Kabaka, an independent sovereign. On that basis the Germans had authorised, or at
least permitted, the purchase. Now the British had got hold
of Mwanga, and the Kabaka wanted delivery specifically in
order to get rid of his new masters.

Lugard had told Stuhlmann, in Kampala at Christmas,
that Stokes meant to smuggle in guns to the Catholics in
Buganda. He warned the German that serious consequences
would follow any attempt to do so, and wrote a note to the
same effect to Stokes. On 5 February 1891 Stokes arrived,
fresh from celebrating the German Emperor's birthday at
Bukoba. Lugard and his second-in-command, Captain
Williams, civilly invited the trader to dinner and asked him
what he intended to do about the arms. (The only account
of this meeting is Lugard's, and may of course be as untrue
as some of his other stories.) Stokes at first denied having
any weapons at all in his store. Then he admitted to having
a few loads of gunpowder which, he said, were consigned
not to the Kabaka but to the IBEA company. Pressed for
details, he left, insisting that the matter would best be dealt
with in writing. He further enraged Lugard by apologising
for the delay to the civilian supplies; meanwhile, he said he
could supply a small but sufficient quantity of goods from
his own stock already in Buganda, and named an extortionate price for it. Lugard had no choice but to pay. In a rage
he signed an IOU on the company's agents in Zanzibar,
and got the cloth he needed for immediate survival.

Stokes, by letter, then made a formal offer to sell the
IBEA company a whole arsenal: 250 muskets, four 30-kilo
manloads of caps for muskets, and 30 loads of gunpowder
– almost a tonne, enough for a decent little war. He was
frank about the price. Good German gunpowder was
packed and sealed in 5-pound kegs, so a manload was 12
kegs. Each keg could be exchanged in Buganda, where powder was much in demand, for one *frasilah* of best ivory,
weighing 35 pounds and worth £17 in Zanzibar market. So

16-17 King Leopold II acquired as his personal dominion the largest share of tropical Africa, and misleadingly named it the Congo Free State. His agents and white mercenaries there employed local fighting men, known as 'friendlies': the pair here are Manyuema from Aruwimi province, photographed about 1900.

18 Emin Pasha, photographed in 1892 by the British agent and correspondent of *The Times*, Ernest Gedge.

20 H. M. Stanley (above), the Welsh-American explorer who ended his life as Sir Henry Stanley, MP, in 1890, after his arrival at Zanzibar following the expedition to rescue, or capture, Emin Pasha.

19 and 21 The Kabaka Mwanga of Buganda (right) inherited his kingdom in 1884, at the age of nineteen; his father, the imposing Kabaka Mutesa (left), had reigned from 1857 to 1884.

THE BLACK BABY.

MR. BULL. "WHAT, ANOTHER!!—WELL, I SUPPOSE I MUST TAKE IT IN!!!"

22 *Punch*, with this cartoon by Sir John Tenniel, showed that Mr Gladstone's Britain did not necessarily welcome the expansion of Queen Victoria's African empire.

each manload of powder was priced at £200. (For comparison, the usual charge for transporting a manload of cloth or other civilian goods from Zanzibar to Buganda was about £6.) For the whole consignment, muskets, caps and powder, Stokes asked an all-in price of about £10,000. This was outrageous.

Lugard was under political pressure, but he had no money with which to buy off the extortionate Irishman, even had he wanted to. Stokes did not care about the politics, or for that matter about the weapons. He wanted to be sure of a huge profit, plus compensation for the damage his reputation would suffer if he failed to keep his promise of delivery to Mwanga. The Kabaka might well refuse to do any more business with a trader who failed to keep his promises: since Mwanga was the richest source of ivory in Africa, and Stokes was his main connexion with the market at Zanzibar, this was a grave commercial risk. Lugard believed he had the right and the duty to keep weapons out of the hands of black people. He wrote sternly back to Stokes, warning him that the arms must not end up in Mwanga's hands.

Stokes was a careful, not to say a cowardly, man. Many people far braver than he had been scared stiff by Lugard's piercing eyes and brusque infantry manner. He decided to keep the arms and ammunition safely out of harm's way, under German guard at Mwanza. But Lugard made a quite different, and highly implausible, claim: 'He [Stokes] appeared to think the temptation to secure the great profit accruing from the sale of powder in Uganda would be hard to withstand, and begged me, if I would not buy the powder and arms, to store them for him in Kampala. I was delighted at the proposal, and made him promise faithfully to place them under my keeping. He promised also to send his boat up with a cargo of cloth we so urgently needed.' This was simply untrue. Whatever he said at his meeting with Lugard, Stokes wrote twice after it to confirm that, in view of the dangerous situation in Buganda, he had decided not to deliver either the cloth or the weapons to anyone.

Lugard next wrote a personal letter to Emin Pasha, as Reichskommissar for the frontier areas, asking him not to

let Stokes's guns pass into British territory. By the time the
letter arrived at the Bukoba base, Emin had set off towards
the Congo. The German officer who received Lugard's
message was Lieutenant Langheld. He very much liked the
British, and owed them some favours: for example, one of
Lugard's boats had lately rescued Feldwebel Kühne, who
had let himself get cut off on the lake-shore without
ammunition, after a skirmish with tribesmen. Anyway,
Langheld's job was to control the Anglo-German border.
He had every interest in good relations with his neighbours.

Langheld sent a polite reply to Lugard's request that
Stokes's guns should be held. Lugard wrote again, asking
if he might collect the cloth belonging to the IBEA company, and the guns with it. Langheld agreed. Lugard sent
a young assistant, Stephen Bagge, down to Mwanza with a
great fleet of Buganda canoes, and brought up Stokes's
stored property, cloth and guns. After his brief protection
by the Germans, when they needed him most, Stokes was
on his own again. The administrations of the two great
powers had combined, as they were bound to do, against
the independent trader.

The British haul from Stokes's store was even greater
than expected - 300 new muskets and over 2,000 kilos of
good German powder. This precious stock was conveyed to
Lugard's little fort on Kampala hill. Beneath it he had dug
an underground store for explosives. In the constant rain of
that lush district it was damp. But the guns were not to be
left to rust. Lugard pretended he wished to keep the arms
out of the hands of irresponsible Africans, who would use
them for harm. In fact, he would soon be handing out those
same weapons to the Baganda Protestants, for use against
their Catholic fellow-countrymen.

For Stokes, the loss of Mwanga's arms was disastrous.
He had forfeited a big investment in stock-in-trade, and the
chance of bargaining it into a far greater fortune in ivory.
The British and Germans had ganged up against him.
Worse yet, his failure to deliver Mwanga's order had
spoiled his carefully established reputation as a reliable man
of business operating free of political control.

On top of that, Lugard deliberately blackened his name

in Europe. In his report to the IBEA company, Lugard of course presented his own version of the transaction over Mwanga's arms. In a private document, that would not have done much harm. But by this time the survival of the company was the subject of a political battle at home in England. The company desperately wanted a government subsidy, justifying its claim by presenting itself, in a vigorous public relations campaign, as the only safeguard for innocent African Christians, who lay at the mercy of cruel Arabs, scheming Catholic priests, and greedy commercial exploiters like Stokes.

The feeble Ernest Gedge, who had so inadequately acted as the IBEA company's caretaker in Kampala up until Lugard's arrival there, was found a useful role at last, as Mr Gedge, the *Times* correspondent, acting as the channel for information from Lugard to the great mouthpiece of the imperialist tendency in British politics. Through Gedge, Lugard leaked the report in which he described Stokes as a gun-runner, profiteer and ally of the French priests and their puppet Mwanga. With added malice, Lugard asserted (and it may have been true) that Stokes was fed up with his German employers, and asking for a trade concession in British territory.

Guns and powder had been normal articles of trade since Stokes first came to Africa. Now he was publicly pilloried in *The Times* for trading in them. As soon as he found that Lugard had used Gedge to blacken his name, he wrote in protest to the new consul-general in Zanzibar, Sir Gerald Portal, in terms that indicate the high opinion he now held of himself: 'I want to tell you, on my honour as an Irish Gentleman, the statement and inference in *The Times* against me, by the correspondent writing for Captain Lugard is not correct ... On my honour, before God, Captain Lugard did have no influence in persuading me not to sell my powder to the natives, as I had no intention of doing so ... It is not the good old days when we could call a gentleman to account another way, if it were, such rascally statements would not be made ... '

In his grammar, his oaths and his threats, let alone his claim to be a gentleman duellist, Stokes showed himself every inch the comic Irishman. Of such a man the English would, and did, believe any accusation. He now became famous as a liar and a rogue.

While this dispute with the British was proceeding, Stokes also broke off his formal connexion with the Germans. They had accepted their exclusion from Buganda, so now had no need for an expensive transport officer whose main value was his association with the Kabaka. As a gratifying pay-off, the Irishman was awarded a suitably modest honour, the Order of the Crown, Third Class. His salary was paid in full. So far Stokes had no reason to complain of his treatment at German hands – but complain he did, in correspondence with various British officials. No doubt he wished to ingratiate himself with them once more.

Once Stokes was off their payroll the Germans began to give him trouble. They made it clear that he would henceforth have to pay customs duty on all goods passing through German territory, at 8 per cent for imports of trade goods and 15 per cent for ivory exports. Worse, the *Limi* was taken without leave and used to transport goods between the Mwanza base and the Bukoba outpost. The justification for this was a story by Feldwebel Kühne, Stokes's drinking partner, that he himself had saved the yawl from destruction, when the Kabaka Mwanga's soldiers had put a bale of straw in the boat and set fire to it. This seems excessively unlikely, especially since, if it took place where Kühne said it did, he would have been leading an armed German party well inside the British sector of the lake. Stokes needed his boat but had to hire canoes to collect her from Bukoba.

But still his relations with the Germans continued. In August 1891 he was in Zanzibar, and wrote a formal letter of resignation from the German service to the new Governor, von Soden. At the same time, he took delivery of a large quantity of muzzle-loading guns and powder from official German supplies, destined for Emin in the forest. With them, in defiance of the British, Stokes set off at once. Events were moving fast, and Lugard was part of the action.

For four months after his successful imposition of a treaty upon the Kabaka, Lugard stuck it out impatiently in Kam-

pala. There was a great deal to do – fortifying the British
command-post, dealing with the grumbles of the French
priests and the expostulations of the Anglican parsons (to
both of whom he was impartially rude), being as civil as he
could to Mwanga, receiving calls and answering grievances
from the leaders of every faction in the land. All this he
tackled with ferocious energy. He hated desk-work, but
drove himself at it tirelessly, keeping a voluminous diary
and writing reports to all whom it might concern. He was
startlingly frank.

To the IBEA company he wrote, bluntly: 'The value of
Uganda, *per se*, has been much overrated.' Ivory was a re-
source that could easily be worked out: he was already
thinking about the need to conserve elephant stocks. There
was nothing else to export. Even when, one day, the rich
soil might be planted with cotton and coffee and all sorts of
valuable crops, none of it could be transported economically
to the outside world for as long as the only way of getting
it there was on tops of people's heads. A profitable Uganda
meant building a railway across 900 miles of awe-inspiring
scenery, over a desert, up the mountains, down the Great
Rift Valley, and up again to Lake Victoria. Until that was
done, he said, he could just about administer the place if he
had the services of seven European officials (plus replacements for sickness and home leave), and 500 trained soldiers
under white officers. The interim budget for the civil and
military European officials alone would, he reckoned, be
about £25,000 a year, payable out of revenue the company
had no prospect of raising.

The effect of this in London was startling. The company
had to pretend to its shareholders that the prospect for
profits was rosy. Its own senior official on the spot said this
was nonsense. So the IBEA directors asked for a government subsidy, to 'fight the slave trade, and assist the spread
of Christianity and civilisation'. The government replied
that the whole point of setting up a company under royal
charter was to empower it to carry on the work of colonisation at no expense to public funds. All requests for help
were brushed aside. Lugard wanted soldiers – native troops
under British officers would be best, and not too expensive

– but he needed permission to recruit them from within the British empire. Ideally he wanted the best of all, Sikhs from British India. Permission to recruit was refused. Then he asked for leave from the British-controlled government of Egypt to recruit Sudanese blacks there. Again, on Foreign Office advice, the Egyptian authorities refused.

Lugard knew that the best-trained soldiers in Africa were on his own doorstep, if he could only get them. They were the Sudanese of Emin's old Equatoria battalions, on whose quality Stanley had reported. But Stanley had also reported on the difficulty of persuading them to serve the British. Lugard made no move towards them until he heard the reports that Emin himself was on the warpath out to westward, heading for his old battalions. In April 1891, Lugard left to head him off. At best he hoped to recruit the men for Britain; at worst to prevent Emin getting control of them for Germany, which would put Britain on the losing side in tropical Africa.

Before setting off, Lugard found it convenient to help Mwanga consolidate his hold on his kingdom. Now that the Kabaka's realms had been signed over to Britain, it was to Britain's advantage that they should be extensive. So Lugard, Williams, their Sudanese soldiers under Shukri Aga and their Maxim guns started off with the support of a vast and disorganised army of Baganda (some 8,000 men, with 1,600 muskets) under the command of the prime minister and Protestant leader Apolo Kagwa. They subdued the rebels, slaughtering large numbers of them with their superior weaponry. Then Lugard sent Williams and the Baganda back to Kampala, and continued towards the far west.

Emin had begun to make serious inroads into lands that the British hoped to claim. He had much influence in the neighbouring kingdom of Toro, so Lugard installed a puppet ruler there, whose descendants were to do good service for several generations to the British empire. Lugard was furious to find that the Pasha had given a German flag to the chief of Katwe, beside Lake Edward, where a salt lake is the only source of the vital mineral for hundreds of miles around. The chief was promptly given a Union Jack and told to respect no other emblem; he was also put under surveillance by a platoon of Sudanese, commanded by Lieutenant Fenwick de Winton and housed in a tiny stockade called Fort George. (De Winton soon died of fever: the fort was in 1984 still rotting away in the rain.) Lugard was now without any white companion, and shooting all the elephants he could locate, to provide meat for his soldiers and tusks for himself. He was not at all sure that the IBEA company would be able to pay his salary.

The raiding party wandered far across the watershed into Congo territory, observing as they went that many of the geographical reports made by Stanley – the only ones that existed – were inaccurate, and that some of the chiefs with whom he claimed to have made treaties did not exist. Lugard caught up with Emin's old soldiers on 17 September 1891, just two months after they had rejected their old commander's appeal for support. Exactly where the meeting took place is not clear: Lugard's account is uncharacteristically vague, even in the diary he wrote at the time. But evidently it was very near the settlement described by Emin as Mazamboni's – deep enough within Belgian territory for Lugard's reticence to be understandable. Emin was on his way down the Ituri river, heading westwards with the tiny group of Sudanese who had agreed to follow him. Lugard set down to persuade the remaining majority of soldiers to march for Uganda behind the British flag.

Major Shukri Aga, his second-in-command, interpreted Lugard's speeches from Swahili into Arabic; much more important, he backed the Englishman's plea with his own persuasion. Lugard's offer was that all those who wanted should have free transport, along with their wives and children (but not their slaves), to Egypt, where they would receive their eight years' back pay and be free to rejoin the Khedive's army. Shukri believed this was the best hope for his fellow-countrymen. The Sudanese would not agree to take service under the English crown, and Lugard frankly admired the loyalty to their own King which prevented them from doing so. But the men accepted the offer of repatriation *en masse*.

Lugard took command of an extraordinary army. He had grown used to, and indeed rather fond of, Major Shukri,

despite his exotic taste in dress: Stanley's chief assistant,
A. J. Mounteney-Jephson, had met him in 1888, 'dressed in
a long blue uniform tunic with enormous gold epaulettes,
cherry-coloured trousers, high-heeled French boots, large
sword and fez'. Major Selim Bey, the senior officer of the
group Lugard now took over, had a long line of slaves to
follow him: most worrying were 'several good-looking
young girls in slave-sticks', the yokes used to prevent the
escape of recent captives. The whole force of 932 armed
men was accompanied by no fewer than 3,065 women, 1,153
male porters and slaves, and 2,856 boys and girls of inde-
terminate parentage. Lugard had more than 8,000 extra
people to discipline and organise, in addition to his own
raiding party. Somehow they got through to Kampala,
arriving on Christmas Eve, 1891.

Lugard's safari had been entirely successful. He had even
managed to avoid a direct meeting with Emin Pasha – a
confrontation between British and German officers on Belgian soil would have been really embarrassing. He had extended the frontiers of the British protectorate, acquired
new allies, denied Emin's former soldiers to the Germans,
and amassed a great deal of new geographical knowledge in
a practically untravelled region. He thought he deserved
well of his country, and of the company that employed him,
and he desperately needed a rest. He and his marching
boots were utterly worn out.

As Lugard approached Kampala, carried in a litter
because he was too weak from fever to walk, messengers
came out to meet him, sent by Captain Williams. They
brought disastrous news. The directors of the IBEA company, in London, had decided to wind up the Uganda
operation. The company would try to hold onto the barren
lands of what is now Kenya, and develop them in a modest
way. But the jewel of Africa, where the Anglican mission
had struggled for fifteen years to establish itself as the pre-
cursor of British rule, would be let go. Lugard had permission to take the missionaries with him, if they agreed to
leave. If not, they, and the Baganda Protestants who relied
on their protection, must be left to face the danger alone.

From the financial point of view the IBEA directors had

no alternative. The company's founder and inspirer, Sir William Mackinnon, was a sick man. (He died in June 1893.) The government would not help. Lugard's first, deeply discouraging report on Uganda had reached England at a time when there was not the slightest chance of raising new capital privately in the City of London. Throughout western Europe a financial crisis had broken. Early in August 1891 the most dignified of City banks, Baring's, had in effect gone bust, surviving only because it was bailed out by the Bank of England. (The Barings' mistake had been to make huge loans to developing economies, for railway and similar big capital projects: the borrowers were unable to pay the interest, let alone the capital. All this is too familiar in the 1980s.) The implications for African finance were cruelly underlined by the fact that one of the bank's proprietors was Sir Evelyn Baring, the British official who effectively ruled Egypt.

The letter received by Lugard in December had been mailed from London on 10 August, as the scale of the Baring's disaster became apparent. He and Williams knew nothing of the context. They were simply confident that the British Empire was being betrayed by a lily-livered bunch of liberals and penny-pinchers, while men like themselves were striving to add new garlands to the Crown. The two officers sincerely believed in their patriotic mission. They had never sought high salaries, and would greatly have preferred to be working for their government than for a mere commercial company. Williams had savings of £4,000, set aside for his retirement. He determined to sink the lot in a campaign to persuade the British government to take up the burden that the company was too feeble to bear. Lugard had no money at all, but he resolved to commit to that struggle his special talents for public relations and violence.

Under Williams, Kampala had been peaceful, if uneasy, for the whole eight months of Lugard's absence. Lugard set to work at once to heighten the tension: he realised that the most persuasive appeal he could make at home would be based on a visible threat to the Protestant mission, rather than on accounts of a quiet stalemate in Buganda. Then, just two weeks after the order to withdraw, he received a stay of sentence. On 7 January 1892 a new letter arrived from the IBEA offices in London, where the Bank of England's rescue of Baring's had averted a general financial catastrophe. The news was that a private subscription had been raised to enable the IBEA company to carry on its work; in fact, the dying Mackinnon had dipped once more into his purse. The officers could stay on in Kampala for a year, provided they spent an absolute minimum of money. Meanwhile, the company and the government would see if a way could be found to continue the Uganda operation.

The two officers shook hands – Lugard describes this as an extraordinary demonstration of feeling – and thought what to do next. Lugard decided to return to Britain and argue the case in public for a political decision to keep Uganda British. The worse the crisis he could describe, the stronger would be the argument for British 'peace-keeping'.

That crisis was precipitated by the return to Kampala, on 10 January, of the German-speaking White Fathers, Hirth and Achte. In Zanzibar they had heard about, and now informed Mwanga of, the proposed British withdrawal, which Lugard and Williams had kept secret. The priests warned Mwanga that the British were secretly conspiring to dishonour the treaty of protection they had signed.

Mwanga was furious, and contemptuous of the white men who so easily broke their promises. He continued to take advice from the French priests. But he also turned once again for support to the Futabanghi, the traditionalists who had always urged him to put his trust in his own family and people, rather than in treacherous foreigners. Then violence broke out between the Baganda Protestants and Catholics. The occasion was a murder, and the refusal of the Kabaka's courts to punish the apparent aggressor: so many obvious lies were told about the incident by priests, officers and those involved that it is not worth trying to disentangle the truth.

Faced with an apparent onslaught by the Catholics, Lugard had the pretext he wanted for distributing arms to the Protestants. The cowhide wrappings were ripped off Stokes's muskets in the store beneath Kampala fort, and the waIngerezi went into battle. Neither of the African parties to the conflict did the other much damage: the muskets, loaded with pebbles rather than with lead balls, had a feebly short range and were barely lethal even point-blank. But Lugard made sure that nobody could make light of the struggle.

The Catholic forces assembled around their church and fort on Rubaga hilltop. The range from Lugard's own fort on Kampala hill was about 1,600 yards, ideal for Maxim fire. He and Williams mounted their two machine-guns and opened fire. The heavy slugs dropped down on a high trajectory, slicing along the Rubaga summit and down its reverse slope. The number of deaths is not recorded. Later, when accused at home of indiscriminate slaughter, the two British officers made light of the damage. Williams claimed that his Maxim broke its main swivel-pin just after he began firing, and was out of action thereafter. Lugard said his old gun kept jamming and could not have killed many people. But several Baganda Roman Catholic dignitaries were wounded. ('The Kimbugwe', wrote Lugard in his diary, 'got several Maxim bullets through his clothes, and one through his leg. I wish I had had the luck to bag him.') The members of the French Catholic mission were extremely lucky. Only one of them was killed; he was François Gogé, the medical orderly. Since Gogé was a black West African, this was not regarded as a matter for strong complaints.

The priests surrendered to Lugard: like many others then and later they thought him completely crazy, and all the more dangerous for that. He held them for a while, then let them go without their possessions to rejoin their people, who included the Kabaka. Together, the leaders of the Catholic party withdrew to the usual refuge on Bulingugwe island, half a mile offshore in the lake near the capital. Lugard saw the danger: the King and the priests might get clear away by boat – and the Catholics already had the two likely heirs to the throne, Mwanga's nephews, in safe-keeping in German territory down the lake.

Against the Maxims the offshore sanctuary was no longer secure. This time both guns worked nicely. Williams denied, later, that what took place was a massacre. The firing, he said, caused only about a hundred deaths, plus those who might have been hit by dropping shots, or drowned in the panic rush for the boats, on the far side of the island. A British official, Rennell Rodd, sent up later to report on alleged anti-French atrocities, said that Captain Lugard's reports, 'I fear, must be read as vivid works of fiction ... The general impression here is that the man is off his head.'

As well as physical danger, Lugard heaped insults on the heads of the priests. The most ingenious, at the height of what Lugard called the 'civil war', deserves recording. The priest in charge was now Father Achte, the Alsatian from Emin's party and a man of no great learning. Lugard wished to offer him terms for surrender, but knew no French and not enough Swahili or Luganda to write a letter. So he spent the night composing a message in elaborate Latin, as taught in the English public schools, with echoes of Julius Caesar and Cicero. Achte, although he said Mass in Church-Latin every day, could make neither head nor tail of this pseudo-classical stuff. Lugard laughed at him for his ignorance.

The war against the Catholics lasted five months, and ended in their submission to English power. By the end of June 1892, Lugard felt sufficiently confident of the outcome to leave for home. He carried with him a letter to Queen Victoria from Mwanga. It appealed for help, asked that the IBEA company should be enabled to continue its work, and praised Lugard: 'He is a man of very great ability, and all the Waganda like him very much; he is gentle; his judgments are just and true, and so I want you to send him back to Uganda.' It is easy to guess who dictated that piece of fantasy to the Kabaka's secretary. The letter was quoted freely at public meetings all over Britain, where Lugard spoke and lobbied in defence of the imperial cause.

In the end that cause prevailed. In Britain (as in Germany, with the fall of Bismarck) politics were changing as the enfranchisement of the manufacturing and trading classes worked its way through into new ideas and new leaders. The new men in both parties argued that the work of colonisation was noble and civilising: it also stood to be highly profitable, and if the British government did not do it the French and Germans would. These people wanted colonies for glory, as well as for trade. The most forceful of them, Joseph Chamberlain, defected from the Liberals because they were not tough enough with subject peoples, particularly with the Irish, declaring: 'It is Britain's manifest destiny to be a great colonising and civilising power.'

This was exactly what Lugard thought. He shared his public platforms with a phalanx of missionaries, manufacturers and politicians, not to mention the imperial star, H. M. Stanley. At the Foreign Office the chief clerk, Sir Percy Anderson, agreed that the government should take over East Africa: he did not want the French or the Germans to grab land that might be British, and he knew that the chartered companies were incompetent, or corrupt, or both. The old Queen Victoria summoned her ministers to terrifying private audiences, at which she harangued them on the moral virtues of her Empire. In the end, Uganda became part of it. Much to his distaste, old Mr Gladstone found himself in office when this unwanted gift was dumped on his doorstep, in November 1893.

Lugard never went back to East Africa. The many official reports on his irresponsible conduct in Uganda were patriotically hushed up within the Foreign Office, and the press made a hero of him. Only the French, whose missionaries had suffered at his hands, remembered his reputation. They had good cause to: his next job was in the service of the Royal Niger Company, the IBEA company's West African counterpart, and his rivals on the upper Niger were the forces of France. Lugard beat them back, and stayed on to rule over the new nation of Nigeria, whose name was invented by his wife, the former colonial correspondent of *The Times*. Thus was created one of the greatest reputations of all Britain's long colonial history.

IV

DEATH
or
VICTORY

Chapter 12

~∽~

Stokes Alone

If I made an expedition without your leave as you say it might be the salvation of English rights and flying as I would the English flag (you must know I have one) would Captain Lugard fire on me or what do you mean by your warning, if he did, by God you would find Stokes's body in front of his men and lead them to death or victory.

Stokes, letter to Captain Williams, commanding Kampala Fort (30 November 1891)

Stokes was an Irish protestant, with his country's faults and virtues. He was so violent and excitable that it appeared as though at times he was not quite sane. Rumours said he was *not* courageous. He was very easily swayed to good or evil, was vacillating in purpose and unreliable. The making of money was the motive of his life, and anything which offered opportunity to this end was a temptation he could hardly resist.

Captain Frederick Lugard, posthumous evidence of Stokes's character (31 August 1895)

Charles Stokes, cast as a chief villain by Lugard and *The Times* in their public relations campaign for subsidies to Uganda, had become notorious in Britain. In Africa he fitted more closely than ever into the local scene. His cloth, beads and guns were bought from European importers, and his ivory was sold in the last resort to European exporters. But between these two ends he had as little as possible to do with white people by way of business. His porters were African. Most of his foremen were part-African, part-Arab

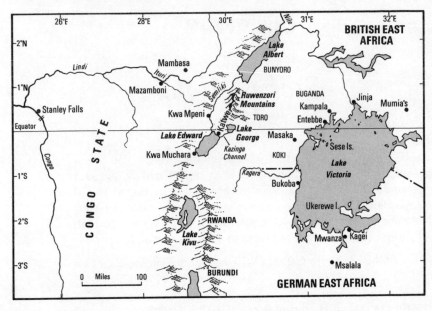

By 1895 the British had established control of Uganda, the Germans had mastered the country round the southern end of Lake Victoria, and the Belgians had strongpoints, served by steamers, on the Congo river. Between the outposts of the three advancing empires lay the hostile terrain where the line of lakes – Albert, Edward, Kivu, Tanganyika – lies along the Western Rift Valley. There (see Map 2, page 62) the colonial borders were still unoccupied and undefined. For the Germans, Emin Pasha had hoped to claim a strip of land between British Uganda and the Congo State, linking German East Africa with the source of the Nile. Charles Stokes, in association with Emin, regarded this region at the Equator as Africa's richest remaining source of ivory, and hoped to profit by trading in it with the Arab warlords who still held sway there. To succeed he needed to keep clear of the armed forces of all three colonial powers. He therefore established his base camp at Kwa Mpeni, on the Semliki river, which was assumed to form the frontier between the Congo State and Uganda. That was his downfall.

Muslims from the Swahili coast. As his business grew, with big contracts for the German administration and for the Anglican mission, as well as the Kabaka's guns-for-ivory commissions, he started to need an administrative staff, and clerks to handle correspondence in Swahili and Arabic, which Stokes could not write himself. The most reliable of these were Juma bin Ali, whose father was Swahili and whose mother came from Limi's home district of Unyamwesi, and Moses Willing, the Nasik-educated African, sacked long since as headmaster of the Frere Town mission school.

By 1891 Stokes was head of a large and far-flung business, with depots at several places along the caravan route from Zanzibar to Uganda. He needed financial backing, and preferred not to write cheques on the British and German trading houses of Zanzibar. (He did not like their snobbish attitudes – and he certainly did not want white people to know the ins and outs of his arms business.) For venture capital he turned to the people who for several generations had financed the trade of the Swahili slave-and-ivory merchants. Dr Livingstone had noted in the 1860s that cheques written at Tabora, on the way to Lake Tanganyika, would be swiftly and accurately discounted in Zanzibar by the Indian merchants there, who were from Bombay, and therefore (in law at least) under British protection: the British called them *banyans*, meaning members of a Hindu money-lending caste, although most were in fact Muslims. The most powerful was Seewa Hadji, who had for many years been banker to Tippu Tib, the leading merchant-prince of the interior. Allidina Visram handled affairs in Zanzibar for the Kabaka of Buganda, and went on to found the first regular commercial bank in British Uganda: he was photographed, probably in 1892, with Stokes and the foremen and escort commanders of the caravan bound for the Congo.

These men were as much merchants as bankers. As well as lending money and cashing drafts, they sought out commercial opportunities, sent out their own goods with caravans for bartering, and took a share of the ivory brought back. (An Italian banker of the sixteenth century would have perfectly understood their business.) They were deep in the trade in slaves and guns, so the British and Germans felt perfectly justified in impeding their caravans and obstructing their agents. If the Indians were to stay in business they needed white men of their own, to stand up to the officials and keep trade alive. That was why they worked closely with Stokes. If he failed to defend their interests, they would drop him.

Stokes in turn needed white men to be responsible for the depots where trade goods, and the ivory bartered for them, were stored. It was not necessary for them to be good at the job: what was needed was a white man to protect the depots from being turned over by a white official, or 'borrowed' from by a white passer-by. At the coast Stokes took into partnership Edward Muxworthy, the lazy man who had been a witness (along with General Mathews of the Zanzibar army) at his wedding to Limi. At Usongo in Unyamwesi Stokes's depot was watched over by Charles Wise, a former CMS lay worker who, like Stokes himself, had left the mission's service in disgrace.

Wise also controlled the new store set up by Stokes at Mwanza, when the Germans decided to make that place their main lake port. It was Wise who, on Langheld's orders, had handed over Mwanga's muskets to Lugard's messenger, despite Stokes's written instructions not to do so. Faced with the German officer and his *askari*, with their rifles, even a decisive person – and Wise, a drunk, was far from decisive – would have obeyed. Stokes sacked him for it, but he got his reward: Captain Williams found him a job as a storeman, to keep him out of trouble.

The old stagers, Wise and Muxworthy, had for a while been useful as go-betweens in the gap between Africans and the inexperienced administrators sent out from Europe. As the officials acquired experience, and the colonial governments began to work together, their time was running out. Langheld's overruling of Wise signified the end of their utility. But Wise and Muxworthy could not rejoin the community of whites. They had taken African wives and 'gone native' before the imperialists had imposed their racial standards upon Africa.

So it was for Stokes and Emin. The Pasha was shy and scholarly, the Irishman was loud and not very bright. But both had African wives whom they acknowledged and cherished, and both had half-African daughters whom they adored. They acted as though merit, not race, would decide things in the continent where they, unlike almost all the other white people, behaved like permanent residents, not short-term visitors. They were misfits: history proved them failures. But they had tried.

Stokes started the year of 1891 as a free agent. He had left his official employment with the Germans, and openly quarrelled with the British who had taken away his valuable stock of weapons. His main asset was his unrivalled connection with the Wanyamwesi and the Baganda. Left to his own devices he could cause the British and the Germans no end of trouble. The Germans prudently decided to have him on their side; they exploited his position, just as they were exploiting Emin's longing to return to Equatoria. In August 1891, Stokes was authorised to purchase from official German stocks large numbers of muzzle-loaders, and an ample supply of gunpowder. With them, he set off to join up once more with Emin.

The British in Uganda promptly got hold of this worrying information. Captain Williams was in command at Kampala, while Lugard swept through the western districts in pursuit of Emin; his informant was Stokes's local agent and sailing-master, Wadi Muftaa, 'a very respectable Mohammedan, looked upon as neutral entirely'. Muftaa gave Williams to understand that Stokes was proposing to travel out to the country west of Buganda, in search of ivory. Williams needed to prevent Stokes from bringing support to Emin, as was obviously his real intention.

Williams sent word, through Muftaa, to Stokes, warning him not to travel through British territory 'on the route of Emin Pasha's recent escapade' – a deliberately insulting phrase. To the insult Williams added financial injury by offering the derisory sum of 250 rupees (about £20) for the guns and powder taken by Lugard from Stokes's store in Kampala. Stokes in turn flew into a rage. On 30 November he wrote to say he was going to Equatoria anyway. This can hardly have surprised Williams, who knew his man. But the style of the letter is bizarre: it reads like, and maybe was, the raving of a drunk. At great length, and with scanty grammar, Stokes swore he was a true subject of the Queen, even if only an Irishman. He had taken employment with the Germans out of pure altruism and family loyalty: 'By doing so I was able to persuade the Wanyamwesi to receive the Germans peaceably, if I had not done so there would have been a fine time in Unyamwesi, can you blame me for wishing to befriend my own people.' Now he would raise the Union Jack again for his march upon Equatoria, whatever Williams said, and in defiance of Lugard, to death or glory.

This flare-up did not last. Maybe Stokes thought it prudent, on reflection, to heed Williams's warnings. Maybe he got the news that Emin had, after all, failed to recruit the Sudanese. Or maybe he just sobered up. By February 1892, he had a far more modest request. He wanted permission to travel to Buganda by lake, then to march westwards through the neighbouring kingdoms of Ankole, Toro and south Unyoro – all in the British sphere – in search of ivory. Once again, Williams sent no for an answer, and this time Stokes accepted the ban. In July 1892, he travelled to Buganda himself. Business was once again taking precedence over dreams of glory.

The *Limi* was laden with cloth and other trade goods ordered by the IBEA company, and Williams was glad to get them. But Stokes's real business was to claim compensation for the losses he had suffered at the hands of the British. For the 300 trade guns and two tonnes of powder removed from the Mwanza store, he claimed $20,000, almost £3,000. At the coast, the price of a reliable muzzle-loader at the time was about 15 shillings, so this was an absurdly inflated demand – although well under one-third of what Stokes had originally asked of Lugard. But he made it clear that he would much prefer the arms and ammunition themselves to the cash. Bartered with the Arabs for ivory, the profit would be far more than $20,000. Williams had two reasons for doing nothing to meet the claim. He was determined that the guns should not fall into anti-

British hands – and anyway, they had been ripped from their rawhide wrappings and handed out in a hurry to the Protestants in the previous December, with no record kept of who had received them. It was impossible to get them back, even if Williams had wanted to.

Then there was a matter of the 3,300 pounds of ivory that Stokes said he had stored at Kampala under Mwanga's care. This, too, he said had been taken without leave by the British, and he wanted the standard price of £1,600 for it. Williams showed himself a skilled bureaucrat, as well as a good soldier. He did not specifically dispute the claim, but produced a counter-claim and referred the dispute to headquarters. Before the ivory was handed over, Williams wanted a storage fee, export duty, and the payment of a special levy to Mwanga, whose fortunes the British wanted to sustain until they knew whether they were staying in Buganda for good or not. Moreover, Williams wanted Stokes to agree that all ivory obtained on British territory should be exported not by the usual route through German territory, but through Masailand and out of the British port of Mombasa. Stokes wrote to the consul-general in Mombasa with a well-founded grumble: 'How can anyone do business with such a duty? 10% to Mwanga, plus 4% to the company for storage, plus 14% on shipment to Usukuma [the German territory where Stokes had his trading post], plus 15% export duty at the coast.'

Williams could not have paid up. He had no money other than for essentials: the IBEA company was effectively bankrupt. Anyway, he thought it his duty to squeeze Stokes out as an independent trading rival to the company – and would no doubt have thought so even had it not been for Stokes's political activities. He was startlingly indiscreet about these, making it clear to Williams that he intended to join up with Emin Pasha once more, out in the far interior. Williams drafted a cable reporting on these transactions, for transmission via Mombasa to London.

The upshot of all this was a meaningless agreement between the two men. Williams agreed that Stokes should be allowed to travel from Buganda as far west as the neighbouring kingdom of Toro, within British Uganda, to buy

ivory. Stokes agreed that if he brought any back through
British territory he would pay duty of 15 per cent on it. In
fact his intended destination was in Belgian territory,
further west again: he only wanted leave to re-enter Uganda
as an escape route from there, in case the Congo Arabs or
the Belgians came after him.

From Kampala he headed back south to German territory, and set off walking westwards along the route that
Emin had taken the previous year. The main body of Wanyamwesi porters carried 300 loads of the usual goods for
barter trade – cloth, beads and brass wire. But 150 porters
carried a more significant cargo of 100 trade muskets, 700
pounds of *Negerpulver* – black powder – and a large
quantity of caps for muskets. On top of that, many porters
were carrying muskets of their own. Interrogated three
years later, Stokes's headman gave a careful account of the
caravan (which he dated to the Muslim year 1309 HJ, corresponding to AD 1892). Rashid bin Ali bin Salim Lenki, a
Zanzibari, stated that the total armament was 600 muzzle-
loaders belonging either to Stokes or to his porters, plus ten
Snider rifles belonging to Stokes, and three shotguns for
game.

The heavily armed caravan was escorted by a platoon of
thirty trained Swahili riflemen, allocated to the job by Captain Langheld of the German imperial army, and dressed in
German colonial uniforms of white baggy shorts and shirts,
with a square naval-style collar behind, bordered with three
dark-blue stripes. The whole party, including women and
camp followers, amounted to some 1,000 people. The rifles
were provided by the Germans, and the muskets authorised by them. There could be no pretence that such an
armoury was for shooting elephants, or for self-defence.
Stokes was unmistakably in command of an expedition
equipped by Germany for warfare in Belgian territory.

The going was tough, even for the experienced Wanyamwesi. The caravan crossed the Kagera river, which winds
back and forth across what is now the straight-line border
between Tanzania and Uganda. Then it turned north,
across the arid hills, where the people might at any moment
prove hostile. The great column of porters skirted round

the desperate volcanic country of Rwanda, and into the Western Rift Valley, where they made camp for a while at the place called Kwa Muchara, after its founder, the son and leading ivory dealer of the great Tippu Tib.

Muchara's village lay on the southern shore of Lake Edward. Then as now, the eastern third of the lake was acknowledged to lie within Uganda: Muchara's was in the Belgian sector. Stokes knew he was in the territory of the Congo Free State, at the head of an unauthorised armed expedition. But the Belgians were nowhere near. The only imperial presence for hundreds of miles around was British, at the north-east corner of Lake Edward, where the tiny Fort George guarded the trade route and the salt deposits of Katwe. The platoon of Sudanese troops there had buried their officer, young Fenwick de Winton, and maintained Britain's territorial rights on their own. Stokes could be pretty confident that they would not interfere with him, but he stuck prudently to the western, Congo, shore, along which he moved on northward.

There were fishermen on the lake, but the country behind it was empty, teeming with wild game that provided all the meat the travellers could eat. Progress was slow: the lake shore was continually interrupted by precipitous gullies crammed with thick bush and fallen trees, so the men had continually to transfer between boats and the shore. So they came to the top of the lake, where the Semliki river surges across the Equator, towards Lake Albert and the Nile. Nobody knew where the border would eventually be drawn between British and Belgian ground in this sector: for the time being the Semliki itself was assumed to be the *de facto* frontier. On its left, Belgian, bank, in September 1892, Stokes came to the village of a chief called Mpeni, which means 'goat' in his own language. There he settled down to await news of Emin, and to do business.

The valley of the Semliki was, and remains, one of the world's strange places. In only fifty miles, from east to west, the traveller moves out of the clear, dry savannah that stretches right away to the Indian Ocean shore, and into the edge of the great rain-forest that covers the land for a thousand miles and more to the Atlantic. The Uganda side is in open land, with thorn-scrub and flat-topped acacia trees, where far-ranging herds of buck and kob are followed by their predators. Moving across the Western Rift, the vegetation takes on a darker green in the volcanic clefts. Patches of dense bush gather beside the track, broken only by the ragged paths that the wild elephants tear as they pass: even today, on the slimy road, giant blue-and-black butterflies seem to revel in the steam that rises from the heaps of elephant-dung, standing fresh on the mud that seeps back into the creatures' monstrous footprints. When the valley haze thins out at dawn, or after a thunder-shower, snowy peaks can be seen to glitter impossibly in the sky to eastward. Right across the Equator, the sky-scraping Ruwenzori mountains run parallel with the valley and its river, holding back the rain-clouds of the west from the dry breezes of East Africa, and dividing the climates of the continent.

In crossing the Semliki, Stokes did more than pass a mere political frontier: he moved into the sickly country of the rain-forest. The river itself is like nothing in East Africa, sucking and bubbling inexorably north, grey and greasy, its eddies half-revealing shadows that may be hippos, or Nile crocodiles, or maybe just baulks of sodden timber that swim up and are sucked down like living things. Today there is a single, crazy, iron bridge over the river, in its whole course of seventy miles. Beside it, amid the putrid undergrowth, can be seen a few rotting house-beams, marking the site where Mpeni's village once stood, and where Stokes settled down, canoes always at the ready for instant flight across the water if enemies threatened.

The immediate danger was from the climate itself, a miasma that sets everything to rot but never completes the process, so that life is a perpetually renewed corruption. The mosquitos hung in clouds; foul crawling things swarmed in the mud. For Stokes's East Africans, from the open plains, it was misery. Even the fever was different from that at home, lingering, sapping the strength. Firewood would not dry, to drive back the shadows and the damp chill of the night.

Out of the forest came strangers with scraps of news, tales of the fighting with the Belgians and the treachery of their own people. Stuhlmann, Stokes heard, had gone away southwards; Emin was camped ahead, or moving slowly to the west, under the protection of one warlord or another. And the visitors, with their news, brought tusks – great teeth of new-killed elephants of a size and quality rare indeed in the well-travelled plains of East Africa, or yellowing relics of long-dead animals, that had for years stood disregarded in the earth at the entry to some forest chieftain's wretched hutment. Sickly part-Arab clerks brought the ivory in under escort of Manyuema fighting men, who looked hungrily at the newcomers and muttered to each other among the cooking-pots. The ivory built into a great pile, stored in a hut alongside Stokes's own tent, and there were promises of more to come, if he could produce the guns and powder that were all the Arab warlords would accept in exchange.

Then, in confusion, three months after Stokes arrived in Mpeni's village, came the news that Emin was dead. Whatever the truth of that murder, Stokes – like everyone else at the time – seems to have accepted that the man responsible was Said bin Abedi. Kibonghe sent to assure the Irishman that their alliance, and the Pasha's plan, would survive the death of its inventor. Stokes would now be Kibonghe's principal partner in the daring plan to find the way across the continent to Kamerun and the Atlantic coast, through the untravelled forest where the European powers as yet presented no threat to the Arabs and their trade.

For the time being the Europeans had their hands full elsewhere. Uganda was in the process of being handed over to the British government (which did not want it) from the bankrupt IBEA company (which continued, despite its fraudulent failure, to demand compensation for every penny it had wasted). Meanwhile the British administrators were pinned down by fighting within the infant protectorate, against the great prince Kabarega of Bunyoro in the north.

The Belgians too were for the time being fully occupied by their fight against the Congo Arabs, which kept them well clear of the wild border. But they knew what Stokes was up to, from their Arab collaborators. Late in 1893 the British vice-consul in the Congo, Mr Parminter, told the Foreign Office of reports that an 'English missionary' was taking forest ivory in exchange for guns. Parminter himself had been threatened with violence, in the upsurge of anti-British, anti-Protestant feeling that followed the reports.

If Stokes was to catch the opportunity for profit that lay in the gap between the advance of the colonial powers, he had to act fast. He had arrived in Mpeni's village in September 1892. In December came the news that Emin was murdered. In January 1893 Stokes left in a hurry for Zanzibar. He was not simply running away from the evident danger of the forest zone, with its anarchic bands of robbers under unpredictable warlords. He saw that there was a fortune still to be made, if he could replenish the stock of goods and guns to be traded for ivory, and bring up a team of porters large enough to carry the ivory away.

His present caravan was in imminent danger, not so much from attack as from weakness and sickness. The foul environment of the Semliki valley had encouraged the spread of fever and dysentery among the men. Then the smallpox arrived – the same infection that had struck Emin's own expedition. Even had Stokes himself chosen to face the risk, he could not expose his men to it: without porters he could make no profit.

He had already amassed a very large quantity of ivory – more than his people could carry away in their weakened state. In exchange for it he had handed over a large number of manloads of cloth and beads. But he had more, and his stock of guns and ammunition was intact. All this he therefore put into store, in two separate villages: 600 *frasilahs* – almost ten tonnes – of ivory; thirty-two and a half manloads of brass and copper wire; twenty-seven and a half loads of assorted glass beads; eighty-seven and a half loads of assorted cloth; fifteen and a half loads of gunpowder; ninety-nine muskets; and a load of ninety-nine boxes of percussion caps for the muskets.

He had struck a bargain with the Arab chieftains. During his absence they would deliver as much ivory as they could collect. On his return they would fix a price, and swap the supplies for the ivory, which he would then carry away as fast as he could. They promised him tusks, he promised them guns. But at this stage he did not actually deliver any weapons to the Arabs.

In charge of his depots, Stokes left his most trustworthy and experienced clerk, Juma bin Ali, whose mother, it seems, was related to Limi. Juma was set up with the ivory in a relatively healthy village, on high ground a little to the north of Mpeni's. As a special mark of favour, Stokes left him one of the pretty young girls presented to him by the Kabaka, called Aminah; with them stayed Suedi wadi Mabruki, Ismaili and two Watoto servants. For their protection they had five muzzle-loading guns, one pistol and a double-barrelled English shotgun, for game to supplement the meagre local diet.

These arrangements made, Stokes set off to walk back to Zanzibar. He took a large amount of ivory with him. (Its value, recorded at the German customs post at Bukoba, was assessed at between £15,000 and £20,000. This is so huge as to be incredible; the German copying clerk probably wrote the sign for pounds when he meant to write that for Maria Theresa dollars, worth roughly seven to the pound.) At Bukoba, having registered his ivory, he handed back to Captain Langheld the platoon of German-trained soldiers assigned for his 'protection'.

Stokes was risking all he had on one last huge expedition. After a call at his home base at Usongo, he was in Zanzibar six months after leaving the Semliki valley, in July 1893. There he set about organising and buying supplies for the great caravan that would collect the Congo ivory he hoped Juma was amassing in his absence. He spent freely in Zanzibar, using the earnings from the initial ivory consignment he had brought down (on 17 July his account book recorded the expenditure of $2,161.12 on Gumpti, Kunguru and Mtama, cloth for trade and grain for the porters – also of $46.06 on two cases of champagne).

Six weeks later he was on the march inland once more, at the head of no fewer than 3,500 porters, with an armed escort and the usual camp-followers. The whole great throng numbered some 5,000 people, straggling in file for several miles across the countryside. Such a procession could not move fast. Because Stokes was constitutionally incapable of turning down business, he added to his baggage-train over 500 loads of goods for the Uganda administration, which had still not managed to get its own line of supply organised by the all-British route from Mombasa. In addition, he agreed to escort a party of Church Missionary Society clergymen, returning to Uganda now that its destiny as a British possession was confirmed. They included two old companions from Stokes's earliest East African days, Cyril Gordon and Robert Walker.

This was extremely indiscreet. The British had every reason to be alarmed at what Stokes seemed to be up to. The Germans obviously wanted to secure a strip of land that would form a buffer between British East Africa and the Congo State. Grabbing the Semliki valley would give them that, and a foothold in the Nile basin too. To send an expedition under their own officers would be a provocation both to the Belgians and to the British, but to help a British subject conduct trade there was a perfect cover. As soon as they arrived in Uganda, Gordon and Walker told the British that Stokes had received massive armed backing from the Germans.

The authorities at Saadani, the German port on the mainland opposite Zanzibar, had issued on 19 September a permit allowing Stokes to transport across their territory thirty-six breech-loading rifles, 300 muzzle-loading muskets with fifty boxes of caps, and twenty-two loads - 660 kilos - of powder. The permit also authorised the transport of 2,200 loads of other, presumably peaceful, goods. From their homes in German territory, at least 200 of this immense horde of porters picked up unauthorised muskets of their own: porters frequently carried arms for their own protection, and sometimes sold them on their own account to undesirable people, in exchange for ivory.

At Bukoba, Captain Langheld again provided Stokes with his escort of uniformed African riflemen carrying Mausers. When signing the authorisation for this escort, Langheld described himself not as an Imperial officer, but as head of the post funded by the German Anti-Slavery Society out of

the proceeds of its lottery in German parishes. Langheld
was indeed acting as the Anti-Slavery Society's agent, since
the society's own man had died on the journey up country.
But he was a scrupulous, even pedantic, servant of the
Reich, and would not conceivably have offered Stokes military support without orders from his superior officers. He
can only have signed on behalf of the Anti-Slavery Society
as a cover-story for what had become a German-backed
invasion of Belgian territory, as well as a giant commercial
raid on the ivory monopoly of the King of the Belgians.

Having lined up the Germans behind his adventure, Stokes
turned to the British. He had a new man to deal with in
Uganda. Colonel Colvile, the new administrator, was an
experienced officer from the Indian army in a thoroughly
awkward position. His job was to see the territory through
the uneasy transition from control by the now bankrupt
British East Africa Company to administration by the
British Colonial Office. There was no established budget:
all money questions were held up in the wrangling between
the company and the government over who should pay for
what. Nothing had been settled about customs dues, taxation, the salt monopoly, transport or military activities: the
borders of the territory were not defined, and there was
fighting well inside them against various insurgents. Colvile
had never met Stokes, but he had certainly been warned to
watch out for the old ruffian.

Unfortunately for the administrator, Stokes had some
genuine grievances against the Uganda administration.
Most had already been listed by Captain Williams, and referred by him to higher authority; but Williams himself had
added extra grounds for complaint. Just before his well-
earned departure for home, with promotion to the rank of
Major, Williams had been joined by Major J. R. Macdonald
of the Royal Engineers, sent out to complete the survey for
the line of rail from Mombasa to Uganda. The two majors
had mounted a final sporting expedition to celebrate the
end of their African service.

Their objective was to put down the last traces of independence among the Baganda people who lived on the

islands of Lake Victoria and obstinately refused to pay customs dues to the British. Their great fleet of war-canoes
posed a threat to commercial traffic on the lake. The two
officers commandeered all the mainland-based canoes they
could find, and put Sudanese riflemen aboard them.
Williams took one of the Maxim guns aboard the company's
steel boat, and advanced with the main fleet towards the
Sesse islands. The islanders took to their own boats, and lined
up to defend themselves, or maybe to paddle away to safety.

Meanwhile Macdonald, a keen sailing man, had
commandeered Stokes's yawl, the *Limi*, and mounted the
second Maxim in her bows under a tarpaulin. In a stiff
breeze the sturdy boat sailed rapidly round the enemy's
flank. At 2,000 yards Macdonald whipped off the tarpaulin
and opened fire along the line of hostile canoes. Hundreds
of islanders died as their boats were struck, or overturned
in the panic. This massacre marked out the *Limi* as part of
the white men's warlike preparations. Stokes complained
that from now on no lakeside community would believe that
she was a peaceful vessel. For damage to his trading interests, not to mention the unauthorised commandeering of
his boat, he claimed compensation of $1,000 (£145).
Williams offered a derisory $200 for the 'hire' of the *Limi*.
Macdonald's subsequent account of the affair shows that
the expedition was regarded by him and Williams as great
sport.

When Stokes listed this and all the rest of his complaints
in a series of letters to Colvile, he did his best to make it
clear that he was a prosperous and wholly legitimate man
of business. He sent Colvile some bottles of brandy as a
gift, indicating that he was prepared to supply a selection
of European luxuries at reasonable prices from his own
stores. In further correspondence he sought permission to
hunt elephants in Uganda, and inquired about rates of duty
payable on ivory, whether acquired within Uganda or imported from outside for transit to German territory. Once
again he grumbled about 'that scamp Gedge', the correspondent of *The Times* (and employee of the IBEA company)
who had published yet more discreditable stories alleging
slave-dealing by an employee, or ex-employee, of Stokes.

23 Charles Stokes at Saadani, the transhipment harbour for Zanzibar island, in 1892, with German officers and his great cargo of ivory.

24 Stokes in Zanzibar in 1892, preparing for his last, fatal journey to buy ivory in the interior. To his right is the Indian merchant banker Allidina Visram, Tippu Tib's financial backer. Behind, with umbrella, is Allidina's private secretary. The men wearing the fez are Zanzibar *askari*, of the caravan's armed escort; in the front row are the foremen who organised Stokes's labour force of Wanyamwesi porters.

25-7 Capt. Frederick Lugard, the conqueror of British Uganda (above left), and his second-in-command, Capt. W. H. Williams. Their only trained troops were soldiers of Emin Pasha's battalions, recruited in Equatoria by H. M. Stanley for British service. Their senior 'native officer', a southern Sudanese, was Major Shukri Aga (left).

28 Nellie Stokes, daughter of Charles, was photographed in Shrewsbury in 1897, at the age of 13.

29 Malyamu Magudaleene Nanjala, mother of Charles Stokes junior, in Kampala in 1958, aged about 80.

30 Limi Stokes, perhaps: this old lady, photographed in 1950 in Dar es Salaam, Tanganyika, claimed to be Limi, widow of Charles Stokes.

31 Mr Charles Kasaja Stokes, junior, son of the trader, at his home in Kampala in 1984, when he was 89 years old.

32 On the road near Kwa Mpeni, in 1984, coffee exports from Zaire to Uganda were still following the international highway that Charles Stokes knew. It had not been much improved in 90 years.

All this made difficulties for Colvile. It was his job to establish order in Uganda, and also to make the place pay. In that, Stokes might be an ally or he might be a rival. For example, he offered to transport goods for the Uganda administration at prices lower than those they were now paying. But the firm whose prices he proposed to undercut was the respected Zanzibar trading house of Smith Mackenzie, practically a subsidiary of the IBEA company (its founder had been the brother of George Mackenzie, the first IBEA administrator). Monopoly capitalists do not welcome price-cutting, especially from competitors with the 'unfair' advantage of a close association with natives. But Colvile could not publicly turn down an offer from a British subject who had done much to develop the region's trade, and whose business might produce a welcome slice of customs revenue.

Then Stokes, typically, threw away his advantage. In May 1894 he was at Usongo, his base in German territory. He knew that the British missionaries he had escorted from the coast were now, or soon would be, in Uganda, and able to describe the huge armed expedition he was leading. He wrote again to Colvile stating that he would shortly be travelling with large quantities of ivory, upon which the British might be entitled to charge customs duty if he brought it through Uganda. He emphasised that he would 'hardly touch British territory', implying that he did not really need Colvile's permission, but that mutual advantage might follow if the rate of duty were low enough to make it worth his while to take the route through British possessions. At the end of this prudent and carefully-worded request, he added a sentence that might have been calculated to set the alarm bells ringing: 'I am going well armed and with over 1,000 natives. Would you like me to retake Wadelai?'

This was a lunatic proposition to put to the British administrator. Wadelai, a wholly insignificant place, had acquired an undeserved celebrity. It lay on the right bank of the Nile, some twenty miles downstream from where the river leaves Lake Albert. Under Emin Pasha it had been one of the strong-points of Equatoria, and had continued to be garrisoned by the Pasha's Sudanese troops after his departure. In 1892 news reached Europe that the place had been captured by Mahdist troops from the Sudan. If true – and Mahdist troops had been there, but had soon withdrawn – it meant that the Islamic regime in Khartoum was advancing into black Africa.

This was the excuse all the European powers needed to make a grab for the upper Nile. The British, under General Kitchener Pasha, were slowly building the railway through Egypt that would enable them to retake Khartoum and reoccupy the upper Nile. From British Uganda, a force under Captain Thruxton was skirmishing around the area. From the Congo, King Leopold had despatched an expedition towards Equatoria, which came to nothing because its commander died on the way. From Gabon, in French West Africa, a tiny but tough expedition under Captain Marchand had set off in the direction of the upper Nile, from which they eventually had to be dislodged by Kitchener's vastly superior force in 1898, in the absurd 'Fashoda incident', which for a few days almost brought France and Britain to war.

The worst thing that could happen to the delicate diplomacy surrounding this dusty place would be the arrival of Stokes with his personal army. If he got there claiming to be British, all the other colonial powers would issue protests. If he arrived as the representative of Germany, the British would be in a rage. Colvile knew that a diplomatic set-to was afoot on the question of Wadelai. He had no idea of the latest state of play. But he could be sure that the arrival there of a freelance expedition, led by a British subject and armed by the Germans, would probably cost him his job and his reputation.

The colonel's reply to Stokes's off-hand suggestion was a splutter of confused indignation, couched in such legal terms as he could muster. He 'viewed with some uneasiness' the prospect of Stokes passing through British territory with 1,000 armed men (Stokes had not in fact claimed that 1,000 of his men were armed). He claimed, mistakenly, that a British post had already been established at Wadelai, on 4 February. Since Stokes had not yet done anything unlaw-

ful, Colvile had to invent a charge: 'I wish to warn you that
I can only treat any unauthorised warlike operations as acts
of piracy.' (Piracy, of course, is an offence that can only be
committed on the high seas: in the quest for a legal framework for their actions, colonial officials in Africa might as
well have been at sea.)

Stokes was in fact not so much a pirate as a privateer,
doing Germany's imperial business without overt imperial
support. As before, he started his journey at the head of his
huge armed caravan by way of Rwanda, ostensibly with the
usual commercial purpose of doing such trade as there was
to be done, and establishing friendly relations with the local
chiefs to prepare for future business. But, although Rwanda
was outlined on the map as a part of German East Africa,
the Germans had done no more than pass through its
fringes. They needed to make contact, and if possible a
treaty, with the principal chief of the dominant Tutsi
people, Rwabugiri, who was rumoured to be falling under
Arab influence. Rwanda's western border lay along the still
uncertain line where German territory met the Congo; any
alliance with Rwabugiri might be an advantage when the
frontier with the Congo came to be defined.

Stokes's caravan was only a part of a determined German
push into Rwanda, all of whose elements were concealed
under innocent-sounding pretences. First went Count von
Götzen, of the German Anti-Slavery Society, with a small
but well-armed party. Then came Stokes and his people.
Shortly after the Stokes caravan marched Captain Langheld, commander of the German frontier districts, on a
'hunting trip' with an escort of his trained riflemen. In the
event von Götzen managed to locate and have a talk with
Rwabugiri, but found him unfriendly and well-armed, so
thought it best to leave. Stokes and Langheld therefore decided not to pursue the Rwanda project for the time being:
they joined up and travelled together as far as 1° south of
the Equator, where German interests stopped and British
claims began. There they said their goodbyes: Langheld
turned back, Stokes travelled on northwards.

Stokes was on his own now, heading, with his soldiers,
his guns, and his porters laden with trade goods, back to

the place where he had left Juma with the ivory. In mid-July 1894 he arrived at the base-camp he had occupied on his last expedition eighteen months before, in Muchara's village on Lake Edward.

Chapter 13

More Fool than Knave

Master Stokes seems to be a sort of old Jew, more fool than
knave.

> Lieutenant Henry, Congo Free State army, to Captain
> Lothaire (10 January 1895)

Stokes was not fond of placing himself in personal danger,
and was most unlikely to be involved in any enterprise involving personal risk. His one aim was to make money.

> Lieutenant Langheld, officer-in-command, Mwanza, to
> the Belgian inquiry into Stokes's death (September 1895)

At Muchara's village Stokes was met by terrible news. The
party he had left behind on the Semliki the previous year
had been destroyed. A band of Manyuema fighters had
come out of the forest, taken away the women and dispersed
the stores. They had killed and eaten Juma bin Ali. The
guns, the trade goods, the precious ivory, all were gone.
The fate of Juma filled the caravan with horror. The loss of
the goods put at risk the whole enterprise in which Stokes's
fortune was bound up. But he could not turn back: he was
gambling for his life.

Stokes knew he was beyond the reach of German protection, and he needed to emphasise that he was clear of British
soil. Colonel Colvile had his eye on him: now that Uganda
was definitely under the protection of the British crown, the
colonel had regularised and strengthened its administration,
removing the government secretariat from Kampala and the
shadow of the Buganda court, and installing it at Entebbe
on Lake Victoria. In this breezy and relatively healthy

location – renamed Port Alice, after a daughter of Queen
Victoria – Colvile had created the beginnings of a proper
civil service. More important, a small staff of British
officials was arriving to man the out-stations of the protectorate.

The key point was Fort George at Katwe on Lake Edward, where salt was evaporated from the brine lake in a
nearby crater, and from which the trade route ran over into
Congo territory. There J. P. Wilson was installed as district
officer. Stokes could perfectly easily have called on Wilson:
in decent weather, a canoe could travel the length of Lake
Edward, from Kwa Muchara to Katwe, in a couple of days.
But the trader was not going to risk putting a toe into
British territory if he could help it. Instead he set out to
ingratiate himself by letters, which he carefully dated from
Kwa Muchara, CFS – Congo Free State.

From this safe distance, Stokes self-righteously informed
the district officer that he had apprehended some natives
armed with Snider rifles for which they had no permits.
The message was accompanied by a small present of brandy
and English books – luxuries too small to rank as open
bribes. Further comforts, Stokes added, might be pur-
chased from the supply in his possession ordered on behalf
of the Arab chief Kilongalonga. He thus presented himself
as helpful, prosperous and well-connected, a useful man to
know.

Stokes also wrote from Kwa Muchara to his old mother
Louisa, in Dublin. He had for many years done what he
could to support her, sending the miserable pittance of £29
a year, regularly remitted by the London office of his Zanzibar agents, Boustead and Ridley. (Mrs Stokes also had
£26 a year in Ohio Railway bonds, and £9 from the Cork
Annuity Society.) On that, she was now supporting
Charles's sister, Josephine, in genteel poverty in a pretty
Georgian house at 18 Sandymount Green, a safe and decent
Protestant suburb just across the road from the dense Catholic slum of Irishtown. These were hard times in Ireland,
and the several Stokes siblings were barely keeping their
heads above water. His other sister, Louise, was married to
Robert Symes, the Bank of Ireland agent at Skibbereen in

county Cork. His brother Alan was employed as a manager
in the Donegall Quarries, at the top of Cave Hill Road, in
Belfast. The jobs were respectable but by no means stable:
Alan was to be sacked the following year. But Protestant
appearances had to be kept up, and Charles now hoped to
ensure respectability for all the clan.

The letter to his mother revealed his hopes and fears.
Charles had made a will, 'as I have a considerable amount
of property'. But his present circumstances were hazardous
– 'I fear I have had a great loss of about £4,000 as I hear
my man has been killed by Arabs and all goods stolen'; this
was a severe disappointment, since 'I wanted to go home in
'95 to see you all'. Meanwhile he sent an order for £50, 'for
fear of accidents of not getting back', and spoke encourag-
ingly but vaguely of splendid orders from the government
of Buganda. Amid the flood of greetings for cousins and
aunts came a piece of news that may have disconcerted the
old lady: 'How are you all in dear old Ireland, you are never
forgotten by your expatriated son, all my people are well
and my little daughter a fine child her name "Louisa".'
This was the first he had told his mother of his irregular
liaisons: whether she was pleased that her name was inherited by a fine child whose mother did not rate a mention we
do not know.

The remaining documents that survive from the last
months of Charles Stokes's life are even more confused, and
deliberately so. He was trying to lie his way out of danger.
The letter to his mother is dated 13 August, from Kwa
Muchara. By the end of the month he had made his way up
to the north end of Lake Edward, travelling along the western shore partly on land and partly in hired canoes, to keep
clear of the British sector of the lake.

The messengers sent to Wilson at Fort George had been
told to rejoin Stokes by the outflow to the Semliki river, in
Belgian territory. They brought back, with other messages,
Colonel Colvile's reply to his offer of an attack on Wadelai,
with the colonel's warning against 'piracy'. Colvile added
that if Stokes wanted to make any move towards the northern districts of Uganda, he must first contact Captain
Thruxton, the officer whom he mistakenly supposed to have

reoccupied Wadelai. Stokes was thus formally warned off British territory.

This forcefully reminded him how much things had changed in British Uganda since his previous trip eighteen months ago, before the completion of the hand-over from company rule to that of the Colonial Office. He replied indignantly that he did not have 1,000 armed men; and that, more to the point, he had formal authorisation from the Germans to carry the weapons for his protection, which would make their possession lawful under the international Brussels convention of 1890.

The next part of the letter made his purpose clear. He wanted to be free, if circumstances made it necessary, to bring trade goods and ivory through Uganda in transit from the Congo to German East Africa, and he did not want to pay duty for doing so. If he sold trade goods on British territory, he was willing to pay the usual duty of 5 per cent. But he argued – and the terms of the Berlin and Brussels conventions supported his case – that goods in transit were not liable for duty. Ivory, he noted, carried a duty of 15 per cent, and this was clearly his real worry: if the British could catch him and make him pay, his profit would be wiped out. He told Colvile his hard-luck story: 'I can only say now my man Juma and his companion have been killed and eaten by the Manyema, but the Arab Abedi has sent me word that my goods are safe and he is willing to pay me for the fault.'

There is something fishy here. The man usually referred to by Europeans as 'Abedi' was Said bin Abedi, the feudal chieftain (under Tippu Tib) of the country Stokes was about to enter. He was generally held responsible for the murder of Emin Pasha, and the men who had attacked and eaten Juma had claimed to be under his authority. But in September 1894 he was not even in Africa. When the Belgians had dropped the charge against him of murdering Emin, he had in exchange put his forces on the Belgian side. The Belgians regarded him as a prize defector, and in mid-1894 they gave him a trip to Brussels, partly to expose him to the power and glory of Belgian civilisation, partly no doubt to get him out of the way. Possibly a clerk was continuing to write in Said's name, so that Stokes was deceived; possibly Stokes himself was falsely claiming to be in contact with Said, as a mark of his own respectability.

In reality, the man Stokes was seeking to do business with was Kibonghe, the former vassal of Said. He was against the Belgians, and had split with his old chief on the question of collaboration with them. Stokes knew this, and was prepared to exploit it for his own purposes, backed up by a precious document – the safe-conduct, in German, signed by Hermann von Wissmann, the former German commissioner, authorising Kibonghe to travel with his ivory free of customs duty through German territory.

But Stokes could not, at this time, make contact with Kibonghe. Subsequent messages signed by the Arab chieftain show that, as Stokes was entering Congo territory, Kibonghe was still journeying in the opposite direction to meet him, on the final stages of the return from German Kamerun, on the west coast. The apparently crazy project upon which Emin Pasha had lost his life was near completion: Kibonghe had traced the route to the Atlantic, and Stokes was returning to join him with the arms and ammunition needed if the new trade route was to be made safe, under German protection, for the export of Congo ivory.

With Said and Kibonghe absent, and under the steady pressure of the well-armed Belgians advancing from the Congo river, the frontier region had fallen into anarchy, under the reign of terror imposed by ranging bands of leaderless Manyuema freebooters, one of which had murdered Juma. Stokes moved on northwards along the Semliki to his old base-camp at Mpeni's village. Out of the woods came the same gang to meet him, 150 men with muskets, gazing greedily at the visitors. They brought with them as prisoners the survivors of the raid on Juma's store, and they were carrying a letter left behind by Kibonghe, before his departure westwards, promising full restitution, in ivory, of the value of the goods stolen, and compensation for Juma's murder.

Mpeni's villagers were terrified at the appearance of these

human predators, and thankful that a well-armed caravan was on their side. Stokes's own people wished to have their revenge there and then upon the wild men who had eaten their late colleague. But their leader saw a profit in the offing. Using all his talent for conciliation, he persuaded Mpeni's people, and his own, to admit the fierce Manyuema to their camp. They had a good meal, delivered their message, and were allowed to leave with their weapons. 'These rascals declare they did not come to fight and as they really have brought my surviving people I let them go. Juma's wife is safe, so I shall get the true story from her', he wrote to Wilson in Katwe. But poor Aminah was as confused as everyone else. Even Stokes did not believe he really understood the wild anarchy of the frontier.

What he did was to draw up a bill for his previous losses and his present cargo, in the hope of reclaiming it from anyone who could pay. Typically, it was grossly inflated, and expressed in the common merchant currency of the region, the *frasilah* of ivory. One *frasilah* was half a man-load, thirty-five pounds, and the established price at Zanzibar was £17 per *frasilah* for top-quality tusks, and a bit less for small pieces and low-grade tusks.

For the trade goods looted from Juma's store he demanded 300 *frasilahs*, the price already agreed. In compensation for Juma's killing he claimed 1,200 *frasilahs*. If these accounts were settled in full, he said, he would be willing to sell his new caravan-loads for 600 *frasilahs*. He was claiming thirty-one and a half tonnes of ivory worth – assuming that two-thirds of it was top quality – well over £32,000 (allowing for inflation, almost exactly equivalent to £1 million in terms of 1985). Even if this was not so much a firm price as a marker for an Arab bargaining session, the commercial stakes were mounting all the time.

So were the personal risks. Stokes had more muskets and powder, more rifles and ammunition, than he could possibly need for a quick trading foray, even into hostile territory. He made exorbitant demands on his Arab suppliers; in return, they produced ivory with a speed, and in a quantity, which makes it plain that they expected more than just cloth and beads in exchange. They desperately needed guns, to

meet the Belgian advance they knew was coming. Stokes
did not actually deliver any guns to them. But he had certainly led them to believe they would get guns from him.
Whether he meant to do as they expected is the big question. On balance, it seems that he probably intended to
cheat the Arabs. That would set them, as well as the Belgians, on his track.

Stokes badly needed a safe way out of the Congo, and he
did his best to prepare one, by sending to John Wilson, the
district officer at Katwe, regular news, albeit of subjects
that did not remotely concern the British authorities. He
told of the incident with the Manyuema, and shortly afterwards informed Wilson that he was about to leave for the
Ituri river, the Congo tributary on which Emin had met his
death, to meet Kibonghe.

The constant theme of the letters to Wilson was customs
dues, and the question of whether they were payable on
goods in transit. He certainly intended to collect all the
available ivory from the Congo, then withdraw across the
Semliki into British territory, safe from pursuit either by
the Belgians, or by any Congo Arabs who might be dissa-
tisfied with his trading methods. Wilson spotted that Stokes
wanted to get British protection without paying British
taxes, and would have none of it. The correspondence took
an angry turn. Stokes made it worse by asking Wilson a
seriously embarrassing question: where did the border between British and Belgian territory really lie?

The treaties establishing the Uganda–Congo border had
been signed in 1884 and 1885. Neither agreement could in
practice be applied, because they were based upon inaccurate maps, and reflected contrasting views of the King of the
Belgians' claims. According to one theory, the Congo state
extended as far as but not beyond the watershed of the
Congo river. Since Stokes was on the banks of the Semliki,
which flows by way of Lake Albert to the Nile, that would
have meant he was not in the Congo at all. The other theory
was that the border ran at this point in a straight line north
and south, along the 30th degree of latitude. That line
would cross the Semliki downstream of Stokes's base at

Kwa Mpeni, so would put both banks of the river in Belgian territory at that point.

Wilson and Stokes both knew about these geographical ambiguities. Wilson's position was awkward. He was a fairly junior official, and he understood that in the end, whatever he did, the frontier question would be decided through diplomatic channels, after an inquiry by an Anglo-Belgian boundary commission, with international arbitration in the event of disagreement. For the time being he had been instructed to act on the reasonable assumption that, whatever the inaccurate maps said, the Semliki should be regarded as the *de facto* border. Meanwhile, any opinion he gave on the question might be taken by some party to the debate either as an admission that Britain had no claim to a particular piece of land, or that Britain was claiming more than its due. Putting any opinion in writing would risk diplomatic complications; to address such an opinion to a known German agent like Stokes would be madness. Stokes never got the clear statement he wanted, that the Semliki was regarded as the temporary border.

There was an extra twist. Wilson knew, but Stokes probably did not, about the Anglo-Congolese draft treaty agreed on 12 May 1894. This agreement was in fact the product of a deal foisted on the Foreign Office by Sir William Mackinnon, in close collaboration with his partner King Leopold; it was in the end never implemented, because Mackinnon died and the French objected. Under it, the Congo State would have leased to Britain a strip of land 25 kilometres wide, extending from the north end of Lake Tanganyika to the south end of Lake Edward; in exchange, the British would lease to the Belgians the so-called Lado enclave on the west bank of the upper Nile, roughly corresponding to Emin's old province of Equatoria.

The British objective in this ill-considered scheme was to gain a north–south right-of-way linking the great lakes, along which one day the fabulous all-British Cape-to-Cairo railway might be built. In reality, the strip under consideration was useless for that purpose, unless the British also obtained rights in the Semliki valley to carry their line up to Lake Albert. But the treaty-makers in Europe did not seem to have considered that point, and were still vague about the actual lie of the land. Great political destinies hung upon the drawing of the border along the fever-stricken valley where Stokes now had his base-camp. In particular, the Germans wished to prevent the British from getting their strip of land, since it would cut off German East Africa from direct access to the Congo and its river transport system.

Stokes, without knowing these details of high politics, was frustrated by his failure to get a straight answer out of Wilson on the border question. But he was continuing to pile up ivory, both in instalments towards the debt Kibonghe owed him from the last visit, and in new purchases. Hadea, one of his headmen, told the subsequent British inquiry that the store at Kwa Mpeni contained 170 *frasilahs* of new-purchased ivory, and 404 *frasilahs* repaid towards Kibonghe's debt. That would make 9,200 kilos (which is close enough to the ten tonnes the Belgians said they found in the store). The total Stokes was aiming for was well over three times as great. For that, he had to await the arrival of his main trading partner, Kibonghe.

Stokes arrived in September 1894 at the unhealthy camp at Kwa Mpeni. It was nearly Christmas before he got news direct from Kibonghe. The chieftain was, he said, desperately short of powder. He was heading for the rendezvous, but still needed time to collect the ivory owed to Stokes. The trader set off to meet his ally, at the forest settlement of Mawambe, two weeks' march to the north-west, where Said bin Abedi's headquarters had been.

Then came a frantic call for help. The Belgians were closing in, wrote Kibonghe, and he needed protection. Stokes had often boasted that he was a friend of the two most powerful nations on earth, Britain and Germany: that he carried their flags, and any caravan under the protection of those powerful symbols would be safe from arbitrary attack by other Europeans. Kibonghe's letter was written by his clerk, Moussa bin Hadji, in the Swahili language and Arabic characters. The text that survives is that of the French translation made by Kibonghe's Belgian captors, but it still conveys the terror of its sender: 'God knows if

you will ever see me come in time. And for you your ivory
has been collected and sent to Pema; it should be with you
very soon. I have more ivory, but I fear that the Belgians
may come and take it. In God's name, in God's name, send
me a flag quickly. The Belgians are coming to make war
upon me without cause; I have not taken their goods, I have
killed none of their people ... In God's name, in God's
name, send me a flag.' Kibonghe signed with his Arab
name, followed by a reminder of the terrible journey he had
just completed – Hamadi bin Ali el Anzagizi *de Cameroun*,
from Kamerun.

Kibonghe had made the crossing that Emin had planned.
He had walked half-way across Africa, through unknown
country, to German territory on the west coast, and had
established that there was indeed an export route that way
for the Congo Arabs' wealth of ivory. But in his absence his
overlord, Said bin Abedi, the murderer of Emin, had been
captured by the Belgians, and had saved his own skin by
going over to their side. Now, on his return, Kibonghe
found the Belgians consolidating their hold upon Said's
former territory, and himself accused of Emin's murder.
His way home was blocked by the ferocious soldiers commanded by Captain Lothaire.

Stokes did not send Kibonghe a flag. Here, on Belgian
territory, it would merely have made things worse, as a sign
that the Arab flying it was in league with foreign powers.
The trader did what he could to save his partner's skin by
sending off a flood of letters into the forest, giving notice of
his presence as a legitimate man of business. To the 'European in command at Lindi' he wrote to request a fair trial
for Kibonghe, offering unlimited bail. To Kibonghe he
wrote a letter of reassurance, on the back of which the clerk
Moussa added his own belief that help was on its way.

But all this was fruitless. At dawn on 30 December 1894,
Lothaire and his men were guided in by a defector to the
encampment where Kibonghe lay sleeping. Next day the
captive was brought to Lindi and examined before the
officers of the Belgian expedition. They were not lawfully
constituted as a court martial, but they did not need to be,
since Kibonghe was a native and so outside the protection

of the law. The officers recorded, truthfully or not, that the prisoner confessed to the murder of Emin.

The following morning Kibonghe was put before a firing squad and shot to death. Lothaire said that the impact of five musket-balls at close range made a terrible mess of the body. He resolved that his soldiers should never see a white man's body subjected to such damage.

Chapter 14

Death in No Man's Land

This is the first occasion on which a European has been executed – for all the world as if he were a native – by order of a military expedition in the interior of Africa.

> Martin Gosselin, British Embassy, Berlin, to Foreign Office (September 1895)

It is a well-known fact that it is impossible in Africa to get ivory without dealing in arms.

> Lieutenant Stuhlmann (October 1895)

When they came to hang Charles Stokes, he refused to play the white man. Screaming through his great red Irish beard, he laid out two of the soldiers sent to escort him to execution. The sergeant, with more soldiers, dragged him to the tree in the darkness, threw the rope over the branch, and tugged the boxes away from under his feet. By dawn the body was buried in an unmarked grave. The bugler of the Belgian detachment blew a salute into the hot, damp forest, and the tropical weeds began to grow over the corpse.

There was no medical certificate of death. The doctor, Michaux, stayed silent in his tent, anxious to dissociate himself from the verdict unlawfully handed down by the 'military court' of the Arab zone. The only acknowledged European witness to the death was Captain Lothaire, president and sole member of the court, and commander of the Belgian forces in the zone. Some African witnesses, questioned much later, swore that another Belgian officer had been present at the trial, and had laughed and drunk champagne with Lothaire after the verdict. The Africans could identify this officer only by his Swahili *nom-de-guerre*, Bwana Lemundu. Amid the cloud of lies put up by the Belgians to protect their officers against the charge of murder of a white man, further inquiries into his identity would only have made things worse. It was clear that Lothaire had ordered the killing of Stokes, and that he was proud to accept responsibility for the deed.

That was on 15 January 1895, at the place the Belgians called Lindi, the main crossing-point on the river of that name which flows through the high forest westwards towards the Congo and the Atlantic ocean, 1,400 miles away. The site is lost. Lothaire's map of the district is hopelessly inaccurate, and there are no roads now into that absolute wilderness. It seems to have been about fifty miles south of the Equator, and ten days' march – about 100 miles on the tangled forest paths – west of the undefined border between the Congo State and British Uganda. Stokes had not been sure there were Belgians at Lindi – but if there were, he had believed he would be able to do a deal with them and come out safe with his ivory. To the end he had assumed that the white man's solidarity would protect him.

But he had not reckoned with the Belgians, fighting their way through the forest with trained African troops whose Mauser rifles made short work of the Arab warlords' tribal musketeers. It was barely a couple of decades since the Muslim traders from East Africa had swept into the forest region, armed with the muskets that gave them an easy dominion over the tribesmen with their bows and spears. Now the Belgians with their own new technology were beating down the former conquerors, and the Arab alliances that Stokes had forged were worthless.

In seventeen years in Africa, Stokes had learned two prime rules of conduct: never hurry, and never start a fight until you have to. Despite the death of Juma and the scattering of his wealth of ivory, the rewards of patience could still be great. He had sat down to repair the damage with his old stock-in-trade of promises, leading his Arab and African suppliers to believe – rightly or wrongly – that if they brought him tusks he would give them guns. So far he had delivered none. By the end of 1894 he still had in his possession all the guns, rifles and trade goods brought from East Africa on this trip. He seems also to have recovered from the robbers the ninety-nine muskets stolen at the time of Juma's murder. Along with the guns, twenty tonnes of ivory had been stolen from his store: he now had ten tonnes back, two-thirds of it in large, high-quality tusks. (The Belgians later assessed its value at BFr. 163,000, about £6,600: the market price was more like £10,000.) He was counting on delivery of more than two and a half times more, when Kibonghe got back from the western forest. Stokes stood, if all went well, to return to the east coast with ivory worth about £35,000, all his own and fully paid for. In present-day money he had over £1 million within his grasp.

The Belgians had other ideas. From their collaborators and informers in the Arab community they had received disturbing reports of Stokes's activities, all more or less true. He was bartering guns for ivory, and thus arming the Arab chiefs whom the Belgians were fighting. And he was escorted by African soldiers wearing German colonial uniforms, and carrying German Mausers, in a district where the Germans were suspected of having territorial ambitions. On both counts, Stokes sounded like a dangerous enemy.

The Belgian forces in the Arab zone consisted of a few hundred African mercenaries, recruited mainly from the Hausa-speaking peoples of French and British West Africa, under a dozen or so white officers and sergeants. Their commander was Captain Hubert-Joseph Lothaire, aged twenty-nine, with seven years of African service already behind him, the acknowledged hero of many battles against the Arabs. He was barely literate, proud, solitary, a martinet promoted from the ranks who spoke even to his white fellow-officers only when duty required it. He had been campaigning continuously, without home leave, since May 1892. In 1893 he had narrowly escaped death in a great battle with Kibonghe's soldiers: Kibonghe got away, but nineteen of his senior associates, and many more of his rank-and-file followers, had been executed on Lothaire's orders after they had surrendered. Like all white men in the forest, Lothaire suffered frequent bouts of malaria. He drank heavily.

Lothaire was a man with a mission. He was determined not only to defeat the Arab warlords, but also to keep all British and German interlopers out of the still unmapped corners of his king's vast dominion. To this end he was prepared to break the ultimate law of the white man in Africa: never harm another white man, for fear the Africans may follow your example.

Even had Stokes not posed a military threat to the Belgians, he was a natural target for Lothaire's rage. By the royal decree of 1893, the frontier zone was *domaine privé*, King Leopold's private estate. All ivory within the domain was royal property: no native or other unauthorised person might possess it, or claim compensation for its seizure on behalf of the King. As a special inducement to enforce the decree, Belgian officers were granted 10 per cent of the value of all ivory they acquired for the monarch. Lothaire had done well out of this provision – his Swahili name, used by his African soldiers, was Bwana Pembe, Mr Ivory. A 10 per cent cut of Stokes's reputed hoard would set an underpaid officer up in style, and probably earn him promotion too. In October 1894, as soon as he had reliable information that Stokes was at Kwa Mpeni, Lothaire set off to intercept him. By mid-December he had set up camp at Lindi, where the main forest tracks crossed the river of that name, and settled down to await his prey. He wanted to trap Stokes. Even more, he wanted to catch and kill his old enemy Kibonghe, to whom he believed Stokes was supplying guns and powder.

On or about Christmas Day 1894, Stokes received Kibonghe's frantic plea for ammunition and a flag to protect him against these new and fiercer whites, and had sent into the forest a wave of messengers, carrying letters. Ten were written by himself, in English, and were addressed to 'The European in command' at various places where he thought the Belgians might pass. They informed the addressee that the writer was a respectable businessman, coming in peace for trade only. A special letter was addressed to the officer in charge at Lindi, where the forest tracks met at the river-crossing, and where the Belgians might most likely be found. It specifically requested that, if Kibonghe fell into Belgian hands, he should not be executed without fair trial: 'I offer bail, of any sum, to give him the full protection of a lawyer of the Independent Congo State.' Stokes further stated that he was himself on the way to Lindi, estimating his arrival there for 12 January 1895.

His letter to Kibonghe was written on one side of the paper in the Swahili language and in Roman characters. It asserted that Stokes was strong, and asked for prompt payment of Kibonghe's debt. 'I do not come to make war,' it said, 'but to get my property back.' On the other side of the paper was a separate message, written by Kibonghe's own clerk, Moussa bin Hadji, now in Stokes's camp awaiting his master. Moussa doubted whether anyone in Kibonghe's party could read Roman writing, so added a text in Arabic script and the Urubi language: 'I can help you, do not fear death, you will not die'. Stokes could not read this, and may not have known it had been added to his letter. It gave the Belgians the impression that he was Kibonghe's intimate friend, sharing a secret language.

The messages got through: that to Kibonghe was found on his person when the Belgians captured him, and was read out as incriminating evidence at the perfunctory trial that preceded his execution. Immediately afterwards Lothaire despatched his second-in-command, Lieutenant Henry, to find Stokes and bring him back. Henry was accompanied by another white officer, Lieutenant Frants Brecx, and eighty black soldiers armed with Snider rifles. They went cautiously along the narrow forest trail, warily scouting around every fallen tree for fear of ambush. The precautions were unnecessary. Two days' march from Lindi they met Stokes, on his way to the rendezvous that he had set in his letter.

Far from being ready for a fight, the Irishman was escorted only by ten of the uniformed riflemen lent by the Germans, and ten porters for his personal effects. He expected the meeting to be friendly: he was, after all, exactly where he had said he would be, and due to arrive at Lindi on time. It was now 9 January 1895. Stokes was surprised, but not unduly alarmed, when the two young officers took him into custody. He knew nothing of Kibonghe's execution, nor that the compromising note from Moussa had been found among the dead man's papers.

Henry and Brecx conducted a preliminary interrogation of their prisoner, in a mixture of Swahili and broken English. He made no favourable impression, but they did not think him dangerous. Stokes fell into the role he usually played with upper-class English officers, acting the simple Paddy, alternately bluff and cajoling. Henry's note to Lothaire gives his first impression of the prisoner: 'As you probably know, Master Stokes [*Maître* Stokes, a facetious title] seems to be a sort of old Jew, more a fool than a knave. I think he has no fixed abode. He is all on his own as an ivory dealer here, and chases up hill and down dale, taking every possible opportunity to squeeze a profit out of anyone with a few elephant tusks.' Lieutenant Brecx wrote to his uncle in Brussels: 'Stokes is a fine-looking man, tall and of distinguished appearance. I asked him a few questions in Swahili: his answers are full of contradictions.' It does not sound like a lynch-party.

From this time on, the Belgian accounts of what happened are full of inconsistencies. Lieutenant Brecx disappears from the tale altogether, despite having witnessed the arrest and written home at once about it. Clearly Lothaire decided – honourably, by his own lights – that he would accept all the praise, or blame, of the affair.

First let us dispose of Lieutenant Henry. Immediately after the arrest he sent Stokes back to headquarters at Lindi, accompanied by his servants and personal bearers, and escorted by fifteen African riflemen under a Hausa corporal called Palet. (In fact Brecx was probably in charge of the escort, but was written out of the story for his protection.)

Henry continued his journey to Stokes's base camp at Mpeni's village beside the Semliki river. There – by his account – he found a squalid scene. The usual population of the village was swollen not only by 1,000 East Africans of Stokes's caravan, plus at least 500 camp followers, wives, slaves and other hangers-on; there were also hundreds of Congolese, refugees from the anarchy in the forest.

The camp was filthy. After four months of waiting in this horrible place, so different from the open East Africa plains they had been born to, Stokes's people had fallen apart, both in health and in discipline. The diseases of the rainforest were rife: malaria, reducing men and women to listless apathy; yaws, producing revolting ulcers, eating down to the bare bone; probably (it had not yet been diagnosed) bilharzia, the debilitating sickness bred from the snails that live in running water-channels. There was smallpox in the camp.

On the outskirts of the village, said Henry, dozens of rotting corpses were thrown anyhow into the forest. Other witnesses confirm that disposal of the dead was a real problem. Usually the local people cleared up corpses hygienically, by eating them themselves or selling them off to neighbours hungry for protein. The East Africans, and the Muslims of Kibonghe's faction, would not allow that horror. But no arrangements for burial were made; and there were many fresh corpses, to add to those who had died of sickness. It is clear that Henry's men slaughtered many of their captives. Witnesses interrogated later in Uganda claimed that the Belgian troops massacred about 100 of their people, until the survivors organised a mass escape across the river in canoes, at night.

Henry had his duty to do, and that meant finding Stokes's ivory. He arrested the caravan headman, Rusambia, and asked him – gently at first, the officer insisted – where the hoard was. Rusambia would not tell. Henry persevered, on his white man's authority, with lies and threats: 'Your master has gone away to Europe, give me up his ivory.' Rusambia was tied up and threatened with death. He told. Lightly buried under the floor of a big grass hut was the biggest hoard of ivory Henry had ever set eyes on, ten tonnes of the stuff.

At Lindi meanwhile Lothaire greeted Stokes with an outburst of rage, mindless and uncomprehending. Even had both men been in normal health and spirits, they would have had problems understanding each other. Stokes spoke English (with a strong Irish accent), Swahili and the Nyamwesi language of his wife's family; he also had some

command of Luganda, and a few phrases of German. Lothaire spoke French, Flemish and Hausa, the language of
his soldiers; his other African languages were ragged Swahili and a little West African pidgin English. The Belgian
doctor, Michaux, spoke English reasonably well, but Lothaire regarded him as a soft liberal and would not pay
attention to anything he said. So, amid confusion, the interrogation began in Swahili.

Lothaire poured out accusations. Stokes, he insisted, had
sold weapons on his own account to the Arabs who were
killing white men. He was part of an Anglo-German plot to
capture Belgian territory. He was stealing ivory that belonged by law to the King of the Belgians. Stokes was at
first baffled, then blustering. He knew there was a damning
grain of truth within each one of these quite different
charges. He asked for paper, pen and a lamp, and was put
under guard in a tent next to Lothaire's to write an explanation. All night he wrote, feverishly, an account of his life,
a justification for his conduct, an appeal for justice, new
instructions for the disposal of his property. Next morning
the trial began.

Lothaire, identified by the African witnesses as Bwana
Pembe, presided. Michaux, the rough country doctor, acted
at the start as interpreter, and was identified as Daktari
Omari. (The mysterious Bwana Lemundu, identified by the
African survivors, was pretty certainly Brecx.) Even by the
standards of a field court martial the tribunal was illegally
constituted: Belgian civil and military law, applicable in the
Congo State, made clear that a court must consist of at least
three officials – judge, prosecutor and *greffier*, or registrar.

The proceedings soon became a farce. Dr Michaux had
long been at odds with his awkward and very sick patient,
Lothaire; now he realised that a verdict of guilty had been
decided upon before the proceedings began. He declined to
interpret and withdrew, thoroughly scared, to his tent. Lothaire carried on in his inadequate Swahili. He was indignant when Stokes denied some of his contentions: lapsing
into French, he declared the defence *inopérante*, 'inopera-
tive'.

The formal charge, such as it was, stated that Stokes had

supplied prohibited weapons – defined as breech-loading
guns, not just muskets – to the Arabs. There was one piece
of substantial evidence. At Kibonghe's capture, a double-
barrelled English shotgun had been found in his hut. Stokes
freely admitted that it was his, but claimed truthfully that
it had been left with his clerk Juma for shooting game, and
stolen at the time of Juma's murder. Far from showing that
Stokes had sold weapons to the Arabs, the shotgun rather
supported the view that he did not. Lothaire did not care.
A shotgun was, technically, a weapon loaded through the
breech, whose supply to Africans was illegal by international convention. The gun had passed, by whatever
means, from Stokes's possession to an African, and that was
sufficient proof of guilt. Stokes begged to be allowed an
appeal to his 'fellow-Christians' of the Congo State. Lothaire refused to listen.

Suedi wadi Mabruki, one of Stokes's Zanzibari servants,
heard Dr Michaux try to cool Lothaire's anger: 'Bwana
Daktari said to Pembe: "Let us tie him up and send news
to Europe", and Pembe, "I won't tie him up", and to
Stokesi, "I will kill you".' Makwera bin Abdullah, a Wanyamwesi of Stokes's party, recalled Lothaire's closing words:
'Kesho uta kufa' – in Swahili, 'tomorrow you die'.

Makwera spent that night with Lothaire's cook-boy, in
the shelter between the captain's tent and that where Stokes
was confined. The Belgian white men, he said, drank late
into the night, making a noise and laughing. 'At 1 a.m. four
askari [soldiers] came with Pembe himself. Stokesi would
not come out and cried out: "If you want to kill me do so
inside." I heard him. Pembe got four more soldiers and
they dragged him out and hanged him ... The askaris
marched around his grave and blew trumpets and beat
drums.' Faudi Ferazi added some details: 'His eyes were
covered. He was stood on top of two boxes: the rope put
around his neck: the boxes were taken away and he died.
He was buried at 8 o'clock next morning. Pembe wanted to
kill us all and Daktari said he must not.'

This evidence, from Stokes's followers, was collected
over a year later, in May 1896, by Major A. E. Smith of the
Uganda administration at Entebbe on Lake Victoria. It is,

of course, not necessarily accurate or complete. Separate evidence, taken informally by the then commissioner for Uganda, Frederick Jackson, tells how Stokes fought off the first men sent to bring him to execution.

Dr Michaux's effort to restrain Lothaire from wholesale massacre of Stokes's people was successful. But the Belgians did their best to prevent news of the murder reaching the outside world. About 100 porters and camp followers were held by them for the next five months. So unhealthy was the district, and so hard the work to which the Belgians put them, that seventy died before the rest were released. The European governments that later exploited the murder of Stokes in order to make trouble for the Belgians did not complain of these other deaths. The victims were only Africans.

Chapter 15

❧

The Stokes Affair

The Germans are merely seeking a plausible excuse for demanding a rectification of frontiers north of Lake Tanganyika.

M. van Eetvelde, Secretary of State, the Congo Free State
(November 1895)

Are we not becoming a trifle too hot in our pursuit of Lothaire? ... If he were to be hanged it would be very inconvenient, as it would make a sort of blood-feud between us and the Belgians.

Lord Salisbury, British Prime Minister and Foreign Secretary (18 December 1895)

In April 1895, when Charles Stokes was three months in his grave, an historic encounter took place in the very middle of the African continent, where the Semliki river flows across the Equator on its course northward to Lake Albert and the Nile. A patrolling officer of the Belgian forces in the Congo Free State looked across the swirling river, and saw on the east bank a neat line of huts of woven branches, with a pair of tents of an unfamiliar military pattern on their upwind side. The Belgians, coming into the heart of Africa from the Atlantic coast, were about to make contact with their British counterparts coming from the Indian Ocean side. The effective occupation of Africa was complete, all along the Equatorial line.

The Belgian patrol, of Hausa troops from West Africa, was commanded by Lieutenant Henry; the evidence of his activities at Kwa Mpeni lay only a few miles off. The British official, at the head of a detachment of Sudanese mercenary infantry, was Mr J. P. Wilson of the post at Fort George. His correspondence with Stokes had ended without explanation, and through his territory the survivors of Stokes's caravan had fled, under the leadership of the Irishman's widow, Limi. Henry could not be sure how much his opposite number knew.

It was the duty of the two men to make contact with each other. By closing the gap between the British and Belgian administrations, they would put paid at last to the risk that the Germans would slip in between them, to link German East Africa with the unoccupied territory of the upper Nile. But neither Henry nor Wilson could afford to make a false move. The boundary between British Uganda and the Congo State was far from being defined by the treaties available to them, which were ambiguous and based upon grossly inaccurate maps.

Tens of thousands of square miles of colonial property lay in the balance. The young officials knew that a series of deals was being worked out between their political masters back in London and Brussels. Both had instructions to make no formal claims or concessions to any representative of another European state, since anything they said might be exploited by a rival claimant. Moreover, any decision taken in Europe could not be notified to them in less than four months, and any query they might wish to make of their governments would take twice that to receive an answer. They were entirely on their own.

Henry made the first move. He sent a Hausa sergeant who spoke Swahili across the Semliki in a dug-out canoe, bearing an invitation to Wilson to come across and celebrate their encounter. Wilson was wary. He thought he knew what had happened to Stokes once he had got into Henry's hands. He sent back a counter-invitation, which Henry accepted. The two men met, shook hands, and soon agreed to continue with the *de facto* assumption that the Semliki should be regarded, informally, as the interim frontier between their jurisdictions. Stokes too had assumed this to be the case. To him the conversation now turned.

The trader had moved on, said Henry; nobody really

knew where he was. Maybe he was heading for Europe by way of the Congo river, through Belgian territory. That had been Emin Pasha's aim in 1892, and it would be a pity if Stokes too were to be murdered by Arab bandits. Wilson revealed that he had heard other stories. Eventually Henry decided that a modified frankness was the best policy, telling the story – as officials do tell each other discreditable news – 'unattributably', and with the nastiest bits left out. Stokes, he said, had been detected selling modern rifles to the Arabs with whom the Belgians were at war, in exchange for ivory whose sale was a Congo State monopoly. He had been tried before a properly constituted court martial, found guilty and executed in accordance with the law. He himself, added Henry, had no personal involvement in the case.

That was enough for Wilson: the confused stories of the refugees were sufficiently confirmed. In his next despatch to the Uganda central secretariat at Entebbe, Wilson described the meeting and the conversation. The commissioner for Uganda, Colonel Colvile, sent a copy of the despatch down to Mombasa by the next caravan. From the East Africa administration offices there, a summary of the information was sent by telegraph to Aden. Thence it was retransmitted to the Foreign Office in London by way of the main cable line between India and the imperial capital.

If the actions of the imperial powers in Africa often seem confused, this is one reason why. Stokes was hanged before dawn on 15 January 1895. Wilson had confirmation of the death in mid-April, and conveyed the news to Entebbe by early May. Colvile's report of Wilson's statement was finally logged into the Foreign Office registry in London on 23 September.

The British government already knew that something was embarrassingly wrong. The first published report of Stokes's death had appeared on 1 August 1895, in the *Kolonialblatt* of Hamburg, the semi-official organ of German colonial interests. The story was garbled. Stokes, it said, had been killed in Congo territory by 'English Waganda' – members of a nation living several hundred miles from where he died, and with whom he was on the best of terms.

But the broad fact of his violent death was true, and of genuine interest in Germany. Stokes had been decorated for his services to the Kaiser's administration in East Africa, and was associated with the enigmatic German hero, Emin Pasha. His home was in German territory, and some of his followers had escaped in that direction from slaughter and imprisonment. Passing the military outposts at Bukoba and Mwanza, they had told what they knew of their leader's end. The Germans there, under Captain Langheld (who had well deserved his promotion), knew more about Stokes's mission than they cared to admit. They reported the rumours to their headquarters at Dar es Salaam on the coast, and from there the story reached Berlin by telegraph.

It was general German policy to stick in pins whenever Britain seemed to be getting comfortable with its continental neighbours. The German colonial lobby was irritated by the apparent good progress of the Anglo–Belgian talks on the Congo's eastern border, which might put an end to their hopes of new acquisitions in Africa. If the Belgians really had killed a British subject, the event could be exploited to make mischief between the British and Belgian governments.

The colonial office in Berlin leaked the rumour of Stokes's fate to the *Kolonialblatt*. A clipping of the story was sent, officially, to the German ambassador in Brussels, Count von Alvensleben. He, on instructions, sent round a copy to his colleague, the British ambassador, with the ostensibly helpful suggestion that the matter might prove of sufficient interest for the two of them jointly to take it up with the Congo authorities. Sir Francis Plunkett, the British ambassador, had a wary respect for German diplomacy. Anyway, there was an implied insult in Alvensleben's message. It was in those days the proud boast of the Foreign Office that any British subject, wherever he might be, was safe under its protection: here a British citizen had been put to death in mysterious circumstances, and the Germans were the first to know.

Plunkett did not take up Alvensleben's offer of a joint approach. Instead, after consulting London, he registered a formal inquiry as to Stokes's fate with the Congo autho-

rities, in their offices in the stable block of the royal palace
at Laeken. The Congo civil servants were mildly inconven-
ienced. Nothing significant was ever done about Congo diplomacy without the knowledge of the King, who kept the
reins in his own hands: in August he invariably went to the
seaside at La Panne, where the submarine telegraph kept
him instantly in touch with the London stock market.

The British Foreign Office, for its part, was unable to act
at all. In June 1895, Lord Rosebery's Liberal government
had been unexpectedly defeated in the House of Commons.
Lord Salisbury's Tories had taken over, led their party into
a general election in July, and won a massive majority. The
new parliament was due to reassemble on 12 August. Meanwhile Salisbury, who was Foreign Secretary as well as
Prime Minister, had no time for foreign affairs. But the
foreign service knew that policies towards Africa were
bound to change. The Liberals, even after the resignation
of old Mr Gladstone the previous year, had retained their
basic anti-imperialism. The Tories and Unionists of Salisbury's new regime were in favour of a wider empire.

So both the British and the Belgians stalled. M. van Eetvelde, the Congo Secretary of State, was polite and helpful.
He reassured his British counterparts that their anxieties
would soon be set at rest. Tragedies, unfortunately, did
tend to occur during the great work of imperial advancement. In that spirit he set his inquiries in train with a signal
to his colleagues in the Congo administration's headquarters at Boma, at the mouth of the river.

What the inquiries began to uncover was the reverse of
reassuring. From Boma came angry and clearly obstructive
replies. British consular officials there began to ask their
own questions, and were rudely sent packing. It was 1,500
miles from the Semliki valley to Boma, but it soon became
clear that the officials there were covering up some atrocity
in the far interior. The Congo bureaucrats in Brussels began
to paint their own coat of whitewash over what seemed an
ugly scandal.

The British Foreign Office knew perfectly well that King
Leopold's regime operated at an unacceptable level of horror. The files were crammed with reports of brutality

against British subjects in the Congo. But nothing was done about them – partly because the British subjects affected were only black men from British West Africa, mainly because the chief objective of Britain's African policy was to frustrate the French and Germans. The Belgians (and for that matter the Portuguese) could do what they liked for as long as their countries were pliable allies.

But three powerful lobbies were aligned against this official quietism, and all three were active within the Liberal party, which had lost the election and felt free to embarrass the new government as much as possible. There were the humanitarians, opposed to the quasi-slavery to which the Belgians were reducing their Congolese subjects; the Protestant mission societies (especially the Baptists, very active in the Congo), who objected to the privileges accorded to their French-speaking Catholic rivals; and the merchants and shipping agents of Manchester and Liverpool, resentful of the virtual monopoly of trade which Leopold reserved for his own companies.

In the mid-1890s the great boom industry was rubber, made hugely profitable by the new technology of the 1890s – particularly the horseless carriage, with its pneumatic tyres. Rubber trees were not yet widely cultivated; but natural rubber grew wild in the forests of the tropical belt, notably in Brazil and in the Congo. In both places the methods used to force the natives to deliver it were appallingly cruel. In the Congo, the rubber trade was an outright royal monopoly. So the commercial and humanitarian lobbies found common ground upon which to attack Leopold's regime. They reminded the British government that the Congo State had been founded under the principles of the Berlin treaty of 1886, and that the Berlin conference had affirmed the basic rules of Victorian liberalism: freedom of international trade, and justice for all. King Leopold was breaking both rules, and now his officers seemed to have murdered a white British subject. Since Stokes was notoriously an Irishman, and the Irish members of parliament could by their block vote at any time make the working of the House of Commons impossible, no British government could afford quietly to forget the affair.

In Belgium, too, the King's regime in the Congo had hitherto faced criticism from many sensible people who realised that Leopold was a scheming crook. The chief critics there were Protestants, republicans, and trade unionists apprehensive of what they called 'cheap nigger labour'. The smooth bureaucrats employed by the King to run his private empire badly wanted to keep down the tone of the public debate.

As an outline of the truth began to appear, the Congo officials in Brussels felt they must do something to pacify the British. They instructed their people in Boma to summon Captain Lothaire back from his campaign against the Arabs, so that they could put him before a court of inquiry which would, they hoped, produce a suitably bland explanation of what had happened. Meanwhile they offered the British government a payment in lieu of compensation for Stokes's death, and in final settlement of all claims that might arise from the incident. The British ambassador, insisting that the settlement was by no means final, accepted the sum of 150,000 Belgian francs, which converted into sterling as £5,922 12s. 6d. To make it look less like official hush-money, it was understood that this payment would be handed over to Stokes's bereaved relatives. Meanwhile the British Treasury held on to it.

The Germans were determined to do as well out of the affair as the British. They too insisted on compensation, and got more – a similar BFr. 150,000 on account of Stokes's death, plus 100 Reichsmarks for each of the African residents in their territory who had died along with him. They used the money shrewdly. German officials in East Africa went to the trouble of tracing eighty-six porters from Stokes's caravan, and paid the 100 marks to their families. Limi Stokes got the big sum of £6,000. The official German account describes her as a 'coloured woman now at Dar es Salaam who had relations with the deceased Stokes'. But she did not know of this insulting phrase, and took the money gratefully. She apparently set up in trade with the capital, and did well. The Germans' generous treatment of the families of the African victims of the massacre had – according to a British Foreign Office report from Zanzibar

- a powerful effect on native opinion in the infant colony, as a sign of the benevolence of the master race. It did not occur to the British to make any claim for compensation on behalf of their own African subjects who had suffered.

The money did not wipe out the offence. The British were angry that the Germans appeared more active than themselves in seeking satisfaction for the death of a British subject. On the insistence of Plunkett, the British ambassador in Brussels, the Congo officials there agreed that Lothaire should be given a formal trial in Boma. The British vice-consul was to be present throughout the proceedings, and if the British government considered the verdict less than satisfactory it was entitled to instigate an appeal against it. The conditions backfired, uniting the white officials and businessmen of the Congo against what they saw as foreign interference.

The accusations against Lothaire were simple. He had denied Stokes the right of appeal to a higher court; he had presided over a court-martial that was improperly constituted since it had no *greffier*, or qualified clerk; and he had inflicted the death penalty upon a white man without due authority and in the wrong form, since a court-martial must shoot, not hang, its convicts. He was formally charged with murder: both he and his accusers were confident of an acquittal on that count. As an alternative he was charged with denying justice.

Lothaire did not contest the charges. He had been promoted in July 1895, as a reward for his triumphs over Stokes and Kibonghe. In September he was wounded in both legs during yet another battle with the Arabs. It was April 1896 before he was pulled back from active service and put on trial at Boma. He was proud of what he had done, and the Congo whites who conducted the trial were proud of him. No member of the Brussels bar was prepared to play any part in the case. The presiding judge of the Congo courts resigned his office to act as counsel for the defence. The president of the court was the lieutenant-governor of the Congo State, Lothaire's superior officer; its members were colonial officials, and traders working for L'Anversoise, the

King's company which controlled, among other things, the
ivory trade in which Lothaire had been so successful.

The evidence was farcical. One African witness had to be
sent home because not a single person in Boma could
understand his inland language. Another, a frightened
Hausa soldier, let slip that Lothaire had said before the trial
at Lindi that Stokes would hang: '*Ne discutez pas*' – 'Don't
argue' – said the court president, shutting him up. At the
close of proceedings Lothaire was declared blameless, and
his judges stood him a celebration dinner.

The British vice-consul in Boma, Mr Arthur, had an
awkward role to play. He knew all about the iniquities of
the Congo regime, and had already been threatened with
violence on account of his reports to London on the subject.
He knew perfectly well that the court would clear Lothaire.
But he was obliged to attend the proceedings on behalf of
the British government, which the local whites angrily
agreed was the instigator of the persecution of a gallant
officer. The court president insisted that poor Arthur sat in
front of the courtoom, to take his notes in full view of the
disapproving crowd of Lothaire's supporters. A brother
officer of the accused, a captain of the *force publique*, was
assigned to 'assist the consul and protect him from public
indignation'.

Arthur's report was nevertheless full and fair. It made
plain that the whole business was a travesty of justice, but
recommended that no appeal be made, since it would only
arouse more anti-British and anti-Protestant feeling, while
having no chance of success. He despatched this advice
towards Britain: it was delayed by an obstructive Belgian
ship's captain. Arthur was obliged to send a hasty summary
by way of the nearest secure telegraph office, which was six
days away by sailing schooner in the Portuguese town of São
Paolo de Loanda, in Angola.

The British government, with time for an appeal fast
running out, decided to request one anyway. But there were
powerful legal arguments against the course that the Congo
government, under British pressure, had agreed to. This
was that an appeal from the Boma tribunal be heard by the
Court of Appeal (*Conseil supérieur*) in Brussels. In law, the

regime in the Congo was nothing to do with Belgium, its courts, or its people. It was a personal venture of the monarch's, conducted (however much in vain) for his personal profit. Belgian officers in the Congo army were technically in the service of a foreign power; rough diamonds like Lothaire and Henry, who had risen through the ranks to become first sergeants, then officers, would pretty surely not have been granted commissions in Belgium's gentlemanly home army. Their formal status was that they continued while on Congo service to gain seniority in the Belgian forces, being listed as 'on attachment to the *Institut cartographique de la Cambre*', the Belgian ordnance survey. This gave them leave to serve and be paid by their King in his separate capacity as *Roi-souverain* of the Congo Free State. Neither the courts-martial nor the civilian courts of Belgium had, it seemed, jurisdiction to try such officers for alleged offences committed outside home territory.

The judges and lawyers in Brussels found a way through this legal conundrum which enabled them to do as they wished. They sent for Lothaire, perfunctorily heard the arguments and read a transcript of the Boma evidence, and dismissed the case out of hand.

Lothaire's counsel hardly bothered to answer the accusations against his client. He sought instead to justify the lynching by showing that Stokes was a rascal who sold arms to the Arab enemies of the King. There were published texts to support this view. Lugard's reports to the IBEA company, published in the Blue Books on Africa presented to the House of Commons, seemed a respectable source (although, as we have seen, they were packed with lies). Stuhlmann's account of his journey with Emin Pasha gave a horrifying description of the arms trade and its consequences, and made it plain that Stokes was a main dealer.

Both Lugard and Stuhlmann were instructed by their governments to put in affidavits swearing that Stokes, whatever they had said in the past, was a peaceable merchant and a Christian gentleman (although, Lugard felt bound to add, 'casual about natives'). These patriotic half-truths were rightly disregarded by the court of appeal. The trial made nothing of the fact that Stokes had been in command of a force of soldiers trained, armed and uniformed by the authorities in German East Africa. All the odium was directed at Britain, as the instigator of the trial, and at the Protestant missionaries in Africa, of whom Stokes was presented as a typical example. Instead of inquiring into Lothaire's conduct, the court blackened his victim's character. The acquittal of Lothaire was a posthumous conviction of the man he had murdered.

Belgium entered a phase of mass hatred for Britain. When a small nation is being pushed around by a great power, none of its citizens can feel happy to side with the bully. Even those decent Belgians who were ashamed of their King and his wretched tyranny rallied behind the Congo lobby, an amalgam of investors in the King's projects, right-wing army officers, Catholic propagandists and news-papers hired by all of these. The Germans, and the French, were waiting to take advantage of the anti-British feeling. But Lothaire himself took the edge off the campaign. While awaiting his appeal, in Brussels, he was lionised by the super-patriots and the King's faction. Instead of behaving as lions should, however, he swaggered about, and when a great rally was organised in his support he failed to turn up; his friends had kept him away, because he was too drunk to appear on a public platform. Then he became engaged to the daughter of a devout and high-born million-aire, but jilted the girl, whose family threatened to sue for breach of promise.

As soon as the trial was over Lothaire resigned from the army to take up a more promising career. Within a year he was back in the Congo as a director of L'Anversoise, the King's own company, and with the concession to extort rubber from the natives of the Mongala river basin. He did so with outstanding brutality, and was rewarded with the title of Chevalier of the Order of Leopold.

Lieutenant Henry, his accomplice in the killing of Stokes, did even better. He continued his campaigning in Africa, and rose in the end to the rank of Major-General in the Belgian army proper. He continued to support the case for Belgian rule in the Congo until his death in 1957. On his retirement, he too had been granted a knighthood: he chose

the title of Chevalier Henry *de la Lindi*, in memory of the
river where Stokes and Kibonghe died.

The British Foreign Office clearly regretted the Stokes
affair, and wished the wild Irishman had been forgotten in
his grave. The last thing the diplomats wanted was to make
an enemy of Belgium. In Africa, let alone in the wider
world, there were more serious problems to face in the late
1890s. In Egypt, an immense army was marching for the
Sudan. In southern Africa, the cheating financier Cecil
Rhodes was organising an illegal uprising against the elected
Boer government of the Transvaal, putting Britain's stake in
the Rand gold mines at risk. Along the southern fringe of the
Sahara desert British officers - Lugard to the fore - were rac-
ing the French for possession of the sultanates of the upper
Niger. Against such considerations the death of one man
of dubious background could not really be allowed to count.
    The Prime Minister, Lord Salisbury, was also Foreign
Secretary, and had a strong personal reason for wishing
Stokes's memory away. Each week he had to stand alone
before the tiny but terrifying figure of Queen Victoria and
give an account of his stewardship. The Queen had received
puzzling letters from her cousin, King Leopold, in whose
charitable work for the Christianisation of Africa she took
a benevolent interest. Leopold had long complained that
British interests were trying to misrepresent and undermine
his great work: feeling was running high among his own
people - he said - about a scurrilous campaign being conducted against his endeavours in the Congo. He was so
indignant that he even cancelled a planned visit to Windsor,
to the Queen's grave disappointment. If hereditary monarchs cannot hold their families together, who can?
    The Stokes papers in their ponderous Foreign Office
cases bear the mark showing that they were, in the latter
part of 1895, included in the boxes sent regularly for Her
Majesty's perusal. What she made of it all is not recorded,
but she can hardly have approved of a man as loose-living
as the late Charles Stokes. The first Empress of India had
no qualms about imperialism in Africa. She wanted action:
retribution against the Mahdi's soldiers for the death of

General Gordon; swift deeds to keep the French off the
Niger; support for Mr Rhodes and his truly patriotic vision
of a continent striped from top to bottom with British red.
Dropping the Stokes business, with its implications for the
Queen's Belgian relations, would bring Salisbury relief
from part at least of the Queen's harangues; anyway, however odious Leopold's regime, the British government
preferred to have the Belgians as friends, if only as a
counterweight to their real rivals, the French. So Salisbury
dropped the case.

In the Foreign Office the affair became a standing joke.
As late as May 1898 the legal advisor, Sir Clement Hill,
was noting down his grumbles about the box of Stokes's
worthless papers, which was still cluttering up his office
cupboard. The bureaucrats could not entirely forget the
matter because a Tory backbench MP had taken it up. He
was a lawyer, H. D. Greene, and member for Shrewsbury,
where young Nellie Stokes – the twice-orphaned daughter
of Charles and his first wife, Ellen – was living with her
uncle, Charles Sherratt. Mr Greene kept putting down parliamentary questions about a final settlement of the affair,
and the officials had to find answers for their ministers to
read out in the Commons.

The Foreign Office had two separate issues to sort out,
apart from the abortive matter of Lothaire's unsatisfactory
trial. One was that of the £6,000 paid by the Belgians as
compensation to Stokes's family. The other was that of the
ivory and other property taken by Lothaire at the time of
the lynching. There was no exact precedent for the distri-
bution of the compensation money. The Germans, we have
seen, had paid their equivalent sum to Limi Stokes. The
British felt no obligation to Limi, a German citizen. They
wanted to placate Mr Greene and Stokes's quarrelsome
Irish family. The most deserving and needy of the beneficiaries were clearly the old lady and the little girl, the dead
man's mother and daughter. But from Belfast and Skibbereen came petitions from other Stokeses, male but
almost as indigent as the women. If they got their hands
on the money, Louisa and Nellie would not see much of it.

Charles Stokes's allowance of £29 a year to his mother,

on which she maintained herself and his sister Josephine, naturally ended with his death. The women were reduced to real poverty, while the £6,000 compensation money gathered interest in a Foreign Office account. A year after Charles's death Lord Salisbury, after anxious consideration, signed a docket authorising payment of £50 per year to the Dublin household, out of the interest. A year later again, in February 1897, old Louisa died, 'broken in health by the death of her son', and the temporary allowance therefore stopped. Poor Josephine had to petition the Foreign Office again for her part of it to continue, and was allowed £10 a quarter to live on. Her letter of acknowledgement said she was very grateful for it. The full capital sum of £6,000 was in the end paid over to Josephine and young Nellie jointly, on condition that Nellie left her uncle Sherratt's house in Shrewsbury, where she had spent all her life, and went to live with her maiden aunt in Dublin. The capital was safeguarded under a deed of trust, on which Lord Salisbury commented, 'Such an elaborate settlement of so small an amount will only benefit the lawyers.'

The lawyers did even better out of Charles Stokes's will, which turned out a greedy advocate's dream. The trader had made and dated it at Kwa Muchara, the village on Lake Edward in the Congo Free State where he had halted before his final and fatal advance towards Kwa Mpeni. Since nobody else in his caravan could read or write English, he did not have his signature witnessed. That was to be the problem, since nobody but a lawyer could have found the document in any other way doubtful.

The will left the farm and store at Usongo to his wife Limi, and disposed of a few other small items of property in Africa to local missionary friends. The main capital worth of the financial property was left in trust to the Church Missionary Society, his old employers, who were to distribute the income in specified proportions to several beneficiaries: the CMS; Louisa in Dublin; his daughter Nellie in England; his African wife Limi; his daughter Louisa, who was living at Mr Hubbard's mission station at Nassa in German East Africa; and 'two girls now with me and known as Nyanjala and Zaria', the two pretty little

slaves presented by the Kabaka of Buganda. Nanjala, unknown to both of them, was at the time the will was made
pregnant with Charles's son.

The main asset of the estate was the hoard of ivory seized
by Lothaire and Henry at Kwa Mpeni – 6,500 kilos of fine
ivory, and 3,750 kilos of small pieces and discoloured tusks.
The quantity was not in dispute, nor was the value,
reckoned by the Belgians, with British agreement, at
BFr. 163,000, or about £6,250 sterling (worth, on a rough
reckoning, just under £200,000 in terms of 1985).

The Congo authorities, having agreed that this sum was
due to the heirs of Charles Stokes, promptly counterclaimed
for the expense of collecting and transporting the ivory to
the coast. This they put at BFr. 191,000. In other words,
they stated that Stokes's estate owed them over £1,000. It
took the authority of the head of the Congo office in Brussels, Secretary of State van Eetvelde, to waive this monstrous counterclaim in the name of Anglo-Belgian amity.
In December 1896 he conceded that the heirs should get
the full sum, less 10 per cent export duty. The Stokes families were due the tidy sum of £5,847 17s. as the reward of
Charles's last and fatal adventure. It looked as though his
sacrifice would bring some reward, at least, for those he had
loved.

Then the lawyers got to work. The will came before the
probate court, which briefed counsel at the expense of the
estate. Since the signature was not witnessed, the will would
have been invalid if made on British soil. But the British
court would recognise as effective a will made on foreign
territory, if valid under local legislation. A Belgian lawyer
was summoned as an expert witness, and gave the court the
expensive opinion that there was no testamentary law in the
Congo Free State, and precious little law at all. His view
was that Belgian law should apply. The court rose to con-
sider the matter, and at last agreed. A fresh Belgian lawyer
was imported, to give the probate court the further opinion
that no witnesses were needed to validate the signature of
a will in Belgium. Once more, after an adjournment, the
court accepted this view. Probate of the will of Charles
Stokes was finally granted in January 1898.

By then, two of the intended beneficiaries were dead. The 'fine child', little Louisa, had died of measles at Mr Hubbard's mission station at Nassa, twenty days before her father. Old Louisa died in Dublin in February 1896. But the survivors did not benefit from an increased share of the estate. Of the original sum of nearly £6,000, the remainder after the lawyers and experts had taken their fees, costs and expenses was £220. So ended the fortune of Charles Stokes.

The hanged man did not know that Nanjala, his beautiful young slave, was pregnant. She was in her early teens, and strong. Through the hazards of the journey she made it back to her old home in Kampala, and was there taken in and looked after by the ladies of the royal house of Buganda. Under their care, on 8 June 1895, she gave birth to a fine healthy boy. He was given the name Charles Kasaja, Little Charles in Luganda.

Mr Charles Stokes, junior, was in 1984 living hale and hearty on the tidy estate beside Bungo hill, in the Kampala suburbs, given in perpetuity by the Regents of Buganda in 1903 as a memorial to his father, the 'friend of the Baganda'. About the same time young Charles was taken under the special protection of the Scottish mission in his country. In due course they sent him to be trained as a medical auxiliary, in Dundee. He recalled to the present writer the courage of the missionary's widow, Mrs Walker, who travelled with him to take ship at Mombasa, by the not-quite-complete railway through Kenya. She was a white lady, travelling in those days with a little coloured boy: 'There was always the danger someone might think I was her own child: that would have been terrible.'

Charles Stokes, junior, served his country for many years as the principal organiser of its blood transfusion service: his own children, grandchildren and great-grandchildren are numerous and happy. One episode in his life stays proudly in his memory. It occurred in 1916, when one of his friends and contemporaries fell gravely sick, and refused to entrust himself to a missionary doctor who would - so the sick young man believed - have done him harm. Mr Stokes nursed the patient through his fever, and saved his

life. Later the survivor came to fame. His name was Jomo
Kenyatta, anthropologist, freedom-fighter, liberator and
first president of the nation of Kenya, whose boundaries
had not been fixed, nor its name established, at the time of
his birth. Thus, across the generations, the Irish adventurer
Charles Stokes did service to the Africa where he lived and
died.

Notes on sources, and some ideas

I do not offer a detailed list of sources for every statement in this book. Instead I here describe its origins, indicate where the evidence can be found, recommend further reading and acknowledge special debts. I also include some odd sidelights on the Africa that Charles Stokes knew, and on what it has become. Scholars might find convenient a select bibliography; but it would be overloaded with standard histories and biographies that anyone can find who wants them. General readers would, I think, find such an apparatus pretentious in what is meant to be an adventure story as well as a tiny piece of history. Anyway, I feel it honest to confess to my own preferences, prejudices and obsessions.

Introduction

'Absolutely no women for the men.' Lieutenant Seymour Vandeleur, DSO, Scots Guards, was deeply concerned for the morale of his African troops when they moved into a Muslim district where the village girls were off limits to travelling soldiers. He wrote *Campaigning on the Upper Nile and Niger* in 1898, and Major J. E. Macdonald of the Royal Engineers published his *Soldiering and Surveying in British East Africa* the previous year. These books, like Alfred Swann's *Fighting the Slave-Hunters in Central Africa* (1910) and Sir Frederick Jackson's *Early Days in British East Africa* (1930), convey the flavour of those times as the pioneers saw them, and touch in their various ways on the story of Charles Stokes. Jackson is described, in his friend Lord Cranworth's preface, as 'the whitest gentleman who ever crossed the shores of Africa'.

There was a lively market for true-life adventure stories in the

final two decades of the last century. The form was established
by H. M. Stanley, a great journalist who is always more readable
than reliable. His reputation in turn was based upon that of another excellent writer, Dr David Livingstone, who understood, as
practically none of his successors did, that the European penetration of Africa was a very odd business. In his *Last Journals* (not
intended for publication as such) he recalls the fascinated crowd
that assembled to see him washing in Lake Mweru: 'One feels
ashamed of the white skin; it seems unnatural, like blanched
celery – or white mice.'

Most of the chroniclers of exploration had axes to grind. They
were trying to raise money for a Christian mission, or finance for
a company, or backing for a campaign of annexation. But they
provide the nearest thing we have to direct witness of events, and
I have relied heavily upon them for this book. It would be tedious
to list all those I have read, and anyway many of those I did
consult were useless. My chief debt is to the wonderful London
Library, which owns copies of books by or about – it sometimes
seemed – practically everyone I mention.

The two most important eyewitnesses are, first, Stanley, the
subject of many biographies more truthful than his own accounts
of his life, but never so thrilling; and, second, Frederick Lugard,
whose own books were frank political propaganda. Dame Margery Perham's biography of her hero (1956-60) is the best account
of the establishment of British East Africa from the imperialist
point of view. Her edition of Lugard's private diaries (1959-60)
is magnificent, and first led me to focus on Charles Stokes. Anyone Lugard so hated could not, I thought, be all bad.

The historical framework for the colonisation of East Africa is
established in three classic works, R. Robinson and J. Gallagher's
Africa and the Victorians (1967), G. N. Sanderson's *England,
Europe and the Upper Nile* (1965) and R. Oliver's *The Missionary
Factor in East Africa* (1957). I found a gold-mine in the volumes
of two symposia edited by Prosser Gifford and W. Roger Louis,
on *France and Britain in Africa* (1971) and *Britain and Germany
in Africa* (1967). Dozens of other histories and biographies provide dates, incidents and personalities; again, it would be tedious
to list standard reference works, and I have not done so.

The main archive material is in the Public Record Office at
Kew. The 'Stokes affair' was the subject of what we would now
call a parliamentary White Paper, whose source material is far

more revealing than the carefully edited public version. The PRO also contains much background material for the reports to parliament of the Imperial British East Africa Company, and there is much of value for my purpose in the reports of the Zanzibar and Congo consulates and of the Brussels embassy.

The archives of the Church Missionary Society are at Birmingham University, where I found much that was revealing to add to the classic history of the CMS by its secretary, Eugene Stock.

I failed to penetrate the East German bureaucracy to see the archives of the old *Kolonialamt*. Nor could I discover what material is still held in Zanzibar, where many relevant documents in German, and a few in English, were until lately said to be located. The Kenya archives, when I visited them in Nairobi, were in what I was assured was temporary chaos.

As for the crucial material on the establishment of British rule in Uganda, I fear all is lost. The British, on leaving, had a big clear-out of material that might be scandalous – and Stokes was always that. But, it seems, much was left. During the rule of General Idi Amin Dada the country grew short of foreign exchange, and therefore of paper. Some enterprising soldiers raided the national archives and took away sheets of paper to sell as wrappings to the market-traders of Kampala. The archives of the Kabaka of Buganda were all burned when President Obote's soldiers attacked the royal palace in 1966. Perhaps nobody could have read them anyway: the records for the twenty years before the Christian conquest were written in Luganda by the old system of Arabic writing, with special signs for the rich vowel sounds that predominate in all Bantu languages.

In Nairobi I found a copy of the monograph by Mrs Anne Luck published by the East African Publishing House in 1972 as *Charles Stokes in Africa*. I have been unable to trace the author, whom I believe to have retired to her native South Africa, so I thank her warmly here – although my facts, and my interpretation of them, often differ from hers. She used the documents on Stokes collected by the late H. B. Thomas, who had explored the East African archives that still existed twenty years ago. Several quotations are directly borrowed from this source.

In Kampala I was vastly helped by my old friend Erisa Kironde, then chairman of the Uganda Red Cross. Amid chaos and sporadic shooting in that wrecked city he introduced me to many people with long memories of the history of Buganda: I recall with especial thanks Mr Eridade Mulira. Mr Kironde has a collection of typescripts on his country's history, which I hope he will one day publish and translate into English.

Erisa Kironde's greatest service was to drive me out into the Kampala suburbs, through the armed checkpoints, to visit Mr Charles Stokes, junior, at Bungo. Mr Stokes was wonderfully helpful. So were other members of the Stokes family, through whom I got in touch with the family historian, Mr Geoff Stokes, of Melbourne. I am glad to have put him in touch with the African cousins whose existence he suspected but was not certain of.

My thanks are also due to a Muganda friend who gave me much wise advice. He was, during the writing of this book, living in exile. Just where the shaky end of the 1985 civil war will leave him is unclear, so I do not lay public claim to our real friendship.

Books involving many names in Bantu languages always have a note attempting to justify the writer's approach to them. On the one side lies pedantry and obscurity to those who do not know how the languages work, on the other inaccuracy and irritation to those who do know. I have tried to dodge the issue, but will sketch it here. Bantu proper names consist of a root-word (for example, -ganda) to which meaning is given by the addition of a prefix. So Buganda is a nation, Luganda is its language, Baganda are its people, Muganda is one person, Kiganda is generally to do with the place. Although all Bantu languages work on this principle, the prefixes are different in different languages. So, the coast is *suahel*, a word of Arabic origin (as in Sahel, the shore of the desert). The people of the coast are Waswahili, their language Kiswahili, their country Uswahili: thus in Kiswahili the country with -ganda properties is called Uganda. The British gave the Kiswahili name to their new colony, which included the old kingdom of Buganda together with several other kingdoms, principalities and districts. So when I speak of the historic kingdom I call it Buganda, and when I mean the British territory I call it Uganda. I understand what I mean, and I hope readers will too.

Another problem arises with names of interest to more than one European country. The pioneers naturally wrote down African names in a form that would be pronounceable more or less correctly by people in their own country: thus the river Ouélé in French is the Wele in English, and the ivory dealer Mihara in English is Muchara in German. I use either the form most familiar now, or the form used in contemporary quotations. When Stokes wrote his will, he gave his location as Kwa Muchara, Muchara's settlement, so I spell it like that. Incidentally, the German philologists who regularised the spelling and structure of the Swahili language did a marvellous job, and as far as possible adapted their spelling to meet the requirements of English-speakers. The main oddity (from the point of view of English) is that a single initial S sounds like a Z in German: so for that sound the Germans wrote a double S. The senior Uganda politician Mr Paul Ssemogerere writes his name thus for that reason. The relics of colonialism in Africa are indeed curious.

Chapter 1

Charles Stokes's own family is dispersed around the world, but their distant cousins in Ireland first put me on their track. Of the eighteen Stokeses listed in the telephone books for Ireland, north and south, in 1983, three were clergymen of the Anglican Church of Ireland, and four had British military ranks, or the initials of British decorations, appended to their names. It was through their courteous replies to my letters that I located members of a family now living in British Columbia, Victoria, California and Britain.

English literature, as well as the British Empire, did well out of the Irish Protestant diaspora of the end of the nineteenth century. Charles Stokes was two years older than Oscar Wilde, four years older than George Bernard Shaw.

The Church Missionary Society's archive at Birmingham has a great deal of correspondence about the East African mission. *A Century of Christianity in Uganda* (Kampala, 1977) is full of a more generous charity than the early missionaries sustained. Its epilogue was written by the Most Reverend J. Luwum, Archbishop of Uganda, Rwanda, Burundi and Boga-Zaire. He was very shortly afterwards murdered on the orders of President Idi Amin.

Dr Livingstone is the subject of innumerable books, and the author of good ones. The same is true of Stanley. There is no way of verifying the information they provide about the peoples they met, since nobody else had ever written about them. Stanley often got angry with his local informants. Livingstone rarely did, but wrote, at the sad end of his pilgrimage, 'It is distressingly difficult to elicit accurate information about the lakes and rivers, because the people do not think accurately.'

The people who saw Livingstone dead sang a mournful song over the body: 'Today the Englishman is dead/Who has different hair from ours/Come round and see the Englishman.' The actual words are recorded: '*Lelo kwa Engerese/Muanasisi ou Konda/To kamb' tamb' Engerese.*' I cannot find out what language this is meant to be.

The British consular papers for Zanzibar are the main source of that island's strange history, at least if one does not read Arabic. Kenneth Ingham's *History of East Africa* (1965), and R. Coupland's *The Exploitation of East Africa* (1939) and *Kirk on the Zambezi* (1928) were of great value to me.

Chapter 2

The rival stories of the Protestant and Catholic missions in Buganda are told in many pious biographies, of which those of Mackay, Hannington, Hirth and Achte are all useful, in their ways.

The special role of Sir William Mackinnon in the East Africa story has to be teased out of clues and half-truths, since he destroyed many of his papers. The selected documents that survive are in the School of Oriental and African Studies at London University.

On the history of Buganda, the explorers' accounts are lively, and are brilliantly summarised in Alan Moorehead's *The White Nile* (1960). Sir Apolo Kagwa's story of the Buganda monarchy, written from a missionary position, is nevertheless invaluable. There is priceless material in the old numbers of the *Uganda Journal*, especially in contributions by Sir J. M. Gray. The *Journal* was written mainly by colonial administrators who loved the country where they served, and thought it far too precious to be handed over to African rule.

Chapter 3

'The missionary is really gaining your experience for you without any cost to yourself ... They strengthen our hold over the country, they spread the use of the English language, they induct the natives into the best kind of civilisation, and, in fact, every missionary station is an essay in colonisation.' Thus Harry Johnston reported to the British South Africa Company in 1888, before he broke with the company on realising what a crook its owner, Cecil Rhodes, was. Johnston (known as the 'galloping consul', and later Sir Harry) was the most brilliant of the generally rather dim British officials who were sent to Africa. Most years of his service he found time to paint a picture and exhibit it in the Royal Academy summer show; he survived the deadly blackwater fever no less than six times; and when given an animal skin by a Belgian officer he recognised that it was something strange, and thus recorded the existence of that strange beast, the okapi, or *ocapi Johnstonii*.

Johnston was an environmentalist before his time, noting in about 1905, 'Undoubtedly the rain supply of Africa has been largely modified by the disafforestation of the country [by native burning] and by the gradual destruction of vegetation by the annual bush fires.' The desertification of Africa began before the white men arrived. Johnston was less up to date in his racial views, believing that Asians should be imported to Africa, since 'there was a great possibility of elevation for the negro by a mixture of Indian blood [to produce] a race superior in intelligence to the primitive black, and in no way inferior in physique.' At the end of his life he went to the United States, met and sympathised with educated black people, and declared that the racist opinions he had learned in Africa were unpleasant nonsense. His life has been brilliantly written by Roland Oliver (1957).

Chapter 4

Mr Donald Simpson, the distinguished scholar and librarian at the Royal Commonwealth Society, showed me poor Ellen Sherratt's letters. He also produced a wonderful little collection of pictures of Stokes. Mr Simpson's helpfulness to researchers is legendary, and his book, *Dark Companions* (1975), on the Africans who worked for the early European travellers, is a model of investigation.

The Hannington muddle is obscured by his pious biographers. He was evidently an arrogant, self-centred man, bent on martyr-

dom or glory. A consular report said he was 'stiff-necked'. Sir
Frederick Jackson described him as 'domineering, very impetuous, and intolerant of opposition ... I was up the Wami River
when information reached me from the coast that he had been
murdered, and I was not surprised ...' But his death, news of
which reached Europe while the Berlin conference was in progress, was a boon to the lobbyists for imperial conquest.

Chapter 5

Quotations sadly lose flavour in translation. King Leopold actually said: '*Le Belge n'exploite pas le monde. C'est un goût à faire
naître chez lui.*' Bismarck said: '*Diese ganze Kolonialgeschichte ist
ja Schwindel, aber wir brauchen sie für die Wahlen.*'

The text of the Berlin Act of 1886 is given, with its map, in Sir
E. Hertslet's *The Map of Africa by Treaty* (1896); so is that of
the Brussels convention of 1890, which put into words much of
what was merely implicit at Berlin. Hertslet provides lists of treaties, and their texts, often with obviously bogus 'rulers' all over
Africa: his book is a catalogue of comic injustices, if you have the
heart to laugh.

Sir John Kirk, the Zanzibar veteran, attended the Brussels conference as a director of the IBEA company: 'It is hard work, all
the dinners, receptions and balls,' he wrote drily.

S. E. Crowe, in *The Berlin West Africa Conference* (1942), gives
a crystal-clear account of what went on there. A. J. P. Taylor's
Germany's First Bid for Colonies (1938) makes them the chief
villains; but then it was written in the 1930s, when all the best
English people wanted to rub out the memory of the times when
Britain and Germany worked together for shared objectives, the
French were the natural enemies, and the Belgians were a useful
cover for British commercial interests. Anglo-German co-operation is still not a fashionable subject.

Neal Ascherson's life of Leopold, *The King Incorporated*
(1963), is excellent. Barbara Emerson's biography (1979) is perhaps fuller on his domestic reign. J. Darcy's *Cent Années de rivalité
coloniale* (1904) puts a French slant on the scramble (which the
French call '*le steeplechase*'). There are of course several lives of
Brazza, that extraordinary man, but in English there is, so far as
I know, only Richard West's *Brazza of the Congo* (1972).

Henry Sanford was a wonderful caricature of a capitalist. He served as American minister in Brussels from 1861 to 1869, then went freelance, representing the United States in various European affairs. Mainly, though, he was a railroad promoter: a town in Florida bears his name, having been developed to create traffic for his line down the Keys. On diplomatic business he always described himself as 'General'. In fact he was an honorary Major-General in the Minnesota militia. During the Civil War he gave the state a pair of field-guns, and received in exchange both the military title and a railroad concession.

Official histories, even of discredited institutions, have their uses. P. L. MacDermott was secretary of the Imperial British East Africa Company, and wrote its version of the story in *British East Africa* (1893). R. S. Thomson did a similar service for Leopold in *La Fondation de l'état indépendant du Congo* (1933). Stanley's *The Congo and the Founding of its Free State* (1885), dedicated to Leopold, prudently tells of adventures but leaves out the politics.

An interesting account of chartered companies and what was wrong with them is Sir Percival Griffiths's *A Licence to Trade* (1974).

Chapter 6

The provisional demarcation line between British and German East Africa is still on the map, including the kink in the line where Peters and Johnston made their rival bogus treaties around Kilimanjaro. When I was last there it was closed to all traffic and trade, as a result of a row between Kenya and Tanzania.

The commercial absurdity of the East African colonies was evident before they were established. The newspaper I work for got it right, of course: 'We do not, apart from surprises, look for any rapid development of either trade or financial success from these territories.' (*The Economist*, 30 August 1890.) J. A. Hobson's *Imperialism* (1902) set out the anti-imperialist case in a way that impressed Lenin. Leonard Woolf, the colonial civil servant whom many regard as a better writer than his wife Virginia, explained the folly of the whole thing in *Empire and Commerce in Africa*, published by the Labour Research Department in the early 1920s.

The Equatoria story, and the character of the anomalous Emin, was told many times over in the 1890s, when he was a popular

hero. His life in the province is exhaustively described by Captain
Gaetano Casati in *Dieci Anni in Equatoria* (1891); Casati was if
possible even vaguer than Emin, and he also had a half-African
daughter. Emin's daughter Ferida lived in south Germany until
her death of influenza in 1923: she was lucky to escape the 1930s.

The German explorer Schweinfurth stayed a while with Emin
in Equatoria, and so did the Russian, Dr Junker. Russia's imperial ambitions in Africa are now forgotten. They ended mainly
because the head of their mission to Ethiopia in 1894, trying to
teach soldiers how to use a Maxim gun, carelessly stood in front
of the party under instruction. Thus he foreshadowed the fate of
some Soviet military advisers in recent years.

The deal between Leopold and Mackinnon over the Lado enclave is obscure, because the parties kept it so. But the British
Foreign Office realised a dirty fix was in preparation, and frustrated it as they had stopped Mackinnon's earlier attempt to turn
Zanzibar into a Scottish monopoly.

The files of *The Times* show how the propaganda in favour of
Leopold's (and Mackinnon's) Emin Pasha expedition was orchestrated. Stanley, who rightly supposed that his book on the expedition would make a lot of money, tried to prevent his colleagues
from writing rival accounts. But he failed. A. J. Mounteney-Jephson, J. S. Jameson (posthumously) and the Irish doctor Thomas
Heazle Parke all published accounts. (Parke's statue is still outside
the National Gallery in Dublin, but nobody there knows who he
was.) H. R. Fox-Bourne, in *The Other Side of the Emin Pasha
Expedition* (1891), attacked the Stanley legend from the point of
view of Liberal anti-imperialism. A thorough modern work on
the episode is Roger Jones's *The Rescue of Emin Pasha* (1972).

James Gordon Bennett, junior, the proprietor of the New York
Herald and Stanley's journalistic patron, has achieved a strange
immortality. In South London (and maybe elsewhere in England)
children today say 'Gordon Bennett' as an expletive or inoffensive
swear-word. But the African lake, river and mountain to which
Stanley gave his name are now all called something else.

The arms trade through Zanzibar was largely hushed up, since
the traders there were clearly selling guns to be used against the
white men. In the period January–June 1888, imports through
the island were 37,441 firearms of all kinds; 70,650 cartridges for
rifles and shotguns; and 69,350 pounds of powder. A single-shot
Snider rifle sold wholesale for 13 shillings, a hunting carbine for

less than 10 shillings. Serviceable cap-fired muskets could be bought for 5 shillings. A manload (70 pounds) of gunpowder, bought in Zanzibar for £4 a load, could be sold to the Arab traders in the interior for £125. The profits were enormous, and the risks of the trade immense.

The Brussels treaty of 1890 prohibited the sale to 'natives' of all guns except flint-lock muskets. By then all muskets on the market had been converted to fire their charge by means of a cap containing fulminate of mercury, rather than by a flint (and anyway there is no flint in tropical Africa). In fact, all parties in Africa agreed that where the Brussels convention said 'flint-lock' it actually meant cap-fired, and that the diplomats who made treaties knew absolutely nothing about their subject-matter.

Stokes's purchase of muskets, and probably of rifles, from the Scottish mission in Nyasaland (now Malawi) is not formally recorded anywhere that I can find, but is commonly referred to as a fact, so I accept it as such.

The race for East African colonies was conducted from Zanzibar mainly because the upper Nile was closed off to European travellers after 1891 by the Mahdist regime in the Sudan. There is a vast literature about the Mahdi Muhammad Ahmad; accounts were written by Europeans kept captive in Khartoum, and by officers of British intelligence, including the brilliant Colonel Wingate – not to mention Winston S. Churchill, who fought at the final battle of Omdurman. The clearest explanation of what really went on is P. M. Holt's *The Mahdist State in the Sudan, 1881–1898* (1958).

Chapter 7

Lugard's diaries (in Margery Perham's edition) are the main source for events in Buganda at this time, together with the highly-coloured accounts of the White Fathers who suffered from his behaviour. Modern Uganda suffers from rivalries more bitter than those of the imperial period. In 1984, President Obote formed the view that the martyrs' shrines at Namugongo were a focus for agitation against him by the Baganda. In particular he claimed that an attack was being planned from the shrines against the nearby satellite earth-station. In August that year his soldiers moved in and massacred at least ninety-three people at the

shrines. It was a non-sectarian killing: the dead included the
Canon in charge of the Anglican seminary, and the Imam at the
mosque. The Christian martyrs of 1886 were praised throughout
Europe. The political martyrs of 1984 were mentioned by only
one British newspaper, in an unobtrusive paragraph.

Sir Frederick Jackson seems to have been a very stupid man.
He later became a highly unsuccessful governor of Uganda. His
first visit to Africa was to shoot lions, and his host then was the
British vice-consul on the trading island of Lamu, Jack Haggard.
Among Jack's later guests was his brother, Sir Henry Rider Haggard. There is no direct evidence that Rider Haggard met Stokes,
but he certainly knew of him, and from that originates the sup-
position that Stokes was one of the originals upon whom the
fictional Allan Quatermain, of *King Solomon's Mines* (1885) and
other adventure stories, was based.

Chapter 8

Carl Peters told his own version of his story in *New Light on
Dark Africa* (1891), a book of comic boasting in which he sets
himself up as a rival to Stanley. But there was nothing funny
about the man's career. After the failure of his Buganda enterprise
he was appointed resident officer for the Kilimanjaro districts that
he had acquired for the German empire: two years later he was
dismissed for atrocities, and reported upon by a German parliamentary inquiry. Its report was used by the British to justify their
claim, after the Great War, that Germany was unfit to own
colonies and that Britain should therefore bag most of them. Ten
years later Peters returned to a more congenial part of Africa -
the British possession of Rhodesia, where beating black people
was an accepted practice. He failed to find the gold he was seeking, and retired home to write about the racial destinies of the
Nordic peoples. Adolf Hitler thought him a great man, and shared
his view that the British empire in India, where a few thousand
white men ruled over millions of 'inferior' stock, was the finest
racial achievement in history. Richard Wichterich's biography of
Peters (1934) is a study in Nazi hagiography, intended to re-
habilitate not only Peters but the whole story of German colonialism.

Peters's Krupp machine gun was of the same design as the

Maxim gun used by Stanley and Lugard. The American inventor Hiram Maxim (later Sir Hiram) had made a manufacturing agreement with Albert Vickers, the arms merchant of Sheffield, in 1884. In 1888, Vickers (who took over the rival Norwegian machine-gun company of Nordenfelt in the same year) licensed Maxim's patents to his friendly competitor, Alfred Krupp of Essen: the international financiers Sir Ernest Cassel and Lord Rothschild made the arrangements. This was a high point of Anglo-German industrial co-operation, and prompted the Liberal MP, Sir Charles Dilke, to tell the House of Commons in June 1894: 'The only person who has up to the present time benefited from our enterprise in the heart of Africa has been Mr Hiram Maxim.'

Zouaves were French troops recruited for service in the colonies, and often rewarded by grants of land there. They wore baggy trousers of a vaguely Levantine cut, as in Delacroix paintings. There is a wonderful description of the social background to the proposal for 'Papal Zouaves' in Zola's anti-Rothschild novel, L'Argent (1891).

The story of Emin's expedition is fully, if confusingly, told in Dr Stuhlmann's Mit Emin Pascha ins Herz von Afrika (1894). Stuhlmann makes out that he never really understood the Pasha's objective, but loyally followed his leader. The German ambition of securing a strip right across Africa, from east to west, is illustrated in a fascinating document shown me by Mr Donald Simpson. It is a map handed by a German diplomat to Sir Percy Anderson, head of the Africa department at the Foreign Office, after the Brussels conference on Africa of 1890, showing German claims to territory from Zanzibar to Kamerun, including Equatoria.

Chapter 9

Lugard's official reports and diaries, and Dame Margery Perham's commentary on them, are the main and often the sole source for his exploits. Stuhlmann's version, and the various CMS reports, shed different lights on events. Joseph Thomson's Through Masai Land (1885) is an entertaining and good-hearted book about what things were like before the invasion of what is now central Kenya.

At this point a reader may become confused between Buganda and Uganda. Buganda is the ancient kingdom of that name, ruled over by the Kabakas. Uganda is a territory taken over by the British, which includes Buganda and several other places and districts as well. Where I quote from sources I naturally follow the form the writer used: they by no means always observe the distinction I have tried to preserve.

The cathedrals of the Anglican and Catholic dioceses of Uganda stand today on the sites of the original missions. On Mengo hill the last of the Kabakas is still commemorated by the prayers of old women, in the reconstructed (and now rather dilapidated) magnificence of the palace compound. On Kampala hill early in 1984 traces of Lugard's trenches could be found amid the rubble and rusted steelwork of an immense but half-finished mosque, whose construction was halted when Saudi Arabian subsidies were withdrawn after the fall of the Muslim President Idi Amin in 1979.

Chapter 10

Conrad's Congo reminiscences are encapsulated and transformed in *Heart of Darkness* (1902). He made clear in *Last Essays* (1926) that it is very nearly a documentary account of his travels: it is, of course, much more than that. G. Jean-Aubry's *Life and Letters* (1927) of Conrad contains the diary entry about Stanley Falls.

Sydney Hinde was, like Conrad, a mercenary in King Leopold's service, and fought with Lieutenant Lothaire in the campaign against the Arab warlords on the Lualaba in 1892. He tells of the scene after the great victory: 'A little later on, when recrossing the battlefield, the only signs left were bloodstained spots here and there, marking the place where the victims of the fight had been cut up in the evening to furnish a banquet to the victorious survivors. Our disgust may be better imagined than expressed, for we found that the camp followers and friendlies made no difference in this respect between the killed and wounded on their own side or the enemy's.' Thus was Christian rule imposed upon the Congo.

Cannibalism is of course a sensitive issue. The first imperialists pretended it was common in Africa. Then a school of anthropologists argued that the whole thing was a white man's slander.

The fashion now is to admit that it did exist, but only in association with the environment of the rain-forest, in which there was
a chronic deficiency of protein at ground level. (There are mon-
keys in the tree-tops. Personally I cannot eat monkey stew, since
if your helping contains a hand it looks just like a stewed baby's.)

The Manyuema, who provided the fighting force for the forest
Arabs, were a remarkable people. Dr Livingstone met them in
1869 and noted that they were cannibals not from necessity but
by taste. He found that surprising since, he wrote, 'Many of the
Manyuema are very light-coloured and very pretty.' Dr Stuhlmann was interested in the fact that the Arabs employed them as
fighters, but did not enslave them. One reason for this, he remarked, was that 'there is not much of a market for the forest
slaves, with their tattoos and their sharpened teeth.' ('*Die Wald-
sklaven mit ihren Tatöwirungen und ihren zugeschärften Zähnen eine
wenige gesuchte Waare [sind].*')

The conditions of existence in the rain-forest appalled the soldiers and porters from East Africa. The effect on European observers was deeply damaging. They saw on the forest fringe, in
what is now Rwanda, among the volcanoes and the snow-capped
Mountains of the Moon, giants, pigmies, cannibals, chimpanzees
and gorillas, all living side by side. To people half-educated in
the great Darwin's theory of evolution, all this seemed evidence
of mankind in transition from ape to human. Somewhere here
might be found the 'missing link' between monkey and man.
Those white people – almost all of them, at the time – who
regarded black Africans as less than human could here contem-
plate their own superiority, and take the degraded condition of
life as proof of the white man's right to rule over Africa.

The introduction of new diseases into populations that have
long lived in isolation, and so have no immunity against them, is
not the least of the disasters of colonisation. Mr Oliver Ransford,
in *Let the Sickness Cease* (1983), has written a fascinating popular
account of how new diseases, and new European cures for them,
have affected Africa in the past century. The introduction of
venereal diseases from the Americas, with the slave trade, has
caused whole populations to rot away. In parts of Zaire today
30 per cent of women are infertile because of sexually transmitted
infections.

Leda Farrant's life of Tippu Tib (1975) is valuable. He
evidently combined great charm and intelligence with his ruth-

lessness, and realised very early that it was no use trying to fight the whites. To Dr Livingstone he showed true kindness: the doctor was rather upset that a slave-trader could be such a decent man.

The horrors of Belgian rule in the forest were told in immense detail during the anti-Leopold campaign, ably orchestrated by E. D. Morel and financed by the British commercial interests that hoped to get a share of the supposed wealth of the Congo. The vile trade in rubber was exposed mainly by the British consular official Roger Casement, who befriended Conrad at the Congo mouth. In 1916, when Casement faced death by firing-squad for trying to ship in German rifles for the freedom-fighters in Ireland, Conrad risked severe censure by publicly supporting his one-time friend from Congo days. It was a brave act by the great writer.

The story of Emin's death is told in an article in the *Century* magazine (February 1895) by R. Dorsey Mohun.

Chapter 11

For as long as the British and German empires ran side by side in East Africa there was close and friendly co-operation between the officials of the two powers. Two world wars obscured that fact; but around the turn of the century the friendship between British and Germans seemed natural. Rhodes endowed his scholarships for the German as well as the British empire. It was the period of Elizabeth von Arnim's *Elizabeth and her German Garden* (1898), of the good Germans of Forster's *Howard's End* (1910), and even of the decent young student in Wells's *Mr Britling Sees it Through* (1916).

The British and German East Africa companies were both ramps, doomed to collapse, and intended only to compel their respective national governments to acquire territory they did not want. The early reports of the surveyors of the Mombasa–Uganda railway reveal the immense cost of the enterprise, and illustrate the prevailing racial attitudes. The railway story, which starts just after Charles Stokes's death, is well told in Charles Miller's *The Lunatic Express* (1972).

Western Uganda is still wild country. The main risk there when I last visited, in 1984, was from soldiers, some of them rebels, some from various government armies and police forces, who lived by taking money from passers-by, at gun-point. I do not like armed men who smoke marijuana. My son Edward, then aged nineteen, was braver than I.

The black southern Sudanese soldiers who served Egypt and were then recruited by Lugard were, after his departure, deceived and exploited by the British. The story of their 'mutiny' against mistreatment is a nasty one, but was not Lugard's fault and does not belong here. The Sudanese had their revenge in the end. President Idi Amin, although affiliated to the Kakwa tribe, claims descent from a Sudanese soldier: people of this origin form a military caste which in practice rules the West Nile province of Uganda – an area roughly corresponding to the old 'Lado enclave', properly belonging to the southern Sudan. West Nile has never been reconciled to rule by Uganda.

The Baring's crash was the first example of how a central bank may rescue an incompetent financial institution. The arrangements were copied in the United States in 1929, and in the 1980s both in the United States and in Britain. It might have been better to let the Barings go bust.

Lugard's misconduct against the French priests was exposed, with some courage, by the Catholic press in England. The Foreign Office did its best to hush up his crazy behaviour, and it did him no harm. Sir George Goldie of the Royal Niger Company thought a man so ruthless was just what he wanted to fight the French. Thus Lugard got a wife – Flora Shaw, the discredited colonial correspondent of *The Times*, adored Goldie. Lugard married her, she invented the name of Nigeria, and together they went off to rule it. Lugard transferred there the system of 'indirect rule' used in the Indian Raj: it did not really suit in Africa, but won Lugard a huge reputation, because it was cheap.

Joseph Chamberlain was an authentic racist: he did not merely look down on black people, but believed that the character of peoples and communities really is determined by 'blood', whatever that may be. Of the white South Africans he wrote: 'Dutch and English, English and Dutch. Most curiously, though sprung from the same stock, the two races do not amalgamate. It shows what a lot of Celtic and Norman blood must be diffused in us.'

The wave of jingo imperialism that arose at the very end of the last century in England has never been satisfactorily explained. It is tempting to blame it on the rise of the popular press, made possible by state finance for education and by the widening of the franchise to almost all adult males. But as a similar spirit arose at the same time in France and in Germany, something more complicated may have been at work.

Chapter 12

The Asians of East Africa have a history which has never been explored, and would be hard to trace. They presumably did their business largely by word of mouth, not in accounts and record-books. The British employed Indians to build the Uganda railway, and many workers stayed on, joining forces with the existing Indian commercial community based on Zanzibar. They did the jobs of clerking and supervising and shop-keeping which would have been uneconomic at white men's rates of pay; this saved the government money on African education, which was rendered unnecessary. So, like the Jews of the old Russian empire, the Asians were hated by the native peoples. Discrimination against them in Kenya and Tanzania, and their mass expulsion from Uganda, gave Britain and Canada the unexpected bonus of an influx of lively and adaptable new citizens.

By far the best book about Africa today, V. S. Naipaul's novel *A Bend in the River* (1979), has as its central character an Asian trader from the east coast.

The deliberate introduction of arms into the forest region by the Germans was a monstrous crime, and they knew it. Dr Stuhlmann in his Emin Pasha book (1893) explained that the Congo ivory trade depended hardly at all on the slaughter of wild elephants, but on the theft by outsiders of tusks collected by local Africans, who were murdered by the thieves: 'Any one of us who plays billiards with an ivory ball, or touches the keys of a Bechstein instrument, has no suspicion that every tiniest piece of this precious substance must be bought with human blood ... The tiniest fragment from the Congo region has cost the life of one man at least, and for the price of a big tusk several villages at least have been destroyed and their inhabitants sold into slavery.'

British officials were strongly opposed to arming the natives; this was to their credit, even though their motive may have been fear that the weapons would be turned on the salesmen. Stokes himself was in theory against arms imports: 'The supply of arms

and ammunition must be stopped at the coast,' he had written
to the consul-general at Zanzibar. But he said he was bound to
keep up the trade in order not to be cut out by his Arab competitors. (This rascally argument is used today by the governments
of almost all the world's rich nations, to justify their traffic in
arms.) Europeans liked to pretend that all Africa's ills were the
fault of the Arab slave-traders. But Europe was the great market
for ivory, and the ivory trade was at least as damaging as the slave
trade. To enslave a human being, he or she must be kept alive.
To steal a tusk it was safer to leave the previous owner dead.

The Uganda–Tanzania border to westward of Lake Victoria is
a straight line 1° south of the Equator, cutting arbitrarily across
the Kagera river which could form a natural boundary. It was
this absurd frontier, and the prospect of redrawing it in Uganda's
favour, that led to the war of 1979 between the two countries,
and the replacement by the dictator Milton Obote of the dictator
Idi Amin.

The Semliki valley today lies entirely in Zaire, and its southern
part is included within the *Parc national des Virunga*, formerly
the Prince Albert National Park. It is a desperately wild place,
with only a single, crazy iron bridge across the 130 miles of river
between Lake Edward and Lake Albert. Well-armed park guards
search every passing vehicle for stolen ivory, which they prefer to
keep for themselves. The bridge is the only river-crossing for
wild elephants, and also the only practicable export route for the
coffee and papain grown in that part of Zaire. The huge Volvo
trucks hauling their loads towards Uganda can take up to six
weeks to dig their way through the mud; for shelter against rain
and wild animals the Somali drivers camp cheerfully under their
trailers, serviced by local women. Their way of life would, give
or take the internal combustion engine, be entirely familiar to
Charles Stokes.

The Zaire government has twice (some say three times) received international aid for reconstructing the old road, which
may one day form part of a trans-Africa highway. The money has
never been used for its intended purpose.

Mpeni's village can still be traced by the rotting beams in the
undergrowth beside the bridge. The village Stokes knew was
closed down about 1910 by Belgian officials, as a health hazard.
The people were relocated on higher and healthier ground to westward, in a new town called Béni, which happens to mean 'blessed'

in French. Its population is mixed. The local pigmies have grown almost to normal size, now that they eat the same food as everyone else. Some of the Manyuema still file their front teeth to points.

Colonel Colvile started as a new broom, writing long despatches to the Foreign Office. The longer he stayed in Africa, the shorter they grew. Major Macdonald recorded his lake trip with Williams in *Soldiering and Surveying in British East Africa* (1897). Stokes's claim for compensation for use of the *Limi* as a machine-gun platform is among the scrappy papers collected to sort out the outstanding debts of the IBEA company, after the British government took over its assets and (larger) liabilities.

The tale of the rival expeditions to grab the Wadelai-Lado lands, and so to control the source of the White Nile, is the subject of many essays in diplomacy. Briefly, the French and Germans became aware that the British and the Belgians were cooking up a deal to make possible a British line of rail from the Cape to Cairo. King Leopold's 'title' to the Congo State stipulated that if he abandoned sovereignty over it, or any part of it, France would have first claim to the succession. The arrangement to lease the Lado enclave to the Belgians, in exchange for a Belgian lease to Britain of land further south, was designed to leave nominal sovereignty in Leopold's name, so barring a French claim. But the British Foreign Office prudently stopped it.

The British, meanwhile, had found the Mahdist regime in the Sudan convenient, although they publicly denounced it. Lord Salisbury wrote to Sir Evelyn Baring, the effective ruler of Egypt, in 1890: 'The Dervishes are rendering us a service in keeping Italy out ... this people were created for the purpose of keeping the bed warm for you until you can occupy it.'

When the government of the Mahdi's successor, the Khalifa, grew weaker, foreign invaders were tempted to intervene. The French launched their drive for Fashoda, on the upper Nile, under Captain Marchand. The British raced through the Sudan, slaughtering the Mahdists by thousands at Omdurman. When the British commander, General Kitchener Pasha, got to Fashoda he found Marchand and his Senegalese riflemen in control, and they might have stuck it out but for the collapse of the government in Paris over the Dreyfus affair. The *Journal de route* (1913) of Dr Emily, Marchand's medical officer, provides the best description of the effect of disciplined rifle fire on native troops armed only with muskets. At Fashoda Emily was given by a British army doctor a copy of the *British Medical Journal* recording the discovery that malaria was linked to mosquito-bites, not caused by 'bad air'.

Chapter 13

The buildings erected by the early British colonial administration, with their wide verandahs and cooling roof-spaces, are far more serviceable than most of what is being put up in the tropics today. There are good examples in the barrack compound at Entebbe, where I once went to see General Amin. The compound is on the lake side of the Entebbe international airport, which the Israelis built for Amin, then raided in 1976; the airport has never recovered.

At Katwe the remains of Lugard's little Fort George were rotting away in the rain in 1984. The buildings are like the stockades occupied by the United States cavalry in Wild West movies.

Captain Thruxton's expedition towards Wadelai seems from the despatches to have been a terrible muddle. The maps were all wrong, and the places described no longer existed when the soldiers got there. The upper Nile settlements, subject to the rise and fall of the river and to constant raiding, are not permanent places even today.

I have done my best to disentangle the letters written by and to Stokes in his last days. The only text available is that of the French translations prepared for Lothaire's trials. I have not been able to trace the originals, and anyway I do not know either Arabic characters or the Urubi language. It seems worth giving the full text of Kibonghe's letter to Stokes:

> Dieu sait si vous me verrez jamais arriver à temps. Et vous votre ivoire a été récolté et dirigé vers Pema; il doît être sur le point de vous parvenir. J'ai encore de l'ivoire, mais j'ai peur que les Belges ne viennent le prendre. Pour Dieu pour Dieu envoyez-moi vite un drapeau. Les Belges me viennent faire la guerre sans motif; je ne leur ai pas mangé de biens, je ne leur ai tué personne ... Pour Dieu pour Dieu envoyez-moi un drapeau.

The translator evidently wrote good French, and was trying to convey the clumsy flavour of the original. An unbiassed reader may think this tends to show that the transaction was an innocent one: but on this evidence Stokes was hanged. The signature '*de*

Cameroun' is evidently ambiguous. I take it that Kibonghe was saying where he came from, rather than claiming a territorial particle.

There is some mystery about the clerk Moussa bin Hadji. Both the letter from Kibonghe to Stokes, and Stokes's reply to it, are attributed to his hand. I take it that he personally carried Kibonghe's letter to Stokes, then wrote back to his master from the Irishman's camp. The Belgian reports make no mention of him: presumably he was done away with in the general massacre.

Chapter 14

The journal *La Belgique coloniale* has several admiring articles about Lothaire, written for the campaign to make a hero of him. There is also a useful potted biography of him in the *Biographie coloniale belge*. This invaluable work of colonial propaganda, of which the School of Oriental and African Studies at London University has a copy, also contains entries on Bishop Hirth and his following of German-speaking White Fathers. The *Biographie*'s account of '*L'affaire Stockes*' (sic) is useful, giving the Belgian version of the many lies told by all concerned. The Public Record Office collection on the affair includes cuttings from Belgian newspapers, including some republican, anti-clerical ones which, while critical of British bullying, were also sceptical of the claims of the King's faction, and opposed to the lionising of Lothaire. When that hero jilted the rich and beautiful Miss van Hecke, one of her cousins, a German officer, tried to get Lothaire to fight a duel. He declined.

Chapter 15

The present-day Uganda–Zaire frontier, as eventually determined by an Anglo-Belgian boundary commission, is an uneasy compromise designed to follow, as far as possible, the line of 30° east that had been agreed at Berlin as the limit of King Leopold's Congo territory. It follows the Semliki for a bit, then climbs along the crest of the Ruwenzori range, and down across the foothills towards Lake Edward. The people of the foothills are thus split by a border right through their tribal lands. Their main business is smuggling. A smooth official of President Mobutu's party, the *Mouvement populaire de la révolution*, sits in Kasindi, where all traffic must pass, and accepts small donations from travellers. He is nostalgic for Kinshasa, the capital: '*Ah, Kin la belle*', he sighs, drinking the excellent beer for which he has, to his distress, no refrigerator.

Limi Stokes may have lived on until 1950. Mr Donald Simpson has produced from his collection of treasures a photograph taken in Zanzibar in that year of an old lady who claimed to be Limi. If so, she was at least eighty, assuming that she was over sixteen when Charles Stokes married her in 1886.

Charles Stokes, junior, was lucky not to have been born in the Catholic Congo. Its founding bishop, Monsignor Augouard, a Frenchman, was once asked by Madame de Brazza to accept into a convent orphanage the girl child of a Belgian official and his African mistress. The Bishop answered: 'I observed to her that the money of the Holy Childhood cannot be used to pay for the consequences of white men's misbehaviour, and that such men should surely be obliged to bear in person the expense of their filthy enjoyment.'

Finally, Charles Stokes was at times pugnacious, at times sentimental. Here are two letters from him. To Captain Williams, on 30 November 1891, he wrote insisting on his right to trade freely where he liked. He protested his loyalty to Her Majesty the Queen of Great Britain and Ireland, and continued:

> I only joined German Service to help the German Government in their own sphere, by doing so I was able to persuade the Wanyamwesi to receive the Germans peaceably, if I had not done so there would have been a fine times in Unyamwesi, can you blame me for wishing to befriend my own people ... I could have war here tomorrow if I liked, so great is my influence, but that is not my wish for poor Africa ... If I made an expedition without your leave as you say it might be the salvation of English rights and flying as I would the English flag (you must know I have one) would Captain Lugard fire on me or what do you mean by your warning, if he did, by God you would find Stokes's body in front of his men and lead them to death or victory.
>
> SITOKESI

To his mother, he wrote on 13 August 1894, from Camp Kwa Muchara, Congo Free State:

My darling mother.

As I get a chance I send this via Buganda to reach you I hope safely. I am longing to hear from you as I have had no news of any sort since leaving the coast last September. I cannot think what my agents are about, perhaps they are all dead or run away.

I fear I have had a great loss of about £4,000 as I hear my man has been killed by Arabs and all goods stolen. I am hoping for the best however and hope it is not true as I wanted to go home in '95 to see you all. I send you order for £50 for fear of accidents of not getting back. In case of anything happening me you are provided for in my will as I have a considerable amount of property. But I am in excellent health and if it be the Almighty's will I shall be home in '95.

Give my love to Pet, Jos, Ack, and wife Elsie Robert and all nephews and neices. I got a splendid order from the government in Buganda before starting and I hope to get more orders for them.

How are you all in dear old Ireland, you are never forgotten by your expatriated son, all my people are well and my little daughter a fine child her name 'Louisa'.

I hope dear George is quite recovered, be sure and let me know if anything is wanted and old Will send him my fond love and I hope he is well.

Send my love also to Mary Ramsay please first chance.

I cannot let myself think of old times, dear old times, never to return after all we were really happy, but as you used to say the young birds fly away. But I never forget you dear mother and you know yourself what a hard struggle it is at home.

Goodbye my darling mother, may the Almighty be your protector ever and all at home.

Ever your affectionate son, Charlie.

Less than five months later he was hanged from the tree at Lindi.

Index

Pearson, Rev. C. W. 30-3, 40
Pema 206
Pembe, Bwana, *see* Lothaire,
  Capt.
Penrose, William 22, 23, 25
Perham, Dame Margery 129, 236,
  245, 247
Peters, Dr Carl: and Kilimanjaro
  72-4, 243; founds Ostafrika
  Gesellschaft 74, 75; competes
  for Emin 87, 88; gets and loses
  Buganda 108-17, 124, 132, 143;
  meets Emin 114, 115; Nazi hero
  246
Philippines 65, 68
pigmies 144, 147
Pinto, cook 53
Pius IX, Pope 12, 117, 137
Plunkett, Sir Francis 221, 224,
  225
Poland 65, 153
Port Alice (Entebbe) 198
Portal, Sir Gerald 163
Portora Royal School 5
Portuguese empire xi, 8, 17, 63,
  65, 67, 81, 116, 148, 154, 223,
  226
Praeger, Rev. E. A. 20
Price, Rev. J. C. 50
Prince Albert National Park, *see*
  Virunga
Protestants: Irish 5, 6, 177, 198,
  199; British 6, 19, 24-57, 85,
  91, 95-104, 117, 123, 134, 179,
  188; Scottish 7-9, 12, 23, 81,
  85, 114; American 9, 10;
  French 11; German 13, 109-13;
  ex-slaves 20-2; Baganda 96-8,
  101-7, 113, 114, 118, 166, 170,
  183, 239, 240; in the Congo
  154, 223, 226, 228
Prussia 65

Quatermain, Allan xiv, 246

railways 165; Uganda 75, 76, 165,
  191, 233, 250, 252; Saint-Louis
  to Djibouti 147; Cape to Cairo
  147, 204, 254; Ohio 198
Ramshaw, Mr and Mrs 48, 49

Rand, the 229
Ransford, Oliver 249
Rashid bin Ali 184
Reading 6
Rebmann, Rev. 109
Red Cross: International
  Committee of the 68; Uganda
  237
Red Sea 30, 35
Rehan 90
Remington rifles 89, 120, 144,
  146, 149
Rhodes, Cecil 147, 229, 230, 241,
  250
Rhodesia 246
Rift Valley, Western 144, 186;
  Great 165
Rio Muni 154
Ripon Falls 32
*Rise of Our East African Empire,
  The* (Lugard's) 135
Robinson, R. 236
Rodd, Rennell 172
Roi des Belges (steamer) 153
Roman Catholics: Irish 5, 198;
  Portuguese 8; in Turkey 38;
  Baganda 95-8, 106, 107, 138,
  160, 240; in the Congo 223,
  257; in Belgium 228; *see also*
  Protestants, White Fathers
Rome 117
Rosebery, Lord 222
Rothschild, Lord 247
Royal Academy 241
Royal Commonwealth Society
  241
Royal Engineers 191, 235
Royal Geographical Society ix
Royal Navy (British) 7, 13, 14,
  16, 21, 81, 110
Royal Niger Company 173, 251
Rubaga 103, 112, 135, 171
rubber trade 152, 153, 223; evils
  of 250
Rusambia 214
Russia 63, 64, 244, 252
Ruwenzori mountains (Mountains
  of the Moon) 186, 249, 256
Rwabugiri 195
Rwanda 143, 144, 185, 195, 249